# Small is Good
Business and Morality among Danish Shopkeepers

Global markets are increasingly dominated by large corporate firms. The Danish economy has followed the same trends, with large corporate firms dominating a growing number of sectors. Small, independent businesses can try to oppose these trends and risk being swallowed up or outcompeted, or they can aim to become larger themselves. In a neoliberal market economy, small, independent businesses represent an alternative to the domination of large corporate enterprises. Based on 12 months of ethnographic fieldwork in Aarhus, the second largest city in Denmark, this book investigates business owners who have taken a stand against current trends. It explores the lives and social values of resilient, independent business owners for whom opposition to corporate capitalism is a key element of identity.

Focusing on family and labour relations, Anne-Erita Berta documents forms of succession and problems related to succession, divisions of labour and family involvement in the firm, views and values concerning work, moral and economic values, structures of ownership and management, and the role played by ideas of justice and equality in creating a conformist state with conformist citizens. The values and moral economic actions of family business owners reveal a combination of the principled rejection of growth with an intimate ethical business strategy. Berta shows that these entrepreneurs are determined to maintain control over their businesses. Their primary motivation is the self-actualization they experience in direct contact with customers and by being involved in production. They are concerned to present themselves as business owners whose primary motivation is not profit or prestige, but the realization of values of community, modesty, and hard work. They act according to the ideas of their moral community. Owners organize their firms according to a shared morality and a philosophy that deviate from the norms of commodity markets. They aspire to create inalienable commodities within networks of meaningful economic exchange. Berta demonstrates how the determination not to grow beyond a manageable size and to act on the basis of values of justice, community, modesty, and hard work form a successful business strategy for shopkeepers who prize their independence.

D1668534

**Halle Studies in the Anthropology of Eurasia**

**General Editors:**

Christoph Brumann, Kirsten W. Endres, Chris Hann, Burkhard Schnepel,
Lale Yalçın-Heckmann

**Volume 44**

LIT

Anne-Erita Berta

# Small is Good

Business and Morality
among Danish Shopkeepers

LIT

Cover Photo: Goldsmith's work desk, Aarhus.
(Photo: Anne-Erita Berta, September 2016).


This book is a revised version of a dissertation manuscript, submitted to
the Faculty of Philosophy I at Martin Luther University Halle-Wittenberg
in 2019.



**Bibliographic information published by the Deutsche Nationalbibliothek**
The Deutsche Nationalbibliothek lists this publication in the Deutsche
Nationalbibliografie; detailed bibliographic data are available on the Internet at
http://dnb.dnb.de.

ISBN 978-3-643-91409-5 (pb)
ISBN 978-3-643-96409-0 (PDF)


**A catalogue record for this book is available from the British Library.**



©LIT VERLAG Dr. W. Hopf
Berlin 2021
Fresnostr. 2
D-48159 Münster
Tel. +49 (0) 2 51-62 03 20
Fax +49 (0) 2 51-23 19 72
E-Mail: lit@lit-verlag.de
https://www.lit-verlag.de

LIT VERLAG GmbH & Co. KG Wien,
Zweigniederlassung Zürich 2021
Flössergasse 10
CH-8001 Zürich
Tel. +41 (0) 76-632 84 35
Fax
E-Mail: zuerich@lit-verlag.ch
https://www.lit-verlag.ch


**Distribution:**
In the UK: Global Book Marketing, e-mail: mo@centralbooks.com

In Germany: LIT Verlag Fresnostr. 2, D-48159 Münster
Tel. +49 (0) 2 51-620 32 22, Fax +49 (0) 2 51-922 60 99, e-mail: vertrieb@lit-verlag.de

# Contents

# List of Illustrations

**Maps**

**Plates**

**Figures**

**Tables**

**Sources:**

Map: Google map of Wintec City Campus Hamilton, https://www.google.
com/maps/place/Danmark/@56.1549059,7.0557458,6z/data=!3m1!4b1!4m5
!3m4!1s0x464b27b6ee945ffb:0x528743d0c3e092cd!8m2!3d56.26392!4d9.5
01785 (retrieved October 2018)

Plates 1, 3, 4, 5, 6 were taken by author [2015-2016]
Plate 2: Reproduced with permission by by Dansk skolemuseum (2017)

# Acknowledgements

There are many to whom I owe debts of gratitude in relation to this book. First, I would like to express my sincere gratitude to Steven Sampson for editing expertise and to Chris Hann, head of department and principal investigator of the ERC-funded REALEURASIA project of which my project formed part. Thank you for academic guidance, patience, immense flexibility, and for supporting me throughout. I would also like to thank Lale Yalçın-Heckmann, our project coordinator.

I would like to express thanks to my colleagues in the department *Resilience and Transformation in Eurasia* and especially to Luca Szücs, Laura Hornig, Sylvia Terpe, and Matthijs Krul in the REALEURASIA team for collegiality and support. Thank you also to Deborah Jones for comments, and to Brenda Black and Bettina Mann for assistance with translation. Anke Meyer and Berit Eckert helped enormously with various administrative tasks in the last stages. Together with Michaela Rittmeyer, Berit played a crucial role in turning the text into an actual book. At the Max Planck Institute, two individuals have been of special importance. Diana Vonnak and Giuseppe Tateo have stimulated me intellectually, socially, and anthropologically. More importantly, they have been my Halle family, with whom I shared an office as well as food, worries and dreams. They have gone out of their way to open their homes and hearts to me and my family and I shall forever be grateful to them both. Another important mentor along the way is Chris Gregory: a stimulating advisor and a friend, he was a continuous source of insightful comments, encouragement and support. I also drew inspiration from Monica Heintz, who shared her work and thoughts with me.

In Aarhus, I cannot even try to list all those who helped me. I could not have written this book without the people who talked to me and invited me to take part in their work and lives. First and foremost are the business owners who shared their lives, aspirations, successes and failures with me. It is with humble appreciation that I dedicate this book to them in an attempt to repay some of my debt. The two families who opened their homes to me and incorporated me into their lives, deserve a special thank you for their trust, care, and attachment, though I shall not name them. Karen, Christian, Rikke, Carola, Bent, Iben, Anders, Marianne, Tine, Per, Klaus, Anne: thank you.

I also want to thank my colleagues at Moesgaard Museum and the Department of Social Anthropology in Aarhus for stimulating conversations and friendship, especially Anders Emil Rasmussen, Natalie Forssman, Jeanette Lykkegård, Katy Overstreet and Spencer Orey, and my dear friend Mathilde Højrup. Mathilde not only shared her enthusiasm and engagement in anthropology and my project; she also helped me to take my first steps into the field and provided a roof over my head. She and her family have helped me in so many ways, but most of all, she has been an invaluable friend and interlocutor throughout the gestation of this book. Ditte Maria D. Hiort was my first informant and she opened her home to me when I needed it the most.

The Department of Social Anthropology at the University of Oslo included me in seminars and workshops and numerous colleagues helped me in various ways. Thank you Signe Howell for pushing me through this project and your continuous inspiration and support. Susanne Brandtstädter, Eirik Bischoff Riis Anfinsen, Audun Bie and Theodoros Rakopoulos provided helpful comments on my text. Lena Gross got me started; Marianne Lien, Elisabeth Schober, Harald Beyer Broch and Keir Martin helped me to keep going.

Thank you to Alex Golub, Kate Lingley, and the boys for all the help in Hawaii.

Last but not least I need to thank my friends and family, above all my mother and sister for their support, encouragement, and understanding. Thank you to Wenche and Erik for support. And thank you to the most enduring, critical, supportive, encouraging, loving, adaptable, and understanding anthropologist, friend, husband, and co-parent Ola Gunhildrud Berta. Thank you for everything you have done to make my PhD become a reality. Thank you also to my son and field assistant, Edgar, for being the most patient, enduring, and adaptable child a mother could wish for, and to Ela for patience and presence.

# Chapter 1
## Introduction and Methodology

In the introduction to the ERC-funded research group Realising Eurasia: Civilisation and Moral Economy in the 21st Century (REALEURASIA), of which this book is part, our research director, Chris Hann, wrote that the overall purpose of the project was to 'assess how far the major civilisations of Eurasia differ in their economic ethic'. With the overall topics of moral economy, religion, and kinship, the REALEURASIA project sought to address the issue of whether religion, or rather, the Protestant work ethic proposed by Max Weber in the early 20th century, has had, and still has, an influence on the moral economy of business owners and families in middle-sized cities of seven different Eurasian countries (see Hann 2015, 2016 for discussion of Eurasia).[1]

In the introduction to *Nordic Paths to Modernity*, Jóhann Páll Árnason and Björn Wittrock (2012) claimed that scholars have argued for an early capitalist spirit in Denmark, and that Denmark was among the most modern countries of 12th century Europe. In 1947, the Norwegian historian Christen Jonassen (1947) argued for a Protestant ethic and a spirit of capitalism in Norway, as did the Norwegian anthropologist Marianne Gullestad in the late 1990s (Gullestad 1996, 1997). According to Max Weber (2001 [1905]), the capitalist spirit was born out of the spirit of Christian asceticism and the idea of the calling, but long after Christian asceticism had been marginalized, the associated work ethic continued to exist.

Today, Danes generally consider themselves a secular society, such that one might think that the Protestant ethos of hard work had disappeared. However, whenever a foreign observer or Danish commentator criticises the Danes for being lazy because they work shorter hours and take long vacations or for complaining too much about stress, they encounter vehement objection from the Danish public. Thus, Denmark seems to be a

---

[1] Besides Denmark, the individual case studies of the REALEURASIA project were carried out in Hungary, Russia, Turkey, Myanmar, China, India, and Germany, under the direction of Chris Hann at the Max Planck Institute for Social Anthropology.

good site for evaluating Weber's hypothesis as it applies to a modern, secular society.

Although Weber's ideas comprised the foundation of our REALEURASIA project, other components deserve attention in the Scandinavian context. It is not my intention to assess whether Weber was correct in his thesis that Protestant asceticism was or not instrumental to the growth of capitalism. Instead, this project considers the everyday lives of a group of small business owners and their families in the Danish city of Aarhus. Specifically, it asks *how the cultural values (highlighted in the Nordic ethnography) of homogeneity, justice, and secularism relate to perceived and enacted moral values within the business activities of small, independent firm owners.* By reviewing the state of these cultural values, I present what I can consider the best case for showing how (Protestant) ethics and (capitalist) spirits interact in an advanced capitalist economy.

Inspired by the ideas of Max Weber and his thesis of the development of capitalism as a consequence of Protestant asceticism, Karl Polanyi's criticism of economic man, and his idea of the 'double movement', as well as by E.P. Thompson's studies of the moral economy, I was one of seven PhD students who carried out fieldwork in different countries beginning in the late summer of 2015 (Polanyi 1944; Thompson 1963; Weber 2001 [1905]). As one of the researchers in this group, my aim was to obtain access to and follow the daily rhythm in five to ten small-to-medium-sized Danish firms in various branches, all with direct relations to customers. According to the overall project, the firms should preferably be family firms, that is, firms owned and operated by one or several individuals who were related by either marriage or kinship. Some firms were generational firms, meaning that ownership had been passed from minimum one generation to the next.

Denmark presented itself as a suitable location to study small businesses in Northern Europe for many reasons. It represents the protestant part of REALEURASIA with a state where Protestantism, historically, has been a central part of political life and the development of the social democratic welfare state. The country is now considered secular, but most Danes view themselves as cultural Christians (*kulturkristne*), meaning that they baptise their children and marry in church, but they do not practice religion in their everyday lives.

Moreover, Denmark is in many ways more European than the rest of the Nordic countries (Mønnesland 1995: 136). It is geographically located more towards Europe than the other Nordic countries (via its longstanding EU and NATO memberships), it borders Germany by land, and is involved with the European landmass to a larger extent than for example Norway or even Sweden. However, Denmark is also interesting as a small peninsular country on the northern tip of the central European continent. It is composed of the Jutland peninsula, the two large Islands of Funen, and Zealand, the formerly Swedish island Bornholm and an additional 70 smaller populated islands. Greenland and the Faroe Islands form part of the Danish commonwealth. While Denmark is now a small, Scandinavian nation, it was also once a larger empire, having once ruled all of Norway, southern Sweden and Schleswig-Holstein, in addition to colonies such as the U.S. Virgin Islands. While Denmark has had a vibrant fishing industry and offshore oil exports, the Danish economy was traditionally based on agricultural export (pork and dairy products), shipping (Maersk) and is today a leader in windmill production, technology, and various business services.

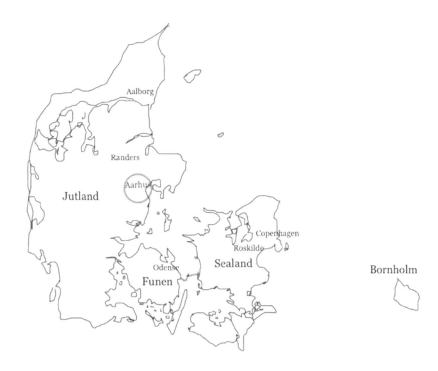

Map 1. Map of Denmark showing the field site of Aarhus.

I spent a year of field research in Aarhus, Denmark's second largest city with approximately 350.000 inhabitants. Aarhus was an appealing field site because of its long history as a centre for commerce, and now a business centre serving the Jutland hinterland as well as national and international markets.

## Key Questions

Prior to commencing the fieldwork, I produced several research questions as a guide for my work. I asked myself whether it was useful to argue for a (Protestant) work ethic and a moral economy among contemporary Danes. However, the common topics from REALEURASIA changed during the course of my work, and I ended up becoming more concerned with small business owners rather than with family firms. As the project developed, I discovered that the firms I studied were all niche firms whose owners expressed a sense of hostility toward large, corporate capitalism, most visibly the large retail chains selling food or household products. It struck me that these niche firms had many odds against them in an economy increasingly dominated by large corporate enterprises, but that they somehow managed. Similar businesses had either closed or been acquired by large corporations, but the business owners with whom I worked seemed confident that this would not happen to them. This inspired me to set out to answer the question: *What motivates the small, independent business owners to persist in a seemingly difficult economic environment where international corporations increasingly dominate the business landscape and what strategies do they use to supply in this landscape?* The businesses I studied all seem to represent success stories, and my thesis might have been different if I were dealing with businesses that had been forced to close down even though they shared the same ethic. I sought to explore the motivations and value orientations of these business owners. I found a network of community solidarity and a valuation of freedom, hard work, and frugality, values which certainly resonate with the (Lutheran) Protestantism that developed in Denmark (Thorkildsen 2006; Jakobsen 2017). However, I would also find that the desire for control, particular control over everyday business routines, was just as much a driving force among these business owners. Moreover, I found that their desire for control, which has positive features when we talk about attention to detail, could also become an obstacle in their search for freedom (to control their own lives). Too much control also means that they lacked trust in anyone but themselves and immediate family. The combination of a motivation for self-employment, being your own boss combined with the aim not to grow and control all areas of the firm were important to their success as resilient, small business owners.

Prior to undertaking fieldwork, I was initially inspired by British historian E.P. Thompson's 'moral economy of the crowd'. I had hoped to apply Thompson's ideas, based on the British working class to contemporary Aarhus (Thompson 1963). However, I found that rather than 'moral economy', it was a broader concept of values that proved to be more applicable. I discovered that the business owners shared a set of values that I could group together under the concept of morality. The morality of their business activities involved more than ideas of justice and fairness limited to the economy, as in Thompson's terms. Instead, the kind of 'morality' I encountered among the Aarhus business owners involved ideas and values concerning all aspects of their lives, both business related and personal. Morality contains ideas about right and wrong, and I therefore sought to explore informants' ideas about corruption, unregistered work, tax evasion, and informal economy. However, in-depth knowledge about these issues generated sensitive data, which for ethical reasons (not wanting to harm my informants) has not received much attention in this thesis.

With my emphasis on the total moral spectrum of life, economic and otherwise, I thus sought to map out the involvement of family members in business, and the division of labour and power between family members in the businesses. I focused especially on trying to discover whether there was a stronger sense of mutuality between family members with businesses than those in a purely wage-earning household (Gudeman 2009). My work was aided by many of the valuable insights of and conceptual frameworks developed by Scandinavian ethnographers. Egalitarianism is one such conceptual framework, which in the discourse of equality (*lighed*) is understood as sameness. As I discovered how the shopkeepers spoke and acted, it became relevant to focus on the role played by the presumption of homogeneity in Scandinavian business life.

Initially, I was interested in the place of religion in a secular society, and its role in how people acted and thought about morality. In my data, however, religion turned out not to be a significant aspect of people's everyday lives. Most of my informants were not concerned with religion or religious issues. Nevertheless, they constantly emphasized doing what was 'good' or 'right' or 'important'. This led me yet again to follow the focus on morality and values as principal analytical categories of my research. The shopkeepers of Aarhus may have been economic agents, but they were also moral actors who judged themselves and others predominantly in terms of moral uprightness rather than economic success.

## Methodology

The methodological pathway to answering these questions and concerns follows the method of ethnographic participant-observation developed and promoted by Bronislaw Malinowski in the early twentieth century (Malinowski 1935). Participant-observation requires the ethnographer to participate as much as possible in the daily lives of the people whose lives the researcher is studying. In a bounded rural community or village, the task and limits are clear-cut. If the ethnographer were studying labourers in an industrial plant, she would observe them both on the shop floor and then go home with them, eating and spending free time with them, laughing and crying with them (Murphy and Murphy 1985: 59).

Malinowski has been criticized for promoting an idealistic and unrealistic perspective on fieldwork that is not necessarily applicable in all fields of study, and certainly not in modern, urban Scandinavia, with its strict divisions between home, workplace and leisure pursuits. However, the core of ethnographic fieldwork, whereby the ethnographer seeks to understand the life-world of those she studies in the complete context of their situation, remains an essential objective of the ethnographic enterprise (Stoller 1989). We '*search for interconnections* between phenomena normally treated as separate and distinct in common sense understandings' (Gullestad 1992a: 25). Ethnographers also have the task of elaborating how people perceive the world, that is, people's representations both of their world as it is, and for the world as they think it should be. These representations act as mutually constituting discourses in the given community (Stoller 1989: 51).

Moreover, the ethnographer goes far beyond her own comfort zone to enable herself not only to observe what the locals experience, but to participate in their experiences and aim to, as far as possible, obtain a deeper understanding of these processes as a lived experience herself. The degree of success implied in this method varies, as it is difficult to escape from our own personal and ethnographic bias (Briggs 1970). Although we strive to participate in our informants' everyday lives, our aim is not to 'go native'. Rather, ethnographers seek to 'exist much like the people, living in their dwellings and eating their foods' (Murphy and Murphy 1985: 51). In researching the small business households in Aarhus, my type of participation consisted of accompanying people while they carried out such mundane activities as cooking, chatting, cycling, praying, picking up groceries, working (various tasks), just sitting quietly, or watching TV. Participant-observation means that while taking part in all these activities – I should attempt to do them the same way my informants do them. I should try to pay attention to the details of the task as well as the context and interaction. This was not always possible in the given situation. Sometimes, my interlocutors neglected to inform me where they were going and simply disappeared before I had the chance to invite myself to go along with them. On other occasions, the informant might have a purely personal errand or activity and did not want the ethnographer to join her (Stoller 1989).

Although my field site resembled my own native Norway (a country geographically close to Denmark with a language similar to Danish), I constantly had to remind myself to 'remember to forget' (Gullestad 1984: 59). In other words, I continually tried to negate or question what I already thought I knew about Danish social norms and regulations. I tried to re-learn what I thought I knew about Danish values and customs in order to avoid a native bias and pre-judgement. I tried to ask the kind of 'silly questions' to which the interlocutor ordinarily expects you to already know the answer (Lien 2001). Although my native Norway in many ways resembles Denmark in its social, political and economic system (small, relatively homogenous, highly developed welfare states), I still had to learn the Danish language, norms, and practices just as carefully in Denmark as I would in a more exotic field site. I did not need to endeavour to ask the silly questions. Nativeness is relative. Even when working with people of the same language and nationality as yourself, it does not necessarily make you native when the life you live as an aspiring academic differs greatly from the lives they live as small business owners (Lien 1997). I was certainly not Danish, and I was in no way native.

My plan was to move to Aarhus and spend a full year in the world of the small business owners and their families, as well as their employees. Although there is a tendency in Scandinavian ethnography to accept and defend fieldwork even when the researcher does not dwell in the same site or neighbourhood as her informants, a more holistic approach is possible. While much good ethnography has come out of such fieldwork, where the ethnographer does not cut herself off from her own private, everyday life, I argue that it is possible to do so-called 'village ethnography' in a modern, Scandinavian setting. For example, Kathinka Frøystad (2003: 36) has argued that it would have been 'meaningless' for Marianne Lien to live among her informants when she studied a workplace where the interlocutors only socialised during working hours. Although I agree that Lien certainly gathered much useful data from observing her interlocutors' lives only at their workplace or workplace-related activities, much additional valuable data could have been collected had she also spent time with her interlocutors in their homes or in their free time. By looking beyond the workplace, she would have achieved a broader understanding of the complexity of the whole person, and this could certainly have benefitted her understanding of their roles and actions at work. When Gullestad made a conscious choice *not* to dwell in the neighbourhood where her families lived but to instead follow the social network of her key informant, the result was a very solid ethnography. However, it would be wrong to dismiss the value of an approach where the researcher decides to move her own life and family into a neighbourhood and participate fully in one area (as does Frøystad 2003).

Ethnographers could and should always strive towards a holistic approach, even if we are interested only in specific aspects or areas of social life. Individuals are never only an employee, or only a business owner. In order to fully understand the role or group whom we are studying, we need to have more information and more well-rounded insight into multiple areas of our informants' lives. Part of being a good ethnographer involves acknowledging our limitations. We cannot always cover all the areas we want, but this should not lead us to dismiss the ethnographic project as a whole. Ethnography is still possible in a modern, urban context, as Frøystad (2003) underscored.

In my view, one of the strengths of the anthropological approach lies in our concern for uncovering the dissonance between how people perceive the world and how they act in the world. We are concerned with the difference between what people say they do, and what they actually do: because it is in this dissonance that we find the reality of what we seek to learn (Geertz 1973). To discover and analyse how people experience reality we need to strive for an immersion into our field that is as complete as possible. Through listening, seeing, feeling, experiencing, and taking active part in the everyday life of our interlocutors, we have the opportunity to gather the widest range of information about their realities (Wikan 1992).

When I first arrived in Denmark, I had in the back of my mind the Norwegian slogan '*Det er deilig å være norsk, i Danmark*' (It's wonderful to be Norwegian - in Denmark).[2] In contrast to the Swedes, who are perceived by Danes as arrogant and rule-bound, and often subject to ridicule and put-downs by Danes, Norway, which until 1814 was part of the Danish Kingdom, is generally perceived as Denmark's little brother (see Jenkins 2011). With this awareness, I therefore arrived with a perception that it would be somewhat easy to be Norwegian in Denmark. My first encounter with Aarhus, however, made me feel anything but welcome. Coming from my academic institution in Halle, a small, German town where consumer and rental prices are relatively low, Aarhus was extremely expensive. A harbour town, Aarhus was cold, windy, and rainy. Aarhus was also home to a major university, and since Danish universities do not have dormitories, there was an acute shortage of inexpensive rental housing. For a foreigner without

---

[2] The slogan derives from a commercial first aired in 1989, trying to attract Norwegian tourists to Denmark.

connections, it was almost impossible to find a reasonably-priced room or apartment. I had been warned beforehand that Aarhus was very expensive, and that housing was limited.[3] After three weeks of borrowing a colleague's room, I ended up in a bed and breakfast 12 kilometres outside the city. I had planned to move into a neighbourhood and get to know the neighbours and their daily lives. I had also planned to spend time in different firms and observe how people conducted their daily business activities. However, not having a proper place to live, my romantic image of being 'in the field', of taking an active part in all aspects of work and life of family firms, proved challenging to achieve.

The housing situation in Aarhus and the impossibility of finding accommodation took up much of my initial period of entry into the field. To make matters worse, my request to spend time with businesses was rejected by many of them. All this made initial encounter with Aarhus much like the initial meetings most anthropologists have described on entering the field (Wadel 1991). The feeling of being unwelcome, isolated, and left out was very much present, and it was not until October that I finally received a 'Yes' from a business owner. After six weeks of searching for a suitable home and asking in different shops if I could 'hang around', I finally found my first firm.[4] It was an old family firm of fishmongers, and the store manager allowed me to stay and work every day for as long as I wanted and to participate in all the firm's various activities. I went every day to this 'workplace' and slowly got to know the owner, his family, the floor manager, and the employees.

Here, a second challenge emerged. It turned out that Danes did not necessarily understand Norwegian (as I had hoped in the spirit of Scandinavian communication). Nor could they understand my attempts at speaking Danish.[5] My initial weeks of fieldwork were thus filled with misunderstandings and slow conversations until my Danish improved enough so that informants became more accustomed to my Oslo-Danish accent.

---

[3] In order to access available housing listings, I had to register on a website and pay just under €50 per month just to see the listings. I had to send a personal application to the letting agency in the hope that I was among the few lucky prospective tenants to be invited to a viewing. I started applying and searching in April 2015 and arrived in Aarhus in August. Despite sending in an endless number of rental applications, I was never invited to any viewings.

[4] My friend and colleague with whom I shared a house outside the city had tipped me about the firm.

[5] Some dialects of Norwegian, such as the old Bergen dialects on the west coast, are closer to Danish, while other dialects, such as the Oslo dialect that I speak, differ markedly from Danish in both vocabulary and phonetics. Also, the Jutland accent spoken in Aarhus differs from the standard Danish spoken in Copenhagen.

I had planned my project as one of living together with a Danish family and taking part in their everyday lives. However, I was well aware that this might not be possible in a Scandinavian setting, as so many Scandinavian ethnographers had experienced before me; various colleagues had so warned me that this kind of intimacy might turn out to be impossible (Gullestad 1984; Hastrup 1987; Frøystad 2003; Bruun 2012). However, after less than a month of spending every day in the fishmonger firm, Polly, who owned the firm together with her husband, invited me to live with her family, consisting of her husband Poul and their three children.[6] I had posted a note for employees describing what I was doing in the firm. In the note, I also mentioned that I was interested in taking part in all parts of everyday life, also at home, and that I ideally would like to stay with a family. Polly told me that she had read the note, and that they had an extra room in their house, which I could have, free of charge.

This stroke of good luck changed my whole plan for fieldwork. It gave me unique access to this firm and the family. Polly, Poul, and their three children, with Poul's parents just across the yard, opened their homes and lives for me almost from day one. I quickly found my place in the family, somewhere between daughter, sister, and confidante, and I became involved in nearly all aspects of their lives. Polly and Poul made sure that I was always part of any activity, both those they did separately and those they did together; moreover, they always expected me to be present. One of several challenges with this very warm inclusion was writing field notes. If I tried to sneak away to my room in the evenings, only a few minutes would pass before someone knocked on my door and asked me to come downstairs to watch TV or hang out. If I wanted to visit employees outside of working hours, interview other, unrelated informants, or see friends privately, Polly and Poul would give me the impression that they were disappointed that I was not joining them in their activities. However, they happily drove me around and picked me up from these interview appointments.[7]

I had been living with Polly and her family for about two months when my husband first came to visit (he was living in Oslo, we had no children). It was the first day of Christmas, and the entire family was at home. It was one of the few days of the year when the fish shop was closed, and the whole family stayed home together for the entire day. Their expectations were high about my husband's visit. They had all heard about this mystery man, but it was as if they did not fully believe that he existed

---

[6] 'Polly' and all names are pseudonyms.

[7] The persistent feeling of disappointing them and not choosing to be with them on such occasions, might have been a constructed idea that existed only in my head, but nonetheless, I ended up spending 24 hours every day with them in their household for nearly my entire stay.

before they had seen him with their own eyes. On this day after Christmas Eve, we all just sat and watched TV, the children played on their computers, and we all had our regular cereal breakfast at different times. In the hours leading up to my husband's arrival from Oslo, we tidied up the house, lit candles in the rooms to create the famous Danish hygge, put on something else than our usual jogging suits, and prepared a festive meal with all the best our fridge had to offer.[8]

Waiting to feast on all this good food, when he finally arrived, we were all ecstatic. The children accosted him with questions and offered him homemade gifts. We all gathered around the table and sat there for the entire evening, eating, chatting, and having a good time. The event made me think about when I first arrived. The children had made small presents for me as well, and when they had gotten over their shyness, they asked many questions. The following day, we woke up to the unusual smell of warm bread rolls. I was a bit surprised that we were having warm bread rolls for breakfast. Bread rolls were something we usually saved for special guests. Again, the table was set with festive food, and instead of the customary instant coffee, Polly had brewed coffee in the coffee maker.

My family kept surprising me with their hospitality all through my husband's stay. They all behaved completely differently around him. The mood was always bright and happy, we ate proper meals together three times a day, always with the best we had on hand, and Polly and Poul took special pains to ensure that the children behaved properly. They all acted as if my husband was a very special guest for his entire stay. Seeing the way our home environment changed with the presence of my husband made me realize that I was part of the family. As soon as my husband left, we returned to our regular routine, eating cold cereal for breakfast, each at different times, the children leaving the table early, with no specially prepared meals for lunch or dinner, and with family members talking and even arguing with each other in a more natural, at times impolite manner. I was part of the daily routine, and the family members did not restrain themselves in their behaviour around me. This realization was important for me in order to ensure that my role and involvement in the family was of a deeper character. I had not reflected upon all this until I saw the significant difference in the way they behaved around the guest.

---

[8] *Leverpostej* (pig's liver pâté), various kinds of homemade herring, shrimp salad, smoked fish, *remoulade* (sauce), and other fish products from the shop.

## A New Start

In February 2016, after having spent six months in Aarhus, I returned home to Norway to give birth to my first child. When I returned with my infant and husband four months later, I planned to focus my study on other enterprises and families. This meant starting fieldwork all over again, with new housing complications and new feelings of failing.

Returning to Aarhus, I was now more familiar with the city. But my fieldwork was more 'multi-sited', to use Marcus' terminology, because I focused on multiple businesses across the city (Marcus 1998). Some scholars have claimed that all urban fieldwork is multi-sited, in so far as there are no clear groups or boundaries, as would be the case in a small village (Gullestad 1984: 49). People and objects constantly move between a variety of different places, social groups, and moral universes (Marcus 1998). I did not settle into a village. In fact, I ended up living in five different places in Aarhus, and only once did I feel even a little bit part of a neighbourhood. However, my fieldwork was also multi-sited because I moved between different environments. None of the firms I worked with belonged to the same local community, and they each operated within quite different branches, from fishmongering to a goldsmith to a bakery. As Marcus suggested, I followed the people, but I also followed the metaphor, given that the same moral worlds and value systems (as the metaphor) bound together my various individual interlocutors (Marcus 1998: 90–3).

Six different firms agreed to let me follow the rhythm of their business for a day or two per week. I started in a goldsmith's shop, and for the first few weeks, I spent almost every day in his combined workshop/shop. I quickly branched out to spend one day per week in a yarn shop, and another day in a café. My strategy for locating these firms was the same as during my first time in Aarhus. I simply walked around the city and asked different shop owners if I could study them. I had the same explanatory letter with me that I had presented to Polly and Poul the year before. I eventually ended up with the three firms mentioned above – fishmonger, yarn shop, café – plus a bakery, a toy shop, and a jeweller where I spent one to two days per week. In each of these firms, I took part in their everyday routines and assisted in those work tasks where I could. I spoke with shop-owners, employees, and customers, joined lunch breaks, and took part in the occasional social event. Unlike my stay with the fishmonger family, I worked with these firms mainly during their opening hours, with the exception of some home visits and social events.

While I visited these firms weekly and strived to take part in the firm's many activities, the nature of the various businesses and their owners required me to approach them differently. At Sally's toy shop, I followed

Sally whenever she was present in the shop. I followed her when she did her office work, made phone calls, travelled around to buy goods, and when she met people, a routine often accompanied or interrupted by coffee and cigarette breaks. In the bakery, I helped with various baking and sales tasks together with the employees, and accompanied everyone at their solitary lunch breaks. At the goldsmith, I sat at the unoccupied work desk and chatted with Julian the goldsmith all day long while he performed his craft work. Julian involved me by showing me what he did, and I assisted him where I could. He even allowed me to try out some elementary goldsmithing tasks. I was present in the shop when customers arrived, and the small size of the shop allowed me to interact with customers, asking questions and sharing ideas. In the café, I helped with dishes, cleaning, and other simple tasks, and I accompanied Lillian in her tasks, all the while conversing with her. In Lillian's interaction with customers, I usually remained in the background. In Pernille's yarn shop, as well, I was always present, participating in all Pernille's tasks and interactions.

In addition to the six firms, I travelled around the city and interviewed 32 other firms as part of a common survey carried out by all the researchers in our REALEURASIA project. Although my main purpose in these visits was to collect data for our survey, I extended the interviews with additional questions and conversations relevant to my own project. Some of the business owners agreed to follow-up meetings, enabling me to conduct from two to nine follow-up interviews.

## Interviews

It would be an exaggeration to call the conversations I had through the course of my fieldwork 'interviews'. 'Interview' connotes the kind of formality and distance that I as an ethnographer sought to minimise. Although I certainly tried to steer most of the conversations I had with the shop-owners and other interlocutors toward questions or themes that I had planned beforehand, I endeavoured to keep conversations casual. My success in doing so may be summarised by one business owner who asked me about halfway through fieldwork if I was ever going to ask her any (research-related) questions. When I told her that she had already answered several of the questions on my list, she was surprised, 'But you have never interviewed me!' I explained to her that of all the conversations we had every day, most of them were guided by me through the follow-up questions I made throughout a conversation, or by a conversational topic that I had initiated.

Whereas she felt that we were just talking, I was constantly conscious of my goal and the questions I sought to answer.[9]

This incident touches on several methodological challenges. First, it illustrates the problem any ethnographer confronts in relation to informed consent. I had properly informed Lillian of the purpose of my presence, explaining that I was part of a research project and giving her a concise introduction to how anthropologists work. I explained participant-observation and gave her a note that should keep her reminded of the purpose of my presence. My relationship with Lillian evolved in such a way that we got to know each other very well, and she stopped viewing me as a researcher – or perhaps more correctly, she thought that I was a bad one. It is extremely difficult to explain to our interlocutors what it is we do. Lillian was a well-educated person, and unlike most, she was familiar with anthropology; nevertheless, she did not really grasp what I was doing or why I was there.

Instead of taking time out of these people's lives to sit down and perform an interview with a list of questions and a notebook, in a formal interview style, I made a point of being present in their everyday lives. I took part by simply being there, helping with tasks, and having seemingly casual conversations. Discussing politics, religion, economy, money, wealth, health, family relations, personal motivations, life goals, and so forth seems natural when getting to know someone. That all these questions and topics were blended and merged with conversations about business-related tasks, cleaning or tidying up the shop, or whatever activity we were doing made the conversations relaxed and casual, and Lillian and other informants found our conversations to be indistinguishable from normal social interaction.

In situations where I asked questions, I sought to collect not only the verbal answers but to decipher how they replied. I paid attention to my interlocutors' bodily expressions and to the reactions of others (Stoller 1989). This entails confronting certain ethical challenges. Is it ethical that I learn about Lillian, and make judgements about her values and actions, in this 'undercover' way, without the informant's constant awareness of being the subject of research? On certain occasions, especially when we touched on sensitive topics, I would remind the interlocutor that I was a researcher and that I might use their responses in a scientific publication, anonymised

---

[9] Her expectations around what it meant to be researched by someone did not fit with the presence of an anthropologist who seemingly just 'hung around' and chatted. She had not noticed the fact that I had a list of topics and questions in my bag that I occasionally consulted, and she overlooked my note-taking throughout the day. Perhaps because she had gotten used to me withdrawing to write notes or thought that I was texting someone when I was making notes on my phone.

of course. Sometimes the person would withdraw what she just said or hold back. However, my experience is that, often, it only took a few minutes, hours, or days before the individual had forgotten why I was there, and they would serve up the same sensitive information again. Ultimately, it becomes our responsibility as researchers to protect our informants against inadvertently exposing themselves.

I chose this methodological approach because it gives the closest access possible to contrived answers (Rivers 1912). We obtain a more holistic view into the perceptions and ideas of people without the constant awareness about research. I hope and believe that this method has generated honest responses from informants, even when we consider that there is usually a discrepancy between people's representations of themselves and their actions. Moreover, it is my job as an ethnographer to trace these discrepancies and make some kind of sense of them. Revealing such discrepancies may lead to ethical issues, especially if I discover something about their lives or businesses that my informants may not want to be described in my analysis (Besnier 2009: 19).

Another recurring question about ethnographic methods is the constant evaluation of veracity (Stewart 1998). How can we verify ethnographic material? Here, I find it useful to quote Marshall Sahlins:

> No good ethnography is self-contained. Implicitly or explicitly, ethnography is an act of comparison. By virtue of comparison, ethnographic description becomes objective. Not in the naive positivist sense of an unmediated perception – just the opposite: it becomes a universal understanding to the extent it brings to bear on the perception of any society the conceptions of all the others (Sahlins 2002).

Anthropology is first and foremost a comparative science, and the only way we can achieve veracity is by comparing different cases and assessing whether there is any consistency in our arguments. Sometimes that means comparing with similar groups in other parts of the world, other times it means sending another ethnographer to the exact same place and seeing whether they come up with the same findings. However, this brings us to the challenge of temporality and the fact that individuals and groups change. They change their behaviour, attitudes, and even values. Therefore, in the end, the reader must have confidence that the ethnographer has provided objective observations and real statements by real people, not fiction.

Another important aspect of veracity is transparency. If the ethnographer is open about the methods used to collect and analyse the data and how the conclusions have been drawn, the reader can make an informed

decision as to whether or not the argument is convincing. This process and
these limitations also necessitate the need for continuing reflexivity: the need
for the researcher to reflect upon their biases, presumptions, ethnocentrism
and to assess our own success in dealing with these challenges (Howell
1997a: 9). Raymond Firth provides a useful example of the relevance of
these issues. In his introduction to *We, the Tikopia*, he states that:

> Dr. Rivers regarded the description of Tikopia custom in his book as
> of peculiar importance, and Oceanic scholars may wonder why I
> have made so little use of it in the following pages. On my travel
> through the Eastern Solomon Islands [...] I became increasingly
> convinced of the arid quality of his material, its superficiality, and
> lack of perspective. [...] Forgetful of the lessons of his own field-
> work among the Todas, which demonstrated the prime importance of
> lengthy personal contact with the people, he was content to
> reproduce the material of a single informant, a foreigner, collected in
> a *lingua franca*, without the possibility of check by direct
> observation (Firth 1936: xviii).

As ethnographers, we should always work with the confidence that if
someone should follow our exact path of study, that our material would
remain, if not directly replicable, at least solid.

The next step in achieving veracity is to be open about how we
understand emic and analytical concepts in the societies we study. One such
area is how we understand the economic market in which my interlocutors
act.

## 'The Market'

Market economy is recognised over large parts of the world, but no society
depends solely on market principles (Polanyi 2005: 100). Polanyi defined
market economy as 'an economic system controlled, regulated, and directed
by markets alone; order in the production and distribution of goods is
entrusted to this self-regulating mechanism' (Polanyi 2005: 99). Informal
and gift exchange also play important roles, even in those societies
recognised as having a largely self-regulated market economy (Parry and
Bloch 1989; Callon 1998b). The market principle implies an interaction
between buyers and sellers, and this relationship presumably determines the
prices of commodities and labour (Applbaum 2005: 275).

Denmark is known for its state-regulated capitalist economy, with a
social democratic welfare state. Regardless of which parties are in power, the
Danish welfare state remains entrenched. The Danish economy operates on
well-established free-market principles, but the state has set certain
regulatory standards that prohibit a totally self-regulating market to

develop.[10] The regulatory mechanisms in Denmark involve strict regulation of all three of what Polanyi called 'fictitious commodities': labour, land, and money. For Polanyi these were the principles for a self-regulating market, and he described them as being protected by the double movement of the nineteenth century (Polanyi 1944: 138–9, 2005: 103), where double movement connotes the oscillation between marketization and a counter-movement toward social protection. The degree to which these fictitious commodities are regulated varies over time, and from one society to another. Hence, in recent years, the Danish state has been criticised for moving away from strict principles of state regulation, allowing the gradual development of a more free-wheeling market economy (Lundkvist 2009a; Hall and Campbell 2017; see Bendixen, Bringslid and Vike 2018; Bruun 2018). This turn toward neoliberalism has led to the demise of a number of smaller firms and given growth to oligopolies and monopolies of large corporations (Lundkvist 2009b: 48, 78).

Immanuel Wallerstein argued that economic monopolies could never be achieved in the market, and that states, especially socialist states, created monopolisation only by means of legislation (Wallerstein 1983: 142–3). However, customs, understood as the development of specific tastes in the consumers through marketing and advertisements, is another important element in the growth of relative monopolies (Wallerstein 1983: 144). Our consumer society has developed certain expectations about what to expect from the market. When listening to the business owners criticizing the market, the particular market they are referring to are the large corporations, oligopolies and monopolies. These are increasingly encroaching upon smaller market actors and dominating the liberalised, Danish economy (Gudeman 2009: 26–8). The business owners with whom I did fieldwork saw themselves as opposed to the kind of consumer society that could be manipulated or controlled by this dominant, corporate-run market. They were business owners against the market.

Scandinavian ethnologists are well aware of the distinctions among various market actors. Danish ethnologist Thomas Højrup thus divided the capitalist production among three different actors: the investors, the managers, and the wage-earning workers (Højrup 2002b: 280–1). If we were to place the business owners in my sample in this three-levelled model, they would belong to none of them. They are petty commodity producers, equivalent to farmers or fishermen within what Højrup called self-employed life-mode, a life-mode in which they exploit their own labour power. The business owners are at once the investors, the managers, and the workers in

---

[10] Such regulations involve taxes, regulation of prices, regulations on import/export, property, (foreign) capital, and labour market policies.

their own businesses. Instead of being a temporary structure until the business is profitable enough for the owner to abandon the lower two levels (worker and manager), they choose to remain tied to their business enterprise. This is a tendency, Højrup argued, characteristic of the small, independent business owner who intends to remain small, since their project is not wealth or career, but autonomy (Højrup 2002: 280–1). Following Højrup, the Aarhus business owners are not capitalist. Højrup's point is that the actors in the self-employed life mode are noncapitalist actors who exist in a capitalist economy.

## The Small Business Owners, an Introduction

Are all business owners capitalists? Højrup (1983), in a study of fishing boat owners in the Danish west coast, distinguished between what he called life-modes. The three life-modes that were important for his analysis were what he called wage-worker, career professional, and the self-employed. The wage-worker operates with a clear distinction between work and leisure and is paid by the hours. The career professional is characterized by blurred lines between work and leisure, and their work requires constant production of creative ideas. In the self-employed life mode, work is embedded into (private) life. For the self-employed farmer, fisher, craftsman or shopkeeper, the work and leisure are not separated from work (business). Moreover, the self-employed, in contrast to the career professional, controls his own time and production and owns his own creative ideas. Hence, he does not need to constantly produce and invent new ideas. The Aarhus business owners encapsulate the self-employed life mode while retaining some of the innovation spirit of the career professional. They seek the freedom from wage-labour, the freedom to control their own firm, but they also seek the freedom to unfold their creativity and leave the company (and start a new company) if they want to pursue another creative idea or desire. However, they are not entrepreneurial capitalists in the conventional meaning of the word as innovators who want to expand their firm into a giant enterprise.

Most of these small shopkeepers come from other backgrounds: they have tried other kinds of employment, which in most cases involved higher salaries and material wealth. As such, deciding to become small business owners was a conscious choice rather than some kind of trap that they fell into or were compelled to take on. Most of my business owners made a conscious change of careers from wage-labour to running their own business. One common feature is that their initial motivation to start a business was rooted in their desire for non-material benefits such as more freedom (*frihed*), creativity (*kreativitet*), and sociality (*kontakt med mennesker*). The business owners also shared backgrounds and upbringing, characterised by relatively low material wealth and an emphasis on personal autonomy. None of the people in my six case studies attended business school or expressed any interest in business literature or theoretical business strategies. They invested little effort in developing marketing strategies or speculating on, or trying to predict the future in any sort of market assessment (Lien 1997). One of my business owners, Ole, claimed in an interview with the local newspaper that while building up their business, they relied on gut feelings, not classical business models. In general, there was little focus on predicting changes or trends so characteristic of the marketing profession (Lien 2004). Moreover, the six businesses where I conducted participant-observation between 2015 and 2017 consisted of only two who were actually married couples. However, they were all 'family firms' in the sense that their business was dependent on a significant effort of family members, both in the sphere of business and private life. In the following, I give a brief introduction to the different owners and their organisation of family/ business/ life. One of the firms, the fishmonger Ikan, is not mentioned here, as they are discussed in detail in Chapter 4.

Marie and Ole were a couple in their fifties. They owned and managed a successful, small bakery in the heart of Aarhus. They both held PhDs in natural sciences, but they had left busy careers when their three children were small, hoping that self-employment would leave more time with their children. Marie and Ole had used their savings to purchase an old farmstead. With funding from various interests groups, bank loans, and their own savings, they turned the farmland into a mushroom farm. They had a shared economy where they – amongst other things – used Marie's state pension savings to invest in the growth of the firm. Their income and expenses all came from shared accounts, and they had no separate, individual economies as do so many Danish wage-earning couples. When their children moved away from home to study, the couple decided to sell their farm and moved to Aarhus in order to start the bakery. They had first lived in a townhouse just a couple hundred meters from the business premises, but when I got to know them in 2016, they had moved to a house in a small town outside Aarhus. They commuted together every morning and shared one car. Marie and Ole did everything together. They were a team, and the one always joined the other, even when one of them was not strictly needed.

Lillian, the café owner, was 28 when I met her for the first time in 2016. Lilian owned the café together with her mother. Lillian managed the daily operations of the café, and she was present from seven in the morning until closing hours at six pm. Her mother came to help for a few hours in the afternoon, a few days per week, and she sometimes baked cakes and pastry to sell in the café. Lillian's parents helped out whenever there was something that needed renovation or for larger projects, but mostly it was Lillian who managed the business by herself. She had no employees, and since she was there six days per week, her mother was also responsible for shopping once a week for ingredients for cakes and pastry. They did not get these ingredients delivered at the door, as is common for larger firms, but simply purchased them in regular grocery shops. Lillian's boyfriend was not involved in the firm, and I never met him. She did not have contact with him during the day, but she did admit that he often cooked dinner. While her boyfriend did not participate, Lillian's café was still a family firm in the sense that her mother was a business partner and co-owner. Lillian's café had been operating for three years when I came to know her in 2016, and in 2023 she still manages the firm without any employees.

Initially, I had included Julian and his goldsmith firm in my sample as a contrast to the family firms, but with time, I realized that his business was not necessarily a contrast to the other family-owned firms. In many ways it was very similar to the other firms I studied although Julian's family's involvement in the firm was minimal and resembled more that which Yanagisako (2002) describes for many of the Como wives that are present but in the background. Julian was a goldsmith in his early 50s. He was married for the second time with two adult children from a former marriage and now two young children with his present wife. The family had moved from an expensive Aarhus town house to cheaper home 30 minutes outside Aarhus. When Julian met his wife, he was working for a large corporation, and earned what he described as a ridiculously high amount of money, managing a firm with thousands of employees. His second wife knew him as a hardworking man who suffered from a lot of stress, working long hours every day. Julian told me that he had longed to do something else. Luckily for Julian, his wife was also successful in her career, earning a good salary. With her approval, Julian quit his well-paid managerial job without having any clue on what he wanted to do next. After a few months of experimenting with ideas, and spending time with his youngest daughter, a toddler at the time, he started training to become a goldsmith. He ended up as a trainee at two major jewellery firms, learning both the creative and marketing side of the jewellery business. Not earning any income during this period of training, the couple sold their three-story townhouse in downtown Aarhus and moved to their current home. In this period, the family was living from his wife's salary and from Julian's savings from the years he had had his corporate job. After a couple of years working at two large jewellers, Julian started longing for creative freedom, and as he felt that he had learned what he could, Julian started researching the possibility of starting his own business. He told me that his main motivation to become independent came from his desire to create something, which he himself had designed in addition to the freedom to control his own working day.

Again, with support from his wife, Julian sold his (80,000 Euros car), found a storefront location and opened a workshop/showroom in the heart of the city. The early years, Julian recalled, were very unstable, and during some months, he failed to earn enough income to even cover the rent of the shop. A whole month could pass without him making more than DK 1000 (€130). But he and his wife had an agreement: the couple would subsist from his wife's monthly salary. In 2016, Julian's firm had existed for four years, and his business was doing 'quite well' according to him. Some months were still better than others, but he could always pay the company bills. Although business was now more stable than it had been, their household bills and purchases were paid through his wife's income, and they had no intention of changing that agreement.

But it was not only economically that Julian's business depended on his wife. The couple had two small children. One had just started school, the other one still in kindergarten. As Julian was operating his shop alone – except for a part-time employee who helped him a few days each week (before she left for a more stable job midway through fieldwork, leaving him completely to himself) – he had to work six days a week, sometimes long past dinner-time. His wife therefore had to adjust her day to fit his. Although adjusting work schedules to fit your partner's is common for Danish working parents, both wage-earners and business owners, Julian depended on the collaboration with his wife on a different scale precisely because there was no one else that could do his job.

Pernille was the owner of a small yarn shop in downtown Aarhus. She was trained as a chef and had worked most of her life in a public canteen. Her grandmother taught her to knit when she was five years old, and knitting had been her great passion ever since. Three years before my arrival Pernille had taken the leap and realised a dream – making a life out of her hobby. Now in her early 50s, Pernille had started her yarn shop. Her husband, Tor, was himself a self-employed business owner of 15 years. The couple had been together since they were teenagers, neither of them coming from families with money. Pernille's mother died when she was very young, and her father, a housepainter was a habitual drinker. Pernille grew up taking responsibility for her younger brother in a home with little means. Her parents left her no assets, nor were they present to help her in her young adult life, but her childhood had equipped her with a strong sense of independence and an ability to get things done. She finished school and got herself a decent job. Her husband came from a family with other struggles, and as young adults, neither of them relied on help from kin. Now, they had a small, but comfortable house in a good suburban neighbourhood, purchased many years ago with a bank loan and savings they had saved up from years of working. They also had a car and two children, both in their early 20s.

When I first walked into Pernille's yarn shop and she agreed to let me spend time in her business, she informed me that her firm was not a family firm. It was just hers, alone. Her husband had a firm of his own, and she could not afford to employ her children, nor was there any need for them. However, the more time I spent in Pernille's shop, the more I witnessed her husband's involvement in her business.

Formally, Pernille owned the shop, and she was there every day taking care of the daily tasks of owning, running and selling. Yet her business could not have survived without the help of her husband. The couple had a shared economy and Tor's firm made profits that enabled capital investment into Pernille's firm. Formally, these investments came from Pernille, as her own private resources. Their shared household economy was in such a sense involved in the economy of the firms. In their household, they shared incomes, expenses, and household tasks. They had shared bank accounts, and Tor had managed their private household economy for many years, keeping track of income and expenditures. Pernille described this as a rational division of household labour. Her husband was 'good with numbers', she was not, and she was glad that Tor volunteered to do what she considered a boring (*kedelig*) task 'I am not good with numbers, but Tor is, so I leave him that responsibility'.

In the initial phase after Pernille opened her yarn shop, she was completely dependent on her husband financially. During the first year, Pernille did not allow herself more than three monthly salaries. She reinvested all the profits from the yarn shop back into the firm.

When Pernille considered starting her own business, she had been worried about keeping track of the bookkeeping tasks and other 'numbers'. Tor supported his wife, encouraged her to start her own firm, and volunteered to take care of the firm's finances. He did the bookkeeping, paid the bills, and made sure that her finances were in order. We can explain such division of labour simply by preference. Pernille preferred mowing the lawn; Tor preferred taking care of the bills. In other families, it was vice-versa.

Pernille sold much of her yarn through her online shop, and every day she had to send out packages from the post office. However, because Pernille was alone in her shop, and she and the post office shared the same opening hours, she was again dependent on her husband, who had a much more flexible day, consisting largely of travelling around the city to visit customers. Whenever Pernille received an online order, she would pick up the phone and call for 'the postman' (a humorous, slightly condescending nickname for her husband). Tor would come by the shop at some point during the working day to pick up the orders and bring them to the post office. This service performed by her husband gave Pernille a double benefit for Pernille and her firm. Tor's firm had a business account at the post office, which gave him discounts. As a good illustration of the entanglement of his business, her business, and their private lives, Tor used his business account when he sent packages for his wife's firm, and consequently, Pernille's mail expenses were tied to her husband's firm, not hers. Pernille thought this was a great arrangement, as it saved her business a relatively large expense. Tor's firm, on the other hand, had a strong enough economy to afford Pernille's packages.

Pernille and Tor's situation illuminates the invaluable importance family plays to the owner and the business economically, through favours and division of household labour. Very much like farmer, fisher and craft households, these ostensibly one-person shops are in fact dependent on family labour as well.

Sally, another of my business owners, was a woman in her 50s. She had a boyfriend, but he was not involved in the firm, except occasionally when his IT-expertise was needed to fix a problem with the web shop or computer system. Sally and her partner lived in an apartment building owned by Sally's mother. Her mother was the former owner of the toy shop, which she now owned and managed. The entire first floor and basement of the apartment building functioned as a storage for Sally's toy shop, although her mother owned the actual property. Sally described herself as one of the many entrepreneurial women in her family. She told me stories of women generations back, who in diverse ways had independently fought their way through a patriarchal, male-dominated society and established businesses. Her grandmother had come from an aristocratic class of landowners (*godsejere*), and thanks to bilateral property inheritance, the grandmother had owned a large property on the outskirts of the city. Sally described her grandmother as a woman who was 'ahead of her time' (*forud for sin tid*). Without a husband, alone with her children, she had maintained her wealth. She bought cheap, old furniture, redesigned them, and sold them as expensive designer furniture. Moreover, Sally comes from a family with 'old money' (*gamle penge*).

Sally's parents divorced in the 1970s, when Sally was a child. Pia, sold the family property in the outskirts of Aarhus and purchased an apartment building in the city. The building included a shop and a large bakery in the basement. Pia transformed the bakery into a storage room, and opened a shop, selling yarn, cloth diapers, and wooden toys on street level with a connected apartment. This was their home and business. In the 1970s, the structure of the city involved a decentralised distribution of businesses and housing properties, with a neighbourhood culture that contained both dwellings and local shops. In time, however, the structure of the city changed, and most businesses becoming concentrated in the urban core. Pia maintained that her business was her life. Her private life and business overlapped, and the thought of moving her business somewhere else than her home took many years to mature. It was only when a friend of hers who owned a shop downtown put down two months of rent on a second business premise next to his own that Pia agreed to try to manage a toy shop away from her home. She kept both shops for a few years, but eventually closed the one in her apartment building to follow developments in the centre of Aarhus. The old shop remained a storage area for inventory. Pia's customers were now familiar with the downtown unit. She explained that the reason why she discontinued one of the two shops was that she could not be two places at once, and that she could not trust 'strangers' (i.e. non-family employees) to manage the business according to her own values.[11]

Close to 40 years after Pia first established her yarn and cloth diaper business, she handed it over to her youngest daughter, Sally. Pia's oldest daughter had a career in Copenhagen, hours from Aarhus, and her son had cut himself off from the family. Pia, Sally, and Sally's daughter, Victoria, now 31, strongly identified themselves as independent women and were proud that men had never been involved in the firm. Sally's declaration that 'No man has ever set foot in this firm, and no man ever will' was characteristic of the way she managed her business. Sally firmly assured me that 'I come from a long line of independent women, and we will remain like that'. However, men were not absent. The women were glad to tell me everything I wanted to know about the male members of their family. Yet they were always careful to make sure that I understood that these men had nothing to do with the firm. However, Sally had worked in her mother's firm while growing up, combined with caring for her younger brother while her mother worked in the shop. Sally's own daughter, Victoria, had worked in the shop since she was a teenager, and the boundaries between business/private life were blurred when mother and daughter spent time together every day in the shop, mixing roles as employer/employee one moment, mother/daughter the next. Sally had acquired the business after her older sister unsuccessfully tried to manage the shop. Sally's sister did not have what Pia and Sally described as 'the right energy', but when Sally took over management, she quickly quadrupled the revenue and proved herself a

---

[11] These sentiments and attitudes will be discussed in more detail in later chapters.

fit successor. Sally was educated both as a schoolteacher and a ceramist, something she believed to be essential to her success: she understood both art and children.

While the Aarhus shop-owners are not entrepreneurial capitalists, they are not unconcerned with profit-making or renewing and inventing new things and methods; these characteristics are not necessarily in opposition to each other. I argue that although the above described, and other factors, might be contributing characteristics — or motivations — to the individuals of this study, they are not the main characteristics that identify them as business owners. The Aarhus business owners fit much of the description of Smart and Smart (2005a) as 'petty capitalists'. As such, they are 'individuals or households who employ a small number of workers but are themselves actively involved in the labour process' (Smart and Smart 2005b: 3). The problem, however comes with Smart and Smart's emphasis on petty capitalists being some kind of intermediate category that is inherently unstable, as growth could threaten their livelihood altogether leading to bankruptcy and proletarisation, if not impoverishment. My Aarhus business owners do not fit this description very well. Several of them could afford to remove themselves from the daily routine of their shops, and thereby the main feature of the 'petty' designation (Smart and Smart 2005b: 4). However, their conscious choice to remain 'on the floor' seems to disqualify them from being simple 'capitalists'. Although the successes these individuals have had could allow them to step out of daily production or sales process, none of them have chosen to do so. The reason why they remain so actively involved in the daily routine of their business or shop lies with their motivation. Their initial motivation to start an enterprise was grounded in a wish to take part in the very production process: fish, yarn/knitting, quality toys, cosy café, unique custom jewellery, etc. Outsourcing this labour by hiring a manager would mean removing one of their main motivations for becoming a small business owner. The pride and self-fulfilment that these business owners achieve from taking part in the immediate production, direct sales, and customer contact takes precedence over material motivations. But this same motivation compels the business owners to remain small. Of course, the business owners are capitalist in the sense that they operate within a capitalist economy; they control their expenses and monitor income, and they channel profit back into the enterprise rather than simply spending it. Hence, they are not conspicuous consumers trying to show off wealth, nor are they motivated by capitalist principles of unrestricted growth and profit maximizing. A true capitalist might move their profits into more attractive sectors; the Aarhus shop-owners remain within their niche.

## Beyond the Suffering Subject

When I started research for this project, I did not set out to answer Joel Robbins' call for an 'anthropology of the good' (Robbins 2013). In his call to go 'Beyond the Suffering Subject', Robbins directed our attention to the tendency in anthropology to focus on the negative aspects of societies: to study the poor, the suffering, the exploited, those without hope, or any chance of ever achieving a good life. As I spent time with my business owners in their firms, I realized that the atmosphere in these firms and families was overwhelmingly positive. All their primary needs were met. They had plenty of food on their table every day, in all varieties, they lived in comfortable, modernized homes, they had jobs that they liked and enjoyed, they were surrounded by people whom they chose to be around, and they were generally happy.

When I finished fieldwork and started writing up my data, I did my best to view all the data from a critical perspective. I reminded myself that 'Yes, their lives were objectively good, but they worked 15 hours a day, they were exhausted, and there must be some discontent lurking somewhere in there'. I looked through my field notes, I scanned through my memories, photos, and all the data I had, in search of tell-tale signs that they were unhappy, that their lives were not as good as they had wanted. Surely, they did not walk around smiling, happy 24 hours a day, seven days a week. Indeed, there were plenty of conflicts, drama, and intrigues in the firms and families I came to know. Nevertheless, all the owners and the families I met focused overwhelmingly on the good things about their lives, not the bad. They had all certainly experienced hardships, loss, and rough periods, but they were not suffering, living in pain or poverty, being exploited, experiencing violence, or in any other way living in the kind of personal or existential crisis of which so much anthropology is focused (Robbins 2013). Nor were they a minority suffering from alienation or an abusive system. They were in many ways the average economic middle-class Danes living the lives they wanted to live (see Gundelach 2004 on the value survey).

Further, I found that the majority of the business owners can be characterised as being opposed to what Anders Lundkvist (2009a) refers to as *Dansk nyliberalisme* (Danish neoliberalism). Liberalism is characterised by privatisation, outsourcing, individualisation of the labour market, commercialisation of the public sector, and a liberalisation of international trade, with liberation of capital at its centre. Neoliberalism is characterised by the transformation of the public realm to fit the needs of the private sector (Lundkvist 2009c: 7). Encouragement of increased competition and opening up Denmark to foreign capital have in turn led to mergers and acquisitions in order to avoid competition and to ensure the survival of Danish firms in competition with international capital (Lundkvist 2009b: 28, 31). The state has approved these fusions under the pretext that they would result in lower prices. However, the result has been growing oligopolies in several sectors. A chart that illustrates how the Danish market has changed towards corporate capitalism (*selskabskapitalisme*) shows this development.

We shall see in the chapters that follow that the small Aarhusian business owners were driven by their conviction that they did business 'morally', and that this moral business stood in stark opposition to neoliberal market practices. I show that the creative and administrative freedom of being their own boss is the main motivation for the shop keepers. They belong to a category of business owners that define themselves as outside the mainstream market. They do not see themselves as having been marginalized; rather, they have consciously chosen not to follow the development of the market. Attached to this kind of morally-based business autonomy are ideas of fairness and trust. Fairness and trust are practices that are acted out in the relationship between merchant and consumer, between supplier and buyer, and as an overall moral guide to how a business should be run.

Although my business owners in many ways fit Smart and Smart's definition of petty capitalists, their opposition to the ideals of the contemporary neoliberal capitalist market economy and their dedicated resistance to liberal economic development restrain me from simply adopting such a term. In search of a concept to describe these business owners, I find the term 'small business owner' to be more suitable as a clustering concept within which all these business owners can comfortably fit. The word 'petty', may encourage negative associations of vulnerability and lack of strength, qualities that do not fit the individuals represented here. However, the word's origin from French '*petite*' (small) is more fitting. As individuals and persons, there is little vulnerability or weakness in any of my business owners. They work hard, they get things done, and *bricoleurs* in ensuring that things will work out.

## Point of View

This is an ethnography. The material presented here derives from ethnographic fieldwork which always aims to represent the native point of view. It aims at analysing the data gathered from conversations, observation, and participation together with knowledge of history, politics, geography, and economy. The analysis is based on the micro-perspective attained from long-term participant-observation, combined with a macro-perspective attained from all the above. Since anthropology is always comparative, another important influence on the analysis of my own data derives from the scholarly literature on similar topics, in this case, literature on 'the market'. In-depth knowledge of theoretical approaches to the market has no value unless we have an idea of how our interlocutors perceive the world around them. In order to avoid unfortunate generalizations, we need to be aware of the internal discourses of the societies we study (Gullestad 1990). How is 'the market' perceived and what meaning does reference to 'the market' have in the context of my Aarhus shop-owners? My argument that these business owners see themselves in opposition to the prevailing 'market' discourse is based on my own fieldwork together with various discussions of the relations between small business owners and neoliberal market capitalism. There are many explanations for the business owners' opposition to the market principles in which they operate. One explanation posits that business owners act within a market that has traditionally been regulated by a social democratic government acting according to principles of universal welfare capitalism (Esping-Andersen 1990). Danish small business owners have grown up in a nation and in an era in which social democratic principles of redistribution, community, and intimacy have been central in the political and public discourses (Andersen 1986; Dahl 1986; Borish 1996; Lundkvist 2009a; Bruun, Jakobsen and Krøijer 2011; Østergård 2012; Bendixen, Bringslid and Vike 2018). This means that certain policies which might benefit wage workers would be hostile to small business. For example, until the second decade of the 21st century, Danish retail opening hours have been limited to prevent shops from having to stay open at nights, Saturday afternoon or Sundays, the rationale here was to protect employees from having to work odd hours. Additional regulations, however, sought to help small shops by preventing the building of giant shopping malls that might threaten small businesses.

Although most of my business owners have degrees from higher educational institutions ranging from bachelor's degrees to PhDs, their educational backgrounds are generally not directly relevant to their businesses. In fact, most of the owners see little relationship between the kind of education they acquired and the business they operate. For instance, Julian, the goldsmith, has a degree in computer science. Marie holds a PhD in natural sciences but now bakes bread and cakes in her own bakery. Pernille was trained as a chef, but now owns and operates a yarn shop. Julian insists that the reason why he became a goldsmith and opened his own shop was that his former computer job had robbed him of the possibility to create and see the results of his creation. Similarly, Marie and Ole admitted that they constantly used their analytical skills, from their background as researchers, to analyse developments in their current firm and products.

Sally was certain that her background as a schoolteacher and a ceramist was crucial to her success in running her toy shop. The degree of informants' awareness of their opposition to the market varies, and reference to the market is mainly an umbrella concept under which I compare these business owners. Common to them all is a motivation to lead 'a good life' which they see is opposed to market principles of profit maximizing.[12]

## Structure of this Book

This book is divided into two parts. Part one focuses on the political and theoretical background of the study, where we present the key questions, methodology, and political and moral background. Part two focus on the two main pillars of running a small business: family structure and moral values. The background, family, and motivations thus constitute the essential components of my main argument: that these independent business owner-operators represent a part of society, which although tied to the market, nevertheless opposes neoliberal corporate capitalism. The historical and political background discussed in the first two chapters enables us to reflect upon the fact that the business owners, with their moral motivations, can afford to have precisely these moral principles because of the political and economic circumstances within which they act. Similarly, we shall see that family bonds are central to the reproduction and generational transfer of moral values.

Chapter 2 provides a historical and political review of topics of Danish historical, social, and political developments that are relevant to understanding the lives of modern small business owner-operators. Of major importance here is the political development of the state, leading to the birth of a social democratic welfare state. Emphasis on the welfare state can help us understand the kind of choices and life situations of the Aarhus business owners. An introduction to the political and economic situation of Denmark and of Aarhus municipality also fulfils this purpose.

Chapter 3 discusses the main analytical concepts applied in my analysis. It discusses morality and values in anthropology and identifies some of the relevant emic concepts used by my informants. The identification of discourses and perceptions about moralities and values involves a discussion of the overlapping concepts that have dominated the ethnography of Scandinavia for decades.

---

[12] There is nothing special about an anthropologist discussing business owners with non-economic motivations. Discourses of a human economy and a movement away from theories of rational man have been prominent long enough for us to be open to accept such an argument, and this thesis will discuss individuals who to a large extent have operated with the notion of a human economy (Hart, Laville and Cattani 2010).

Chapter 4 introduces Ikan, the family fishmonger firm with whom I spent most of my time. It goes through the history of the firm and discusses the possible reasons it underwent a major upheaval, where a younger sibling suddenly replaced the daughter and son-in-law who had been operating the firm. The case illustrates the deviant expectations between generations and the tensions and conflicts that occur when outgoing and incoming generations have different moral perspectives. In this chapter, I review the moral complexities involved, highlighting the importance of following the perception of a shared morality and the consequences that deviation from these norms might entail.

Chapter 5 discusses succession and highlights the challenges and paradoxes involved in the generational transfer of firms. I present the bureaucratic challenges involved, as well as the conflict of interests between the owning and the successor generations. The main argument is that transferring the 'right' values seems to be of utmost importance in the transfer of the physical firm to the next generation. Most of my small business owners are themselves children of small business owners, but most of them did not take over management of their parents' firm. Rather, they started their own niche business. Hence, while having inherited values from their parents, they have nevertheless established their own firm independent from their parents and do not plan for their children to continue the firm.

Chapter 6 discusses work and labour. It addresses the experiences and sentiments related to work and the significance of work and the work ethic to small business owner-operators. Not surprisingly, I find that taking initiative and the relations these individuals have with their work is an embedded part of their very identity. By insisting that the work they do in their firms is not perceived as drudgery, and that work and life cannot be separated, these business owners remain motivated by the freedom and sense of control that comes with self-employment, regardless of their long hours spent in their shops.

Chapter 7 illuminates the various motivations that lie behind the shop-owners' daily activities. The motivations described are directly related to most of the fundamental concepts in Scandinavian ethnography and coalesce with existing, dominant political and popular discourses on Danish values. Motivations thus contribute to the reproduction of what I have identified as a specific type of small business morality among my informants, a morality which one also finds in generalized Danish discourses about identity and personhood. I also argue that by this sentiment that they act as morally-based business people is an important element in their feeling that they are successful business owners, able to stand against the more impersonal, neoliberal market.

The final ethnographic chapter, Chapter 8, elaborates on the motivations analysed in Chapter 7, with an emphasis on the distinction between these business owners and the market in general. Mood, control, and the existence of a sociality inherent in the kinds of good they sell, and how they sell them, are important aspects of their contrast to the mainstream market. I illustrate how these shop-owners value the freedom of being their own boss to the extent that market principles of profit maximization and growth become ideas that they define themselves as being against.

Finally, I conclude that my interlocutors' primary motivation is not to oppose neoliberal market capitalism simply for the sake of opposition. Instead, the business owners grounded their motivation in their wish to protect their own agency of small-scale niche business without the intention of growth beyond a certain scale. The Aarhus business owners were concerned primarily with their aim of living a good life as self-employed, doing something they enjoyed and sharing their enthusiasm with their community and customers. I suggest the global market can learn from the independent business owners and move towards a more ethical and sustainable market, allowing for growth of independent business owners and a reduction of monopolies and oligopolies. But we need more research about what makes these small firms work. Are the sentiments these business owners expressed common for small niche business owners other places? Do small, independent farmers share similar sentiments? These are some of the questions we might seek to answer in further research.

*Chapter 2*
# What's Happening in the State of Denmark? Political Economy and Welfare State Capitalism

Denmark is a highly developed welfare state with a strong social safety net which imposes regulations on businesses and supports a strong labour force. This chapter emphasizes the areas of the Danish economic and political history that is relevant to the Aarhus business owners and their moral way of doing business. This chapter deals mainly with the period from 1800s until today, placing emphasis on the homogeneous nation-state. The political development that grew out of the unification of the Danish *folk* through the Lutheran church, laid the groundwork for the Danish welfare state. The chapter discusses the role of religion in the development of the welfare state. Finally, the chapter presents statistical and analytical data concerning the current financial situation of the Danish market and nation-state. It then reviews current data on self-employment and entrepreneurship, and some of the financial and political implications affecting the business owners directly.

## A Brief Economic History of Aarhus

Although contemporary Scandinavia is renowned for being a unique and separate region in terms of language, economy, and their successful universal welfare states, historians describe the region's long connectedness with the other nations on the Eurasian continent (Gullbekk 2008; Hedeager 2008). In fact, sociologist Johan P. Árnason (2009: 20) criticises civilizational studies for a tendency to think of civilizations as 'mutually closed worlds', and claims that their interaction is 'one of the most fundamental constitutive features of world history' (2009: 20–1).

Aarhus is one of Scandinavia's oldest cities. It was an important location for power and economic activities from as early as the fourth century and far into the Middle Ages (Hedeager 2008). With a large natural harbour, Aarhus became a convenient trading location, enabling maritime goods to reach northwards, southwards and westwards to the whole of

Jutland. After the Reformation, merchants' houses gradually expanded, and by the mid-nineteenth century – with a large expansion of the harbour in 1847/1861 and construction of a railway connecting Aarhus with the town of Randers to the north in 1862, Aarhus became a central location for business and import/export.

Throughout its history, Aarhus has been dependent on the surrounding districts for the export of farm produce. Despite the more recent development of a large tertiary service sector, the harbour, with its characteristic cranes, bears witness to the importance trade in Aarhus economic life. Thanks to the fertile soil of eastern Jutland and the many large farms in the districts surrounding Aarhus, the region was, and is, a major producer of agricultural goods (Larsen 2017). Amongst others, Arla Foods, one of the largest dairy groups in Europe, has its headquarters in Aarhus. The Swedish-Danish vegetable oils and fats company, AarhusKarlshamn (AAK) also has a large processing plant in the area. In fact, oil and fat industry has a long history in Aarhus, starting with the Danish Preserved Butter Company, which exported butter to Asia, Great Britain, and Africa. Aarhus is thus a natural place to establish a business.

## From Monarchy to Union of the Folk

Scandinavia is characteristically perceived as different from the rest of Europe and North America in terms of economy, welfare, and individualist egalitarianism. Why is this so?

One answer, can be seen in the development of social democracy and the welfare state (Mønnesland 1995: 146). Since the industrial revolution in the eighteenth century, the country evolved from a position as a powerful monarchy with control over large and important areas of Scandinavia to a homogenous rump state where the democratic involvement of the people in government decisions combined with sameness (*lighed*) and justice (*retfærd*) have been central objectives.

The Danish kingdom enjoyed prosperity from 1660 until the 19th century, when it ruled over Denmark-Norway and the Duchies of Schleswig and Holstein. In addition, Denmark had colonies in the West Indies, West Africa, and India. In 1814, the kingdom shrank when it lost Norway to Sweden, and later, in 1864, Holstein and Schleswig to Prussia, inducing the lower classes to start organizing for civil rights. The Danish Liberals allied with the peasant movements and formed the political party, *Bondevennerne* ('Friends of the peasant'). By the mid-19th century, demands for a written constitution had been achieved (Østergård 2012). This marked the beginning of the Danish national state, which in a few decades would begin to establish genuine welfare institutions.

Political scientist Gøsta Esping-Andersen (1990a), and sociologist Peter Gundelach (2004a) have argued that the Danish welfare state grew out of the working class's attempt and success in establishing a more cohesive society. The state managed to resurrect and gain support from the people by 'personifying ideals of the Enlightenment thinkers' (Østergård 2012: 52). Focus turned from an orientation towards Europe to an orientation towards the north. This turn inwards, as the Danish historian Uffe Østergård (2012) argued, resulted in a homogeneous nation-state that proclaimed ideals of homogeneity and facilitated the growth of a workers' party. Today, the political discourse indicates that history is about to repeat itself. In the 2015-2017, not just the far right, Populist Party, *Dansk Folkeparti*, but also most political parties refer to Danish ideals of homogeneity and sameness (and Christianity) as part of Danish core values.[13]

Denmark combines its past as a large composite, European empire which following the loss of territories and most of its non-Danish speakers ended up as a small, homogeneous nation-state (Østergård 2012). Other societies and structural models have influenced the development of Denmark as a state, but the governing classes continued to have a close relationship with the inhabitants in the cities and countryside and, in this way, continued to listen to the voices of its people. Due to its small size and population and its decentralised administration, Denmark remains one of the most homogenous countries in Europe (Vike 2016).[14] The Danish right-wing parties, have used homogeneity to argue against mass immigration and recognition of multi-ethnic society, claiming that their interest is to protect a culturally and ethnically homogeneous Denmark through a strict integration policy.

Scandinavian homogeneity is apparent also in the way religion and politics were closely connected and overlapping. From the end of the sixteenth century until 1849, when the king signed the constitution, Lutheranism was the only legal religion in Denmark, as well as the rest of the Nordic countries. The enlightenment theologian, Nikolai Frederik Severin Grundtvig (1783–1872) promoted principles of 'one language, one culture, one belief, one church, one state, and one nation' in the reformed unification of Denmark (Lodberg 2001: 17). Lutheranism developed into an everyday religion that determined one's actions and was meant to fill the individual with a 'tireless enthusiasm' for the benefit of the people and the well-being of all (Koch 1943: 29). Grundtvig's ideals encouraged an enthusiastic work ethic that served the public good.

---

[13] See for example Tulinius (2016), Hovbakke (2017) and Ritzau (2017a, 2017b).

[14] Even taking into account recent immigration from Southern Europe, North Africa and Asia, Denmark's immigrant population of 8 % is among the lowest in Europe (Vike 2016).

Historian, Mette Frisk Jensen (2014), argued that Danish Lutheranism, following the ruling class, transformed the Danish administration towards what she refers to as a Weberian model of bureaucracy. The Weberian model implies a reduction of maladministration, in the form of corruption, and increased state control. Jensen thus credits Lutheranism and a 'Weberian model of bureaucracy' for making Denmark – and Scandinavia – a country with a comparatively low level of corruption.

Protestantism in Scandinavia thus encouraged values of individualism and collective association (Stråth 2012). It encouraged the growth of individualism and liberalism, combined with a sense of unity against the most brutal aspects of the growing market economy (Gullestad 1992; see discussion on egalitarian individualism in Bruun, Krøijer and Rytter 2015).

Today, the church is important in Denmark, not because religion is important to the individual Dane, but because the many church buildings and the church as a public institution offers a convenient venue for community activities. Data from a large Danish value survey indicates that the community church-goers no longer seek the church congregation as such but rather a general feeling of community (*fællesskab*) as family (Andersen and Lüchau 2011). Danish families find it a comforting (*hyggelig*) 'tradition to go to church on Christmas Eve' (Gundelach 2011: 16). These same churches might be nearly empty on a normal Sunday service.

## Welfare State Capitalism: The Development of the Danish Welfare State

We cannot fruitfully compare Aarhusian small business owners with shopkeepers in other Eurasian nation-states without some idea of the role of the welfare state in Denmark. Motivations for a good life, and the shopkeepers' lack of concern for profit-maximizing, are due partly to the fact that these individuals operate within a national state that offers universal welfare benefits, ensuring a certain level of material comfort and social safety net for all its citizens, regardless of their social class, employment status, or geographical location (within the country). All the small business owners were aware that if they failed completely in their business activities, they would still have food on the table, shoes on their feet, and a roof over their head. They would still receive free health services and their children would have the same opportunity for free, higher education. In fact, it is likely that they would be able to keep the same car and house, and if they wanted to, they would probably obtain a new job within the first year of unemployment. My informants thus found themselves within a system of social security that has been placed in the category Esping-Andersen defines as a de-commodifying welfare state (see Esping-Andersen 1990 for different welfare state models).

The Scandinavian welfare states, in contrast to most other welfare states, are categorised as institutional, universal, de-commodifying, and social democratic. They endeavour to ensure all their citizens, independent of their social or economic means, equal rights, full employment, and maintaining a quality of life independent of the market. This extensive welfare state evolved over several decades. Hence, what is described as the unique equalizing strategies of the Scandinavian welfare states emerged only in the late twentieth century (Esping-Andersen 2015).

Although Esping-Andersen described Scandinavian welfare states as among the most de-commodifying, even in Denmark, you still need state approval and control to get maternity benefits, sickness benefits, job benefits and other benefits. However, if you have lived, worked and paid taxes in Denmark, and if you are member of a union (*a-kasse*), you have rights to welfare benefits also when you voluntarily leave a job. Welfare goods involve the right to sickness insurance, unemployment insurance, parental leave, and educational leave, where the individual (following a state certification procedure) receives nearly the same amount as their normal wage for a period of several months or longer. Scholars have tended to categorise Denmark as universal and de-commodifying, but in some areas the policies are considered liberal and means-tested. In fact, the Danish government has gradually introduced new policies, which are influenced by a liberal, commodifying approach to the welfare state (Pedersen 2011). For example, it is now harder to get unemployment benefits if you are not member of a (privatized) workers union (*a-kasse*).

Before World War II, Denmark had a small, but open economy that relied heavily on trade with other European countries. After the war ended in 1945, there began a period referred to as 'The Golden Age' or the three golden decades. This period marking the beginning of welfare state development (Esping-Andersen 1990a; 1996; Andersen et al. 2014). In the Nordic countries, prosperous, growing economies with increased workforce participation inspired a need for the state to take responsibility for areas where family and women had previously played the key roles (e.g. childcare). In fact, scholars seem to agree that female participation in the work force is the main feature that marks the beginning of the welfare state era (see for example Esping-Andersen 1990b, 2015; Andersen et al. 2014).

What distinguished the Scandinavian welfare states from other welfare regimes was a shift at the end of the twentieth century that emphasised equalization of opportunities on two main points: women and children (Esping-Andersen 2015: 125–9). This involved an increased incentive to facilitate female employment and gender equality (understood as equal opportunities and requirements), education reforms, and efforts to avoid child poverty. The development of a universal childcare system involved a very generous child-allowance, parental leave, and a universal pre-school system, where all incentives were focused mainly on enhancing female (workforce) participation (unlike other countries, Denmark did not prioritize part-time day-care centers). Denmark, as a welfare state, has succeeded in creating a dual-earner society with a very high percentage of female participation in the labour force.

These developments have contributed to gender equality in the sense that they made it possible for women to combine career and family (Esping-Andersen 1996a: 13). The encouragement of female workforce participation has been presented by politicians as an incentive to promote gender equality, but, as ethnologist Thomas Højrup noticed it has been equally important as a strategy to enhance economic growth through dual-earner families (Højrup 2002: 289). Of the 27 EU countries, Denmark has the highest number of dual-earner families and the word housewife (*hjemmegående husmor*) is rarely heard (Schultz-Jørgensen and Christensen 2011: 31). Denmark has the highest proportion of working mothers in the world (Schultz-Jørgensen and Christensen 2011: 31).

It appears that Danes have a sense of ownership towards the welfare state, because it originated from the people's own involvement (Esping-Andersen 1990b; Gundelach 2004b; Klitgaard 2007; Vike 2018). The Danish welfare state grew out of the working class's initiative to create a more solidary society. Since the social reforms started in the first half of the twentieth century, the Danish population has grown accustomed to general social security, involving universal education, extensive health services, and publicly financed cultural programs (Bruun, Krøijer and Rytter 2015). The growing challenges facing welfare states involve large, ageing populations together with shrinking contribution years. When the Scandinavian welfare states were fully established in the 1960s, an average worker was employed from age 16 to 65 and benefitted from 7–8 years of retirement (Esping-Andersen 2000: 2–3). Nowadays, workers finish their education and start working full-time when they are 20–30 years old, and early retirement can be as early as 60 (Esping-Andersen 2000: 2–3). As a method to handle these challenges, the state reduced unemployment benefits and it instituted an early retirement scheme.[15] Although the Danish government introduced new

---

[15] The Danish government has gradually reduced unemployment benefits from 8.5 years in 1993 to two years in 2016, now with more strict demands on the unemployed to demonstrate active job-seeking be willing to take job offers that are not necessarily relevant to their education or experience (Beskæftigelsesministeriet). The early pension scheme, for citizens

policies to increase the age of early retirement, the number of contributing years remained shortened and receiving years prolonged due to the population's increased longevity and longer educations. Incentives to reduce social expenditures involve reducing for those unemployed. To encourage workforce participation, active members of the workforce are entitled to 52 weeks of maternity and parental leave, heavily state subsidised day-care for all children below school age, 37-hour work week, and five weeks paid holiday.

Decline in benefits to the elderly and other inactive citizens, in favour of active, contributing citizens, is a strategy known as the 'social investment approach'. The intention is to ensure the future of the welfare state (Esping-Andersen 1996a: 14). However, this approach risks a collapse of full employment when the limits of public employment growth are reached and employment must rely more heavily on the private sector service economy (Ploug 2003).

Although the number and proportion of unemployed citizens is relatively low in Denmark compared many other OECD (Organisation for Economic Co-operation and Development) countries, 'flexibility' is the new word to describe success in the labour market.[16] As long as the worker is flexible, willing, and able to adjust to changes and developments in the labour market, they are more likely to remain within the work force.[17] The introduction of a labour market model known as *Flexicurity* reflects the Danish government's commitment to a labour market built on flexibility and social security. The Danish government introduced *Funktionærloven* (the Act on Salaried Employees) to protect managerial employees from job insecurity. However, employers have their ways of avoiding the Salaried

---

between the ages 60–65, implied an offer of *efterløn* as a reward for long employment. The scheme offered early retirement at 60, with a pension equal to their average salary for the five years preceding the normal pension age of 65. There should be no need to say that although those entitled to *efterløn* had paid a contribution for 30 years or more, the scheme is costly for the state budget. The scheme is therefore being gradually phased out, with small reductions every few years. The *efterløn*-age has been raised to 62, and the individual must have paid *efterløn* contributions for at least 30 years, and receives a maximum of 92 per cent of their salary (Styrelsen for Arbejdsmarked og Rekruttering 2017).

[16] The Danish unemployment rate is at 6.3 per cent of the labour force in 2016, which is much lower than virtually all EU and OECD countries, such as Spain 18.7 per cent, Turkey 11.6, Germany 3.9, Russia 5.4, EU average 8.2 and OECD average 6.2 per cent of the national labour force (OECD 2017).

[17] In order to avoid a discussion of the new precariat, which I leave for others more informed of these debates than me, I use the word 'flexible' or 'flexibility' to characterise recent developments in the (labour) market. The choice of wording is inspired by the Danish government's discourse of what they call *Flexicurity*.

Employees Law by hiring employees part-time and paying them by the hour instead of offering them full-time contracts with fixed salaries.

Since the 1990s, neoliberal ideas have slowly emerged together with growing right-wing populism. The government has promoted privatization and contracting out of public responsibilities, such as healthcare, transport, infrastructure maintenance, etc. Other changes involve an increased focus on cost-effective performance and a more market-oriented welfare state, known as competition state (*konkurrencestat*) (Pedersen 2011). Danish political scientist Ove Kaj Pedersen argued that the Danish welfare state is being transformed into a competition state, promoting neoliberal principles of increased competition at national, international and municipal levels, optimization of each citizen, and increased focus on individual responsibility and adaptation, the idea being that each citizen is responsible for their own well-being. Whereas the welfare state promotes values of stability and security, *konkurrencestaten* is internationally oriented and promotes diversity of response, flexibility and competition for resources (Pedersen 2011: 12).

Pedersen's ideas sparked political debate, with some politicians arguing that the competitive state model was the preferred future welfare state (Bruun, Krøijer and Rytter 2015: 12). Anthropologists have suggested that a better way to describe recent developments in Scandinavian welfare states can be grasped through concepts of *forandringsstat* (shifting or transforming state) and *selvstændighedssamfundet* (independence-society) (Bruun, Krøijer, and Rytter 2015: 13; see also Bruun et al. 2016; Vike 2016). A focus on change as an aim characterises the transforming state. The Independence-society is meant to describe the moral economy that lies at the core of the shifting state (Bruun, Krøijer, and Rytter 2015: 13). The idea that the competitive state shifts from moralism to economism (financialization might be a better word), and from community to individual opportunism is important in this context because it contradicts some of the core concerns of my small business owners.

We can see examples of how the *Konkurrencestat* has evolved in reforms such as the 'Flexicurity' model. Denmark has undergone numerous reforms in the educational system and instituted increased control over new immigrants to make them more integrated and more accountable. A major structural reform of local administration has led to more bureaucratization and a larger gap between the individual citizen and administrative apparatus (Bruun, Krøijer and Rytter 2015: 11). Ethnologist Thomas Højrup argued that those reforms that have reduced welfare and 'economized' the system have been implemented with the support of the people (*folket*) and trade union movements (*fagbevægelser*) (Højrup 2002: 275). Højrup highlighted how, during different reforms and adjustments in welfare, different grass-roots movements have promoted demands using moral arguments about social justice and 'the good life' (Højrup 2002: 275).

There has been a significant change in the orientation of the Danish welfare state, from universality to competition, and this re-orientation began with Social Democratic governments in the 1990s and has continued through both Liberal and Social Democratic governments up to the present (Pedersen 2011; Lundkvist 2017). When the Danish state started to shift towards a more market-oriented welfare model, the government was careful to ensure that the population maintained a feeling that the welfare state was still an aim. Although the state has focused more and more on private economic matters and a liberal market economy, government leaders have never relinquished the principle of the welfare state as the most important element. It is only when the population stops believing in the welfare state, and welfare stops being a goal in its own, that the people governed state (*folkestyrede stat*) is threatened. My business owners also showed their concern for this development, as in the following statement:

> There are almost no small firms anymore. Everyone shops at Føtex or Bilka [hypermarkets owned by large corporations]. It is easier; often also much cheaper. They can make large sale offers to attract customers. They can buy large quantities at a cheaper price. Then they can afford to sell it cheaper, too, and still make a profit. We, for sure, don't have that opportunity (my translation).

This statement, uttered by fishmonger Poul, touches on the essence of the sentiments expressed by the small business owners I studied in Aarhus. In contrast, and opposition, to the large, corporate chains, the businesses I studied, were small, independent, and resilient in a market dominated by large corporate firms. The tensions between us (the small businesses) and them (large corporations) will be discussed thoroughly in Chapter Seven and Eight.

## 'Lige børn leger bedst'[18]: Inclusion and Exclusion

In a small, homogeneous country like Denmark, the involvement of the citizens is possible without the risk of a chaotic situation that could occur if an attempt at the same amount of popular involvement in government decisions took place in a larger, more diverse population group. But Scandinavia and Denmark are not extraordinary egalitarian societies, nor do they lack mechanisms for social exclusion. Historically, the obsession with sameness (*lighed*) has been an actively used rhetoric to achieve homogenic

---

[18] 'Equal children are better playmates', i.e. 'birds of a feather flock together'.

society with a culture where equity ideals are used as control mechanisms in obtaining and maintaining exclusive groupings on multiple levels of society from state level, to social groups of friends (Gullestad 1992). The profound idea that those who are equal (same) should go together contributes to a culture of exclusion.

British anthropologist Richard Jenkins dealt with the early and continuous institutionalisation of Danish children and the strong presence of the state in all areas of an individual's life (economic, health, relationship status, residence, to mention a few). Jenkins viewed this as the mark of a totalitarian state practicing what he referred to as a 'soft tyranny' in the 'watchful and inclusive community' (Jenkins 2011: 200–1). Jenkins is not alone in his perception of the Danish state as particularly watchful and intrusive (see also Vike 2004). Anthropologist, Karen Fog Olwig (2011), similarly described how children start their civilizing project (*dannelsesproces*) as soon as they start kindergarten. The civilizing project is not coincidental. Anthropologists have argued for 'individual egalitarianism', meaning that ideas of egalitarianism encounter ideologies of individualism – understood as independence – by avoiding social groups and contexts that are different, and by adjusting national values of *fællesskab* (community) and *lighed* (equality as sameness) to individual understandings of shared concepts (e.g. Gullestad 1992; Bruun, Krøijer and Rytter 2015: 17). These variations and constitutions of hierarchy and exclusion are important in understanding Scandinavian egalitarianism (sameness), but it is equally important to understand the implications of this kind of conformity for Scandinavian sociality and society. The development of the Danish welfare state has encouraged a growth not of individual egalitarianism, but conformity (Bruun, Krøijer and Rytter 2015: 21–2). What may appear as individualism, an increased demand for independence, is in fact dominated by increased monitoring and standardising, with sameness or homogeneity as the result (Vike 2004; see also Olwig and Pærregaard 2011; Gilliam 2016).

The Danish state has ascribed it as their task and goal to civilize (*danne*) all Danish citizens (and new immigrants) so as to ensure the re-production of Danishness (*danskhed*), which is bound up with nation-statehood. The detail of state involvement is constantly increased and is evident in new laws, reforms, and detailed *læreplaner* (teaching curricula) in both school and day-care institutions (*vuggestue/børnehave*). In 2006, the Danish government started the introduction of the *heldagsskole* (literally full-day schools), with mandatory classroom teaching from 8 a.m. to approximately 3 p.m., five days per week, for all Danish schoolchildren. In addition, various after-school options (SFO [*skolefritidsordning*]) are available for families who work longer hours.[19] This means that Danish children spend between 7–11 hours per day at public institutions, where teachers treat them according to specific pedagogical curricula (*pædagogiske læreplaner*), stressing 'cooperation' and social skills, or what we might term learning to conform.[20]

Although Danishness is far from constant, but rather paradoxical, and as pointed out by numerous ethnographers, in constant negotiation, the state places great emphasis on producing *dannede, lige* citizens who will 'fit in' (see Jenkins 2011; Bruun, Krøijer and Rytter 2015: 22; Gilliam 2016). These pedagogical understandings are willingly accepted and supported by the population, who accept the involvement of the state in nearly all matters of life. If the state and school can help children to 'fit in' better, then parents will accept most forms of control and intervention.

The tradition in the Danish welfare policies, with its focus on flexible and adaptable employment, has been to establish agreements between employers and employees through membership in trade unions or general framework agreements as promoted by the central government (Abrahamson 1992).[21] However, these arrangements, which have universal coverage, are only applicable in the labour market, among the so-called 'social partners' and do not apply to those members of society who belong to other categories. Social policies are generally means-tested and considered as charity, defined by strong social control (Abrahamson 1992). Whereas the Danish model maintains its focus on equality, full employment, and a high level of spending on social security and an active labour market policy, benefits are dependent on union membership or membership in a union-affiliated unemployment compensation fund (*arbejdsløshedskasse*) (Abrahamson 1992; Greve 2004). Full pensions are available only to those citizens who have been active members of the workforce for a large number of years and who have contributed into their union retirement account. The remaining members of society receive a much lower universal standard

---

[19] See Børne- og undervisningsministeriet [Ministry of Education]. *SFO* (https://www.uvm.dk/sfo-klub-og-fritidshjem/sfo/formaal--indhold-og-ansvar) for more information.

[20] I borrow Richard Jenkins' (2011: xv) interpretation of *Pædagog* to be 'the generic title for a range of professionals who specialize in the development of social and other competences'. Pedagogues are trained at special schools and can then specialize in early childhood up to youth age groups; they would typically work in day-care institutions, after-school clubs, youth centers, homes for troubled youth and juvenile detention facilities. *Pædagogiske læreplaner* refer to the official, municipally approved teaching programs that promote a practical approach to socialization in the widest sense (Jenkins 2011: 180).

[21] Examples of policies of general frameworks can be mandatory state labour-marked pension contributions (ATP), the Act on Salaried Employees (*Funktionærloven*), and universal maternity leave.

pension (*folkepension*), along with the possibilities of housing, heating, and other subsidies.

A comfortably, high level of social security is thus available only to active members of society. The fact that unions and business associations are widespread, and that they are directly involved in policy decisions related to the labour market, means that people are directly involved in policy-making through the many trade unions (Hall and Campbell 2017: 33) (about 70 per cent of Denmark's labour force are members of a trade union). Although the government subsidises trade unions, through tax deductions for union dues, those who are not able to work are far less privileged than those who are. Moreover, the strong focus on employment has made the state dependent on labour market participation. This has led those members of the population who can afford it to choose private service offerings instead of having to wait for public care. This development, in turn, leads to an increasing social gap and a move towards a more corporatist than a universal welfare model (Greve 2004: 166–7). However, inactive citizens are still entitled to social benefits, ensuring that no one falls completely through the social safety net. To the business owners, this meant that they were socially secured, and so were their employees. The flexibility of employment worked as a benefit for the employers, who were not responsible for the social security of employees. It was the responsibility of the state welfare system.

## The Meaning of Social Security

The business owners in this study make their life choices well aware of the protection offered by the Danish welfare system. As employers, their decisions regarding employees are also affected by employment laws. In practice, the Danish welfare system entitles any member of an unemployment insurance fund (arbejdsløshedskasse) and who has had full-time employment for 52 weeks or who has just graduated higher education to up to two years of unemployment benefits (*dagpenge*) over a three-year period (Beskæftigelsesministeriet). The insurance covers both employed and self-employed citizens. However, the unemployment benefit programmes have gone through drastic cuts over the last thirty years, from 8.5 years of unemployment benefits in 1993 to two years in 2016, with additional requirements for having had full-time work prior to filing for unemployment benefits. With more restrictive demands on the unemployed, Denmark has a high labour force participation ratio (80% aged 15–65 in 2016 [OECD 2018a: 63]). In relation to this, scholars agree that the Danish government has a tradition of focusing on employment over benefits (Rehn 1986; Nielsen and Kesting 2003; see Jensen 2007; Larsen and Andersen 2009).

It is reasonable to assume that the fact that small business owners know that the public welfare system could support them if they went out of business made them more prone to risk-taking than small business operators in other parts of the world. Simultaneously, it is important not to underestimate the importance of pride and self-fulfilment in entrepreneurial activity. The fact that Danish small business owners are more secure does not mean that they would simply relax and stay home if their business failed. The Aarhus business owners worked hard and possessed a motivation and strong will to succeed.

Moreover, we need to remember that Danes enter childcare institutions from an early age and what are believed to be Danish values, including the high consideration for work and providing for oneself, were thoroughly internalised (see Borish 1991; Christensen 1997; Jenkins 2011; Damm 2015).

Failing in business would certainly be a major blow to the individual's sense of self-worth, entailing great stress for those involved. The business owners would suffer not only materially but also psychologically. Another important aspect of the welfare state that aids us in understanding the mentality of Danish society, and the Aarhus business owners, in particular, is that due to the acute presence of the welfare state, the loss of their business would not deprive them of an opportunity to still have a good life doing something else.

In 1916, when the First World War ravaged across the European continent, Danish poet Jeppe Aakjær published a poem that criticised a mentality in the population that may still be relevant. The poem, titled *The Deepest Well Always Gives the Clearest Water/Som dybest brønd gi'r altid klarest vand,* originally *The Song of History/Historiens Sang,* and, perhaps the most renowned line:

> You weakling country that enjoys hygge in hiding while the whole world is burning around your cradle/Du pusling-land, som hygger dig i smug, mens hele verden brænder om din vugge' (Aakjær 1920).

The poem was a critique of the ignorance shown by Danish civil society towards the ongoing war, which did not affect Denmark considerably. In recent debates, the same poem, and especially this sentence, has been used to describe and criticise Danishness and the Danish tendency to stay on the side-lines of world problems (Christensen 2001; Rehling 2005; Metz 2014; e.g. Buhmann-Holmes 2018; Vestergaard 2018). The perception of being ensconced in the security of the welfare state, and the unwillingness to acknowledge changes in global economy, climate, and demographic mobility may be reflected in the way business owners do not worry about the economy or profit maximizing. The Danish mentality is that 'one need not worry', because Denmark is safe (*tryg*).[22]

At the other end of the scale of security, being self-employed implies adjusting to the welfare state in the form of regulations imposed on employers. Before hiring someone, the owner needs to consider whether there is a need for an employee not just momentarily, but in the long run. Employment protection laws aim at protecting employees from unreasonable temporary contracts and require the employer to consider the need for a new employee before offering a hiring contract. In several branches, such as office work, retail sector, or transport/storage, employers are obliged to give a three months' notice before ending a work contract, even when the employee has only just been hired. However, Denmark's flexicurity model is famous for the ease of which people can be hired and fired because the state takes care of them.

It is possible for most business owners to hire people on temporary contracts. The business owners I worked with commonly solved the challenge of avoiding permanent contracts by either hiring someone as a freelancer – meaning that instead of establishing an employee-employer relationship, the person hired to work at the firm was registered as self-employed and sent an invoice to the shopkeeper for hours worked[23] – or on a flexible paid-by-the-hour-contract. One would think that the amount of money paid for a freelance employee would amount to the same as a salaried worker, given that the independent contractor should calculate all their costs in their hourly wage. However, the employer can save knowing that in periods when less help is needed, there is no obligation to pay a salary, as the state can provide unemployment benefits. However, I discovered that in the firms that I researched, there existed a tendency among the freelancers to request a lower salary package than the 120–135 per cent that is the real labour cost of having an employee (i.e. the wages paid directly to the employee plus taxes, vacation payments and social security paid to the state or various benefit funds).[24]

---

[22] See also Sara Binzer Hobolt about Denmark's peculiar local orientation (Hobolt 2004).

[23] An employee hired as a freelancer is responsible for their own insurances, tax payments, vacation money (*feriepenge*) and pensions savings (Sand 2011, 2013; Moth 2016).

[24] The 120–135 per cent refers to the entire wage package which an employer must pay when hiring an employee. In addition to direct wage costs paid to the employee, the additional 35 per cent covers mandatory employer-paid vacation money, which amounts to 12.5 per cent of the salary, together with 'social contributions' such as the maternity leave fund and labour market pension (ATP). ATP is a compulsory pension savings account intended to ensure that citizens receive a little extra in addition to their public pension (*folkepension*). All Danish firms are obliged to pay for at least two-thirds of their employees' ATP contribution. The employee herself pays the remaining one-third. However, the ATP contribution is minimal,

Social security and high taxes bring financial restrictions and challenges for the business owner, especially when the question of generational transfer of the firm occurs. Various inheritance laws are intended to ensure a more equitable society and have been the subject of debate and policy changes in Scandinavia (Sweden and Norway abolished gift and inheritance taxes in 2004 and 2014, respectively). In the case where a business owner wants to pass on the firm to her children or other close family members, the transaction is subject to taxation as if the business were an item for sale. This means that the entire market value of the firm is due to taxation. Firms registered as a limited liability company are usually taxed at a rate of 42 % of market value (Nielsen 2014b). Even in cases where business owners treat the firm as a gift, the owners must calculate the market value of the firm and pay a gift tax. The state requires a fee of 15 per cent of market value when someone transfers a privately owned firm as gift or inheritance to the children or children-in-law. If the transfer comes from grandparents, they are accountable to a fee of 36.25 per cent. If the owners transfer a firm to someone outside the family, or more peripheral family members, the recipient is subject to a tax as if it were personal income if transferred as inheritance and a fee of 36.25 per cent if given as gift (or anticipatory inheritance).

Because the assets of a firm only rarely are counted as money in the bank, and more often according to the market value of the firm's total assets (including interior, goods, surplus value, potential income, and so forth) paying the nearly 50 per cent tax value is often impossible without deeply indebting the successor at the risk of the firm. Moreover, inheritance laws require equal distribution of the estate assets among all siblings, such that other children than the successor must be compensated (Nielsen 2014b).

An alternative strategy used by business owners who want to avoid the high taxes is to apply for the taxation to follow the successor. This means that the business owner avoids paying taxes when he or she transfers the firm to spouse, children and grandchildren, consensual partner, parents, siblings and their children and grandchildren, or to an employee who has been employed fulltime in the firm for at least three of the preceding five years. This exemption allows the transfer of firms from one generation to the next without bankrupting the previous generation. Instead, the successor generation 'inherits' the tax burden, together with the firm, and is obliged to pay the taxes for the firm only when selling the firm or its shares ('C.B.2.13.1 Familieoverdragelse med Succession' 2017). When arrangements like this are made, it is recommended that the firm be

---

amounting to DKK 284 per month (€40 in 2016) for a full-time employee. Employers must also pay compulsory work-related injury insurance (AES).

transformed into a limited liability company in order to further reduce the tax burden. However, inheritance of taxes (in Danish referred to as *successionen*), applies only to the market value of the firm, and not in the case when the firm, or parts of the firm, is transferred as gifts. In those cases, the firm is liable for tax regardless of other circumstances. The implications of the bureaucracy related to transfer of firms and the Aarhus business owners' solutions to these challenges will be discussed in depth in chapter five.

## Denmark in the World Economy

While Denmark has developed an effective re-distributional economy domestically, where do we place Denmark in the global market? Today, the Danish economy can be described as a 'coordinated market economy' implying a market capitalism governed by public and private arrangements (Hall and Campbell 2017: 33). One of the main questions that this thesis asks is 'How do small, independent firms cope in a constantly growing, competitive economy?' In order to answer this question, I have sought to understand the broader economic picture, of which the small firms in this study are part. In recent decades, Denmark has developed into one of the richest nations in the world with a Gross National Income (GNI) of 51,321 USD per capita[25] (OECD 2015a).[26]

### Yearly GNP growth, per cent

| 2004 | 2005 | 2006 | 2007 | 2008 | 2009 | 2012 | 2016 | 2017 |
|------|------|------|------|------|------|------|------|------|
| 2.3  | 2.4  | 3.4  | 1.6  | -1.1 | -5.2 | 0.1  | 1.1  | 2.3  |

Table 1. Danish annual GNP growth. (Source: Nielsen [2010: 7] and Trading Economics [www.tradingeconomics.com]).

Table 1 above, shows that the Danish GNP declined in the wake of the financial crisis of 2008 but has slowly increased in later years. Denmark's Gross Domestic Product (GDP) has had an annual growth rate of 1.63 per cent from 1991 to 2017 with an increase of 2.6 per cent in the second quarter of 2017. These numbers indicate a growing economic development and

---

[25] Adjusted to current prices and purchasing power parity (PPP).

[26] The Gross National Income (GNI) is defined by the OECD as gross domestic product, plus net receipts from wages, salaries, and property income in addition to taxes and subsidies. Also included are wages and salaries from residents who live and consume inside the country's borders but work abroad either long-term or short term. The focus is thus on cases where the economic interest of the person remains in the home country (OECD 2015b).

purchasing power in the population (see Danmarks Statistik n.d.). Although Denmark was one of the first European countries to impose lockdown due to the global pandemic Covid-19 in 2020–21, the country's economy proved resilient. The GDP declined by two per cent in the first quarter of 2020, expecting to rise to more than four percent in 2021.

Public services constitute the largest part the Danish Gross National Product. This is followed by the production industries and other manufacturing businesses. Service businesses are the third largest contributor.

The Gross Domestic Product in Denmark was worth 306 billion US dollars in 2016 (The World Bank 2017). According to Trading Economics,[27] the GDP value of Denmark, represent 0.49 per cent of the world economy. Considering that Denmark has only 5.8 million citizens,[28] this shows that Denmark has a relatively strong economic position in the global market.

Nevertheless, being one of the richest nations in the world has other consequences. According to Statistics Denmark (*Danmarks Statistik*), Denmark is the most expensive country in the EU, with a price level 36 per cent above the EU average (Andersen and Bosanac 2016). Nevertheless, these numbers tell us nothing about the relative price level in the country, since Danish average pre- and post-tax wages are also significantly higher than those of other EU countries. One way of understanding the relative cost of living in Denmark, is to apply a Purchasing Power Standard.

**GNP per Citizen Based on Purchasing Power Standard in Euro**

|  | **2012** | **2013** | **2014** | **2015** | **2016** |
|---|---|---|---|---|---|
| **EU average** | 26,500 | 26,700 | 27,500 | 28,700 | 29,000 |
| **Denmark** | 33,500 | 33,700 | 34,500 | 35,500 | 36,400 |
| **Germany** | 33,000 | 33,300 | 34,600 | 36,000 | 35,700 |
| **Hungary** | 17,200 | 17,700 | 18,600 | 19,500 | 19,500 |
| **UK** | 28,600 | 29,000 | 30,000 | 31,600 | 31,200 |
| **Sweden** | 33,600 | 33,300 | 33,700 | 35,400 | 35,900 |

Table 2. GNP per citizen, by country. (Source: Jensen [2018]).

---

[27] Trading Economics (tradingeconomics.com) is an international website providing historical as well as current financial status for various countries.

[28] For comparison, Germany has a population of more than 80 million and GDP at 5.59 per cent of the world economy according to Trading Economics.

According to a set Purchasing Power Standard, accounting for differences in living expenses in the different countries, Denmark has maintained a strong GNP and purchasing power (see Table 2 above). Denmark has a relatively high national income, and the distribution of wealth is significantly higher than in other countries with similar or higher GNI. The welfare state ensures that inequality of opportunities is minimal and that no one falls through the social safety net. It ensures all citizens the same quality primary education, free health services, and heavily subsidised day-care for children (80 per cent). This system encourages dual earner households and support for single parents, diminishing the risk of acute child poverty.

The Danish economy has not gone unaffected by fluctuations in the international market economy, such as the global financial inflation of the 1980s, the 2008 crisis and the Covid-19 economic downturn of 2020. Despite these downturns analysis shows that the Danish economy has recovered and continued to grow (Formandskabet 2016), and even under the Covid-19 crisis, most sectors of the Danish economy have remained reasonably robust, and unemployment has only risen slightly.

Furthermore, the Danish government has developed a security system that protects large financial institutions from bankruptcy. After the 2008 global financial crisis, the government took responsibility for corporate loans that would have destroyed most of the Danish economy. As a consequence, the Danish state is in deeper debt, but at least the national banks and financial institutions are now inoculated against bankruptcy (Lundkvist 2009a). Corporate immunity has encouraged large corporations to take greater risks, because they are aware of their protection against bankruptcy. By reenforcing large capitalism more pressure is placed on small, independent businesses; hence, a growing number of oligopolies and monopolies are dominating more and more branches in the Danish market (Lundkvist 2009a, 2017). This is also a global trend that is recognised as a consequence of capitalism (Wallerstein 2004; Tsing 2005). The state is also indebted by an amount that in 2015 corresponds to 54 per cent of the Gross Domestic Product (OECD 2018b). By comparison, the United States holds a debt that corresponds to 125 per cent of their GDP, Germany 79 per cent, and Hungary 97 per cent.

These statistics indicate the health of the Danish economy. Unemployment is relatively low, GDP is high, and income poverty rates are minimal. A report published by the OECD (2016a) includes an overview of basic statistics from 2014, where the labour participation rate for citizens in the 15–64 age-group was 78.1 per cent, six per cent above the OECD average of 72.7 per cent, and putting Denmark in first place in terms of employment rates. Furthermore, long-term unemployment (one year or more) in Denmark is as low as 1.7 per cent, far below the OECD average of 2.5 per cent.

Although Denmark as a nation is in good financial shape compared to many other OECD countries, maintaining a welfare state remains a costly affair, requiring constant adjustment to global market developments and to local conditions (Esping-Andersen 1990a, 1996a, 1996b, 2000, 2002, 2009). According to the national economic advisory board's quarterly report, the slow growth in Danish economy, reported from earlier years, is still relevant. However, after the United Kingdom voted to exit from the European Union, Denmark now has a higher rate of growth than most other European countries, which are more cautious after 'Brexit' (Formandskabet 2016). Recent Danish reforms have lowered personal taxes, but increased municipal taxes and lowered pension benefits, leaving the state with long-term positive numbers. With the aim of a structural balance, the financial advisory board predict an increase in the workforce, a strengthened economy, and a release of some of the current pressure on the labour market.

## Aarhus Business Life

Aarhus, as a municipality and an urban environment, views itself as a business centre of international standards. This carries important consequences for the small businesses in this study (Landström 2005: 104). In a 2015 report, Aarhus municipality expected to spend 25 per cent of the net communal budget on social transfers (Aarhus Kommune 2015). The local government stated that it focused strongly on employment and closely collaborated with local businesses in order to reach their aim for employment.[29]

Access to goods on the global market, a well-developed infrastructure, type of competition, and a group who are conscious about where goods are produced and under what circumstances, are among the important factors that affect the success of small businesses. Several of Denmark's largest industries are located in Aarhus. Aarhus based Vestas, the world's largest windmill producer, had a revenue of € 7.2 billion and 15,500 employees worldwide, of which 1730 were in Aarhus (in 2013). Søstrene Grene (The Sisters Grene) is another example of an Aarhus firm that has enjoyed great international success. As a cheap 'bits and bobs' chain, offering everything from candles to small furniture, Søstrene Grene's success in Scandinavia has spread rapidly across the world. Aarhus based Arla Foods, has more than

---

[29] Some of their aims include accumulating 2000 new jobs each year and ensuring that 95 per cent of youth obtain secondary education; they also plan to reduce long-term unemployment and work in closer collaboration with local firms (OECD 2016b).

19,500 employees around the world (1500 in Aarhus), and revenue of DKK 73.6 billion (€9.86 billion) (in 2013). Denmark's largest supermarket corporation *Dansk Supermarked* with its headquarters also located in Aarhus, with revenue of € 7.29 billion and 43,000 employees (in 2013).

National statistics tell us that Aarhus is second after the capital of Copenhagen in the number of self-employed persons across most industries. At the same time, an EU report from 2014, revealed that Denmark has the third lowest proportion of self-employed of all EU-countries (Danmarks Statistik 2014). Why would Danes rather be wage laborers than be their own boss? Considering the fact that wage work (*lønarbejde*), and especially public sector jobs, comes with social benefits that does not apply to the self-employed (*selvstændig erhvervsdrivende*) (such as pensions savings, holiday pay [*feriepenge*], and parental leave), that the public sector employs 30 per cent of the workforce and the growing numbers of oligopolies, these statistics are hardly surprising.[30] Another statistic shows that the main industries for Danish self-employment are trade and transport, 'other business services', agriculture, forestry and fishing, construction and real estate (Udenrigshandel 2014). The business owners I worked with all belonged to the category 'other business services'. Statistics from 2011 show that most independent firms in Aarhus offer services within the health sector, wholesale retail, trade, and consultancy (Antal beskæftigede personer bosiddende i Aarhus Kommune pr. 1 januar 2011 fordelt på erhvervsgrupper og arbejdsstillinger. 2011). Available statistics on self-employment also include a category for 'self-employed and helping spouse' (*selvstændig medhjælpende ægtefælde*), indicating that the self-employed are likely to be assisted by their spouse or life partner. This was also the case for nearly all the business owners I worked with in Aarhus. They were dependent on their family, in one way or the other, in order to successfully manage their firm. In Aarhus, 5.9 per cent of the active population are in this category (Budget og Planlægning, Borgemesterens afdeling, Aarhus Kommune 2014). The statistics do not clarify what is meant by a 'helping spouse', but Danes in general are familiar with the concept from the farmer household. They know that it refers to a spouse who may or may not be employed elsewhere, but who dedicates a significant amount of their time helping in their partner's farm or business, with or without being on the payroll.

As one of their main developmental goals, Aarhus municipality is seeking to increase the number of entrepreneurs. They have formed a committee for this new project, the goal of which is to encourage and work towards an increase in the number of newly and existing businesses, with the

---

[30] Average in the EU was 14.3 per cent, whereas Denmark measured 8.3 per cent (Eurostat 2003).

goal of creating more jobs (Aarhus Kommune 2011). One of the initiatives included in this plan is that of offering municipally supported funds to entrepreneurs (*iværksættere*) in need of initial capital to start a firm.[31] Nonetheless, the municipality also mentions 'networking' as an incentive to introduce new entrepreneurs to investors and national and international money lending institutions, such as Accelerace.[32] Both Aarhus and the capital city of Copenhagen have benefitted from an increase in entrepreneurship following the financial crisis in 2008 (Pallesen 2014). Whereas one in every 20 registered self-employed went out of business after the global financial crisis of 2008, Aarhus had a growth of 6–9 per cent during the period 2009–2014. One explanation for this growth lies with the encouragement of the municipality, which has entrepreneurship on its core list of municipal objectives. Will we see the same trend, post-Covid-19? The fact that Aarhus is an important city for tertiary education, with the highest proportion of students to the total population, has also contributed to the growth of entrepreneurship in Aarhus.[33] With support and encouragement from the municipality and a number of institutions directed toward encouraging entrepreneurship, entrepreneurial students are encouraged to remain in Aarhus after they finish their studies and establish a business there.[34]

Nevertheless, the focus on local, small-scale entrepreneurship in Aarhus and in Denmark generally has been a polarising issue. Along with incentives to encourage start-ups, national financial development has created a challenging environment for new, independent firms now that large corporations are protected by national security and liberal economic policies, thus allowing a growing number of oligopolies in certain sectors (see e.g. Albæk, Møllgaard and Overgaard 2003; Lundkvist 2009a; Vestergaard and Linneberg 2018). Take for example the organic industry in Denmark, which was initiated by small, independent producers. Today, the market for organic products is dominated by large corporate conglomerates and privately-owned businesses that maintain a monopoly (Vestergaard and Linneberg

---

[31] Such start-up institutions include the *Vækstfond* (growth fund) such as *Vækstkaution* (growth investment guarantee) and *Kom-i-gang-lån* (get started loans) (Aarhus Kommune 2011).

[32] Accelerace is an innovation company that offers support for start-ups, help with innovation for companies 'take great technologies of tomorrow and even greater teams under our wing to make them fly' (www.accelerace.io).

[33] With approximately 335,000 inhabitants, Aarhus has 50,000 students (Business Aarhus 2017).

[34] The branches most likely to succeed are those within manufacturing, especially of products suitable for export, but also welfare technology (Pallesen 2014).

2018). In Aarhus, oligopolic corporations dominate more and more of the downtown commercial area.

Plate 1. Bang & Olufsen, a successful large, Danish electronics firm making its way into one of the Aarhus areas dominated by local, independent shops.

Denmark's international trade connects it to many different countries inside and outside the European Union (EU). Denmark's most important trading partners are Germany, Sweden, and Great Britain. Trade with countries outside the EU, such as USA and China are also important for the Danish market, but here it is imports that dominate exports. The most important commodity groups for export are machines, foods, medicine, and dairy products and eggs – mainly arriving from Arla Foods – which accounts for around half of all exported goods.

The business owners in this study provide their goods and services locally within and around Aarhus. Simultaneously, nearly all the firms were dependent on online sales, through which goods were sent anywhere in the world if the customer was willing to pay for transport. In practice, however, most of the online orders came from within Denmark and even Jutland. On rare occasions, the business owners sent their products abroad, and some firms had regular customers in the neighbouring countries of Norway and

Sweden. In a survey published by the Aarhus municipality, 26 per cent of 500 Aarhus businesses reported that they exported their goods.

Overall, import is larger than export in Denmark, and fruits and vegetables are the main import products on a national scale. Among the business owners in this study, all were dependent on imported goods, though to varying degrees. Even firms that were dedicated to using local products received many of their ingredients from abroad as these ingredients were unavailable on the Danish market.

## Conclusion

The aim of this chapter has been to describe the broader framework in which the individuals of this study live and work. In order to arrive at a composite image of the past and present system of the nation-state, and the financial development into a global economy in which the Aarhus business owners take part, I started with a brief look at the development of a homogeneous nation-state and a distinctive Scandinavian system of welfare, built on ideals of sameness, universalism, and full employment. The universal welfare state developed with a focus on female workforce participation, abolition of child poverty, and reduction of benefits and means testing directed at inactive citizens. The business owners in this study have grown up in a welfare state with free medical help, free education, and ideas of sameness and homogeneity. I have shown that the welfare state is important for the social security of citizens, providing a security net that ensures a relatively high living standard for all and comparatively low levels of inequality.

I have situated Denmark on the global financial map and shown that despite its small size and population, Denmark holds a relatively strong economic position in the global market. The small, open market economy is increasingly dominated by large corporations and oligopolies in several sectors. Why have the business owners in this study decided to leave wage-labour to benefit from the freedom of being their own boss, leaving behind welfare benefits including sickness benefits, paid holidays, and rights to paid parental leave? The following chapters will discuss why the Aarhus niche business owners chose a life of self-employment, establishing small, niche firms in a country where wage-labour and large corporations are trending. But first, we shall look deeper into the moral background of these small, independent business owners.

# Chapter 3
# Moral Background

In this chapter, I shall focus on the main theme of this thesis: moral values. What are the business owners' primary areas of moral concern? From where do these concerns derive? What factors underlie their judgements of right and wrong, good and bad? In order to better understand the ideas and actions discussed in the following chapters, I shall bring in insights from ethnological and ethnographic studies of Scandinavian society and cultural history, including religion.

Dealing with the values of business owners involves dealing with people who confront moral choices in their everyday lives as producers, sellers of goods and services, as employers, in interaction with customers and suppliers, as well as in their behaviour as private persons. Although the business owners I worked with hardly qualify as elites in the context of Danish society, owning and managing a small business nonetheless places them in a position of moral responsibility that differs from the moral demands placed on their employees and customers. This is especially true in a social democratic political culture such as Denmark, where the central figures are the 'ordinary worker' or the 'socially vulnerable' person, and where 'doing business' sometimes brings forth connotations of dishonesty, tax cheating, or unearned wealth (some of this attitude has become more sympathetic in the wake of the corona virus and the economic hardships of so many small businesses during the pandemic).

The small business owners in this study are subject to moral decisions when they purchase supplies, negotiate salaries, set working hours, decide which products to offer, and how much they should cost. All these arenas channel moral economic values as the community understands and deals with them. These moral arenas are not limited to prices and markets, of course (Rapport 1997; Widding 1997). They also ramify through family life and other social relations (Howell 1997a: 9–11). In their everyday lives, the business owners make moral choices in both business and ordinary living. Some are conscious decisions over which they reflect, others take the form of embodied concepts of morality (Howell 1997a: 9–11). As part of the way to successfully understand and analyse the meaning of these moral domains and their content, this chapter begins by reviewing some anthropological approaches to moralities and values. This review of the anthropology of morality is then followed by a discussion of dominant values and morality as it has been reproduced and distributed in the Scandinavian political, cultural, and social science discourses.

## Anthropology of Values

The concepts of 'values' and 'moralities' are closely interrelated, and while often used together, they are not necessarily synonymous (Heintz 2009a: 3–4). Chris Gregory mentions some of the many forms the concept of 'value' can take and the many different contexts where values matter. Gregory distinguishes several dichotomies: between 'economic values such as use-value and price […], [between] familial values such as respect and familial love; religious values such as purity and auspiciousness; [and] moral values such as virtue or vice' (Gregory 2015: xxxiii). Gregory also adds that the conception of 'the Good' envisions a future in which people live good lives (ibid.).

Anthropologists were originally not concerned with the commodity aspect of value (Gregory 2015: xxxiii). Traditionally, they have discussed values from a perspective that sought out the existence of universal values. It dealt with the question of whether humans are inherently good or evil (Kluckhohn 1951; 1956; 1958), gift exchange and reciprocity (Mauss 2002 [1950]), and later on, from a structuralist view of hierarchy or meaningful difference (e.g. Sahlins 1976; Dumont 1980).

In a call for a more critical view of value as a phenomenon in need of constant evaluation. David Graeber discussed theories of value and values (Graeber 2001: 2). Graeber distinguished between three conventional ways of understanding value(s). First, there are values in the sociological sense, which is the way anthropologists traditionally have dealt with values as, 'conceptions of what is ultimately good, proper, or desirable in human life'. A second understanding is that of value (singular) in the economic sense, i.e. the degree in which objects are desired and measured and how much people are willing to sacrifice to get them (Graeber 2001: 1). Although this second approach is ascribed to economists, theorists discussing anthropological studies of value have dealt with value in its singular sense in the study of markets and commodities (i.e. Carrier 1995; Gregory 2015). However, this approach was often combined with a discussion of values in the plural sense, dealing with social and moral values in relation to material and economic values (Gudeman 2008: 4; Gregory 2015). Finally, Graeber's third understanding of value is linguistic, whereby value is a 'meaningful difference', as in the Saussurian understanding associated with structuralists (Graeber 2001: 2). The Saussurian understanding of value perceives values in a hierarchy. Different components of the same whole contribute to the distinction of one over the other, and the value of one can only be understood in relation to another (Dumont 1980). Graeber further developed his own theory of value where he was concerned with what people think is good. He suggested we answer this question by looking at how people devote their creative energy to specific projects. Graeber's focus was on people's actions, and he suggested that we can understand the meaning and value of objects in the material world by observing people's actions in relation to these objects and the broader social relations in which they are involved.

Although Graeber's contribution to theories of value is of importance, we will use the term 'values' in this book in a more straightforward fashion. In line with Kluckhohn, we will invoke 'values' as perceptions about what is and should be desirable. Social values are the conceptions about what we ought to want, and they become moral values when they are guided by principles of right and wrong, good and bad (Heintz 2009a: 4). The '*ought*' is central because anthropology has demonstrated the common discrepancy between what individuals desire and what they ought to desire (Robbins 2012: 117). People's actions become important as one of the means to grasp the 'oughts' and desires, accompanied by the same and other individuals' pronounced sentiments.

The challenge with any study of moralities or moral values lies in the fact that the meanings given to values are multiple. Although every social community contains a general or dominating set of values and moralities, there are also wide variations depending on subgroups or situations (Graeber 2001: 56). In the words of Chris Gregory, 'values describe and prescribe' (Gregory 1997: 5). Children live by values created by their parents and grandparents and by other significant persons who influence them; as adults, we are both 'subject and makers of the values that guide human actions and influence human destiny' (Gregory 1997: 5). Because people have different values, conflict is inevitable, and the values 'of the dominant usually, but not always, triumph at the end of the day' (Gregory 1997: 5). If we agree to a set of dominant values within a given historical time and region, these limited set of values represent a cultural unity (Gregory 1997: 5). We can study this cultural unity, while remaining aware of how this unity is contested by alternative values.

In society, there are dominant values and a contestation of these values, such as left-wing versus right-wing political parties. The two political wings have two different sets of values about the individual, the state, about solidarity, about individual responsibility. Distinguishing which is the dominant depends on which part the individual identifies. Our problem, then, becomes one of how to distinguish the dominant values in our specific field of study. More importantly: to what degree do the values of our interlocutors overlap with the dominant values in the society? Do the small business owners in Aarhus reflect the dominant values of their sphere or are they contesting these values? The business owners I studied belonged to different political orientations, but they shared the conviction that small, niche businesses were 'better' (morally good) than large corporations.

This chapter deals with the search for these dominant sets of values in areas of social life that might influence the ways in which my Aarhus small business owners and their families act in the world. There are different interpretations of what my interlocutors understand as dominant moral values. The variations may differ according to their social or class backgrounds, employment situation, education, and current economic situation, to mention a few main variables. There are also differences in the expression and interpretation of values. And, as Pierre Bourdieu argued in 1977, the expression of these values may vary with regards to the kinds of social, economic, and cultural capital that the individual possesses, (Bourdieu 1977). Differences in the expression of values might also appear in different social contexts and in interactions between different persons, whether they be family members or business partners. Moreover, values are made and remade through cultural and community discourses *and* the interpretation and expression of them may vary according to personal aspirations (Heintz 2014: 13).

My aim is not to provide an ethnography of Danish moralities, or even the morality of Danish small business owners. Rather, my aim is to document and analyse the different levels of which expressions of morality become apparent and highlight the similarities between them as a contribution to the comparative understanding of human sociality. On that note, I insist that there is no such thing as '*a* value' or '*a* morality' in any sociality. This means that when we as anthropologists attempt to distinguish and understand these concepts, we are always dealing with multiple values and multiple, often competing moralities (Gregory 1997: 5; Howell 1997a: 4; Heintz 2017). However, the constant justification of moral actions is made with reference to what is perceived as generally good and bad. For example, it is generally conceived as morally bad to commit tax evasion in Denmark (and it is also illegal), but there are local and subjective variations in the perception of what is tax fraud and just stretching the rules. For business owners this could mean buying fish directly from a local fisherman instead of at regulated auctions, engaging in friend's favours involving the products of your business, or receiving gifts from customers. In order to understand this justification-practice we need to become familiar with what may be understood as dominant values and moralities.

## Moral Anthropology

The anthropology of morality, or moralities, has its roots in moral philosophy (Howell 1997a: 2; Laidlaw 2002: 312; Fassin 2012: 1–2; Laidlaw 2013). Anthropology dealing with moralities can be divided between two main approaches, one arriving from Émile Durkheim, the other from Michel Foucault or Aristotle (Zigon 2011: 6–8; Fassin 2012: 7).

Didier Fassin criticised the anthropology of moralities for de-contextualizing the study of moralities from politics and for not being sufficiently reflexive. Fassin asserted that, 'moral questions are embedded in the substance of the social; it is not sufficient to analyse the moral codes or ethical dilemmas as if they could be isolated from political, religious, economic, or social issues' (Fassin 2012: 4). Fassin thus called for an anthropology of moralities or what he called a 'moral anthropology' that is more reflexive and which relates to political issues (Fassin 2012: 5, 10). Fassin criticised several contributions to anthropology of moralities for lacking concerns about political, religious, and economic issues (e.g. Howell 1997b; Heintz 2009b), but his criticism is misplaced. In fact, Signe Howell emphasized that in studying morality, the contributors to her edited volume have 'identified arenas, which they consider highlighting local morality. That includes the moral significance of the use of exemplars; of sexuality; of cross-and same-sex relations; of gossip; of guilt, honour and shame; of showing respect; and of passages from scriptural texts' (Howell 1997a: 4–5). Although the focus of these authors has been on one or more of these arenas of moral significance, this does not mean that they are isolated from each other. Arguing that these are arenas of moral significance, in fact, acknowledges the importance played on all these arenas in the construction of moral meaning. Further evidence to dispute Fassin's accusation of lack of reflexivity is a quote from Howell where she argued that anthropologists must be conscious about their own 'failure to understand the priorities of our contemporaries who live in different social worlds from ours and who orient themselves according to different moral priorities' (Howell 1997a: 9). She stated that 'continuous reflexive probing of our own ideas, values and practices is heralded as an integral part of the process of interpreting alien forms of human life' (Howell 1997a: 9). A clear statement that anthropologists *are* reflexive. Similarly, Monica Heintz opened her edited volume with a reflective note on how anthropologists can avoid cultural blindness and moral judgements when studying morality (Heintz 2009a: 1–2).

While there are also recent contributions to the methodological study of morality, both Howell (1997a) and Heintz (2009a) pointed out the most important methodological and analytical challenges that we need to be aware of in order to successfully approach an understanding of morality in any given society. First, they highlighted the obvious challenge facing the researchers' own internal moral orientations as we attempt to describe other moral realities (Howell 1997a: 9; Heintz 2009a: 1–2). The primary method for avoiding the researcher's own bias is the simple awareness of its existence. Second, and perhaps more important, is the recognition of the fact that morality is an analytical concept and not necessarily something to which our interlocutors relate in their everyday lives (Howell 1997a: 6–8). The perhaps biggest challenge is then to identify what concepts or discourses might be characterised as 'morality' and what these concepts and discourses actually mean in the given society (Howell 1997a: 4–5). How can we distinguish social acts and ideas as *moral* acts and ideas in the given society? How do we avoid conceptualising morality in a way that makes it either too narrow or too nebulous? These are the challenges dealt with by the contributors in both these two edited volumes; they are also the major questions in my own work with the Aarhus business owners. We are all trying to locate the drivers of moral behaviour, while we understand that morality can itself be the driver.

In her introduction to *The Anthropology of Moralities*, Howell (1997a) attempted *not* to define morality. She invoked the anthropologist and moral philosopher couple May and Abraham Edel (1959), who distinguished between 'ethics wide' and 'ethics narrow'. Ethics wide refers to moralities that are 'part and parcel of the whole field of human endeavour and striving' (Edel and Edel 1959: 8). Ethics narrow refers to obligations or duty, which 'ought to be or ought to be realised' (Edel and Edel 1959: 9). In other words, moralities contain and express both discourse and practice, and they contribute to constituting individuality and making of action in the world (Howell 1997a: 3–4).

Moralities have been understood to involve a set of principles and judgements based on common beliefs in actions that are right and wrong, and these actions are culturally and temporally situated (Munn 1986: 15; Heintz 2009a). Furthermore, these actions and beliefs can be understood as a combination of choice and routine (Robbins 2012: 118–19). Dealing with moralities thus implies dealing with people's motivations to act morally. Why do people choose to act according to the contested or the dominant morality?

Durkheimian approaches to morality have been broadly accused of spreading 'morality too thinly over society, making it everywhere present but almost invisible in its role in shaping social life' (Robbins 2009: 62; see also e.g. Heintz 2009a: 2). Joel Robbins suggested that by acknowledging that moralities are rules, which therefore involve a freedom of reflective choice, we can grasp morality more easily than if we view it as everywhere present (2009: 62–3). I agree with Robbins (2009) that we need to limit our definition of any analytical concept in order for it to make sense in a given social context, and to apply it analytically. I also agree that morally-based actions are always subject to varying degrees of individual choice. Nevertheless, the theories of moralities proposed by Durkheim in the early twentieth century, particularly those concerned with the role of desire in morality, continue to be relevant to contemporary studies of moralities. In fact, Durkheim specifically argued that '[o]bligation or duty only expresses one aspect abstracted from morality. A certain degree of desirability is another characteristic no less important than the first' (Durkheim 2010: 16).

This is the link between morality, doing what's right, and values, doing what is desirable. A simplistic understanding of Durkheimian morality understood as 'rules of conduct' may lead us to view morality as just another word for culture (Heintz 2014: 6). However, by adding desirability, i.e. 'values', as a second important aspect of morality, Durkheim and Robbins's approaches to morality come to resemble each other. Although people have the freedom and choice to act against or at the limits of the moral codes of their given community, individuals are subject to moral judgements made both by the self and imposed on them by the community, even when they are not fully aware of their actions (Zigon 2011: 7). This is certainly the case, as we shall see, with our Aarhus business owners. However, acknowledging freedom of choice is a crucial element in analysing how morality operates at the day-to-day level of social life (Laidlaw 2014).

## Some Methods for Studying Values and Moralities

Among the methodological approaches to the study of morality, and especially if we are to investigate all the complexities between the ought and the is, one of the most useful approaches is that of narrative, understood as 'articulations of the embodied struggle to morally be with oneself and others in the social world' (Zigon 2012: 205). It has already been established that moralities are not necessarily shared between individuals in a group, at least not entirely (Robbins 2009: 63). The narrative – the individual story told by an interlocutor – could tell us about how individuals negotiate moralities within a social group. In other words, we can understand narratives as 'the articulation of the ethical process of attempting to regain moral comfort in the world by charitably negotiating moral breakdowns. What is articulated, then, is not a concern for meaning or mutual understanding, but rather the embodied struggle once again to be with others comfortably in their mutually inhabited world' (Zigon 2012: 205).

Moreover, narrative stories tell us not only of individual differences within the moral universe, they are also 'considered a primary means by which meaning and moral values are publicly articulated, transmitted, adopted, and reworked' (Zigon 2012: 206). When studying morality, therefore, we need to acknowledge the existence of multiple realities, not just on cultural, social, or community levels, but also at an individual level (Zigon 2011). However, application of the narrative approach as one of several channels to understanding local moralities must be done with awareness of the communicative biases between researcher and informant (Heintz 2014: 10). Poul, the fishmonger, was an excellent source to understanding moral values through narratives, when he made moral judgements on colleagues or employees who did not work as hard as they should, or spent too much money on the wrong things, while he simultaneously compensated for his own lack of 'real work' (manual, on the floor labour) by habitually make reference to all the manual work he had performed earlier in his life. Poul's attention to hard (manual) work indicates the importance of hard work. His emphasis on hard work yields an anticipation that not living up to the expectations of high work performance could lead to moral judgement.

Another methodology for studying morality derives from the suggestion that morality is easier to identify in times of crisis (Robbins 2009: 68). This approach is not sufficient on its own, but it is obvious that times of crisis and extraordinary situations might be moments that highlight moral values, as these are also times of transformation and change. Because of this transformative potential, the picture we get of morality during a crisis situation may differ from what we might observe when studying the 'ordinary' (Heintz 2014: 14). In my fieldwork among small businesses in Aarhus, I found that the crisis in a family firm highlighted the values of hard (manual) work. Another supplementary approach to the study of morality, arrives from Thomas Widlok (2009), who has suggested that we construct different moral scenarios to test how our interlocutors make moral judgements. This method suffers from numerous potential biases that might occur from such surveys. Not only do we face the bias of presenting an individual with a moral dilemma in the presence and surveillance of an anthropologist, but we also create an artificial situation where the individual has time to reflect and act in ways that are far different from an actual situation. In addition, the individual will be biased by factors such as time, place, mood, and relationship with the interviewer that might affect the result in a negative direction. To deal with this variation, I have conducted a values-oriented survey with 32 participants, and the data from this survey has been used as complementary support for my ethnographically grounded arguments.

## Values and Religion

Religion provides guidelines to determine what is right and wrong behaviour in a community. The relationship between secularism and religion has received much attention in the Scandinavian sociological and historical literature. The historical literature has been extensively concerned with the transition from pagan Vikings, with belief in mysterious Old Norse gods,[35] the gradual Christianisation of Denmark marked by the reign of Harald Bluetooth,[36] the Lutheran Christian Reformation that was popularized by the Danish theologian Nikolai Frederik Severin Grundtvig in the 19th century, and the modern insistence on Denmark as a secular state, where people routinely define themselves as 'cultural Christians' (*kulturkristne*).[37] How have these religious ebbs and flows affected the development of moral values in Scandinavian society?

Danish anthropologist Jeppe Trolle Linnet (2011) and the Swedish-Finnish historian Henrik Stenius (1997) agree on the importance of the Scandinavians' egalitarian/secular revolt against the established hierarchies and ritual forms of the church, they emphasised that Lutheran Christianity in Scandinavia cultivates an inner, individual faith. Similarly, Norwegian anthropologist Marianne Gullestad (1991) and Thomas Luckmann (1967) argued that by studying the intimate confines of the home we can find that religion carries meaning through inherent moral values that have developed from Christian morality.

Although I have not strictly defined morality in a broad Durkheimian way, it is certainly true that morality or moral orientations are influenced by society at large, as articulated through political and religious institutions and practices (Laidlaw 2002: 317; Laidlaw 2014). The dominant values of society, in which individual values are often guided, are likely to derive from influential religious and/or political domains (Gregory 2015: xxxiii). However, while there is a clear influence of Christianity on existing understandings of morality, we must be cautious about automatically

---

[35] For example Hastrup and Löfgren 1992; Gräslund 2008; Hultgård 2008; Raudvere 2008; Sundqvist 2008.

[36] See Lodberg 2001; Brink 2008; Rosesdahl 2008.

[37] See P. B. Andersen and Lüchau 2011; Reeh 2013; M. F. Jensen 2014; A. M. Nielsen 2014.

assigning too much credit to Christianity for the moral lives of contemporary Danes, or for any society for that matter. Although some moral values and judgements are encouraged, imposed, and maintained through religious observance, many of these orientations can be understood as part of any form of sociality, independent from religious affiliation, if not inherently human (Firth 1953: 148). One example from the world of alcohol: while Denmark, Sweden, and Norway all have dominant Evangelical Lutheran churches with pietistic elements, the libertarian attitude toward alcohol differs profoundly from the more restrictive, state-controlled alcohol distribution in Sweden and Norway.

Anthropologists have provided evidence that social communities in all corners of the world act and behave within moral social communities, although the meanings, understandings, and actions related to these values sometimes differ greatly (see for example Munn 1986; Humphrey 1997; de Sardan 1999). Danes are exposed to Christian religious moralities throughout their educational system, starting already in day-care institutions from age nine months until University. But they are also exposed to social democratic and national ideas through school history teaching and exposure to political campaigns.

In *The Protestant Ethic and The Spirit of Capitalism in Norway*, Christen T. Jonassen (1947) claims that the Norwegian Lutheran reformist Hans Nielsen Hauge adopted some concepts from the Lutheran religion and gave them new meaning, value, and vitality, transforming them into more or less the same behaviouristic premises as that of Calvinism (Jonassen 1947b: 681). We can make a similar claim about the Danish theologian and Enlightenment thinker Grundtvig. Grundtvig transformed Lutheranism with influence from the French Revolution and Enlightenment ideas in a way that appealed to Denmark's peasant population, adding ideas of freedom, community, and equity (values that were not encouraged by Luther [Stjernfeldt 2017]). I suggest that regardless of whether the 'Danishness' ascribed to values of community (*fællesskab*), work ethic (*arbejdsmoral*), and sameness (*lighed*) existed before or since the introduction of Lutheranism, the effort of Grundtvig and other reformists emphasized and reenforced these values and presented them as both Christian and Danish.

Although Grundtvig should not be credited with the introduction of these values (Østergaard 1997; 2012), Grundtvig, as a Lutheran theologian, philosopher, educator and prolific writer, successfully managed to enlighten the Danish people with ideas of freedom, self-sufficiency, and independence, together with principles of 'one language, one culture, one belief, one church, one state, and one nation' (Lodberg 2001: 17). Grundtvigianism encouraged people to act together with other community members in a variety of associational configurations.

In Aarhus, I encountered Danish associations and organisations that are an important part of community life today (Bruun 2011; 2012), such as community meals (*fællesspisning*). These community initiatives grew out of the encouragement from Grundtvigianism to come together in *forsamlingshuse* (village halls), folk high schools (*folkehøjskoler*), and establish *foreninger* (voluntary associations) that encouraged teamwork and co-operation around shared activities (Jenkins 2011: 57; Hall and Campbell 2017: 30–3).

Grundtvigianism is said to have succeeded in making Protestantism a religion which determined people's actions and filled the individual with an enthusiasm for the benefit of other people and the well-being of all (Koch 1943: 29). In the same movement, the Evangelical Lutheran Church, *Folkekirken*, has evolved into a democratically governed folk church driven by the belief that the church should be a church, both for and of, the people (Thorkildsen 2006). Grundtvig also established the first folk high schools (*folkehøjskole*) a network of adult education institutions offering people the right to further civic education, all of which were important steps towards the equity/sameness ideals of the modern Danish social democratic welfare state (on the folk high school movement and modern folk high schools see especially Borish 1991).

Generally, Scandinavia and Denmark are viewed as secular nations. Few people attend church (beyond baptism, confirmation, weddings and funerals), and in nation-wide surveys, few Danes admit that they are religious or believe in God.[38] I am concerned with the influence religion might have had on moral and social values. There is no doubt that Grundtvig and his followers had great influence and mobilized the Danish population under the ideas of the folk (*folket*) and a broader *folkelighed* (national-based). Regardless of the origin of Grundtvig's ideas, his ideas concerned

---

[38] According to the European Value Study (EVS) 2008 (see Nielsen 2014: 264) 88 per cent of the population viewed themselves as members of a religious denomination whereas 40 per cent claim they never attend religious services, and 40 per cent claim they attend less than twice a year. Accordingly, 10 per cent say they attend several times per year, only 2.6 per cent once a week, and 7.4 per cent once a month. According to the same EVS survey, 63.6 per cent of the Danish population profess a belief in God, whereas 72.3 per cent consider themselves religious. With the variables of asking people more in depth about their belief in God, only 13.4 per cent stated that they with certainty believed in God (A. M. Nielsen 2014: 266). According to these statistics, Denmark has many believers and Christians; they are only not very active in the community of religion, at least not the official community. In addition, they are very ambivalent as to how they perceive religion. Statistics show that 20.9 per cent of the population stated that religion is 'not at all important' to them, and an additional 49.1 per cent stated that religion was 'not important' (A. M. Nielsen 2014: 267).

decent compassionate behaviour towards other members of the community (*fællesskabet*) could very well stand on their own, without the message of God or Christ being involved. The forum for spreading these ideas was thus religious, but the content builds more on being human than being religious.

## Moral in Danish

The definitive Danish language dictionary, *Den Danske Ordbog*, defines the Danish word *moral* (Engl. 'morality') in three ways. First it is defined as 'the perception of what are good and bad ideas and actions, especially related to a person or group's set of norms' (translated from Den Danske Ordbog 2018). Second, it is described as 'a behaviour or ability to behave according to what is perceived as proper and acceptable' (ibid.); and finally, *moral* is defined similar to the English '*morale*', i.e. as courage or 'fighting spirit [*kampgejst*], discipline, and ability to maintain courage and hope, also in adversity' (translated from Den Danske Ordbog 2018). One of the examples the dictionary gives to how the word moral can be used in a sentence regards tax avoidance, 'the children observe their parents' lack of *moral* in relation to black labour [off-the-books work] and cheating on taxes' (my translation). In this sense, lack of *moral* and unethical behaviour is synonymous. Other examples where the concept of moral is in use, is 'Christian *moral*', 'bad/good *moral*' and 'public *moral*'. As an example of good *moral*, the dictionary offers the sentence, 'the Danish *moral* was so good that the national team could fight their way back into the game'. Here, the word *moral* is the equivalent of the English word 'morale', as in fighting spirit. This definition and the examples following them, gives us an impression of how Danish society understands and uses the term *moral*. We see hints of national pride and clear directions for what values Danish society should be protecting and cultivating in their shared moralities. Similarly, the moral judgement condemning cheating on taxes encourages solidarity and community in the re-distributional project which is the welfare state.

We can identify guiding principles or dominant values in various historical, political, and religious sources about Denmark. In what way have these dominant moralities influenced the moral orientations of small, Aarhusian business owners?

Spending time with Danish shopkeepers allowed me to identify various value orientations that I have narrowed down to four main concepts that make them analytically comparable. These are the concepts of equity (*lighed*), community (*fællesskab*), justice (*retfærd*), trust (*tillid*), and the value of hard work (*arbejdsmoral*). The same five concepts are cited by Richard Jenkins (2011) as components of 'Danish identity' in his monograph from Skive, Jutland (see also Jenkins 2006: 373). These themes also reappear in various Scandinavian ethnographies, in historical publications, in political and public debates, and in international media reports on Denmark and Scandinavia regarding trust, civil society, social equality, well-being, and happiness.

The broad acknowledgement of these value orientations in local as well as national discourses qualifies them as core themes in any study of values and moralities in Danish or Scandinavian society (Bendixen, Bringslid, and Vike 2018a: 2). I recognized the presence of these sentiments in the priest's Sunday sermon, in conversations between shopkeepers and customers, and in the commentaries diffused in the public media. I could trace them in social relationships within families, and between neighbours and friends. What effect does the constant exposure to these sentiments as characteristic of national identity have on people's moral sentiments and actions?

The amount of attention equity (*lighed*), community (*fællesskab*), justice (*retfærd*), trust (*tillid*), and the value of hard work (*arbejdsmoral*), have received throughout modern history in both scholarly and public discourse (and some argue they have 'penetrated the state' [Bendixen, Bringslid, and Vike 2018b: 4]), makes them relevant as concepts to be subjected to analysis and critique. Indeed, these concepts have been subject to critical assessment by several scholars. However, their continuing reappearance in Scandinavian social anthropology has contributed to their reproduction as symbols of Scandinavian values (i.e. Lien, Lidén, and Vike 2001a; Bendixen, Bringslid, and Vike 2018a). In fact, egalitarianism (or rather sameness) is recognised by anthropologists as one of few uniquely Scandinavian regional concepts (Bruun, Jakobsen, and Krøijer 2011: 4). Some scholars have argued that some of these Scandinavian 'public values' have been threatened by the penetration of 'market values' (T. B. Jørgensen and Bozeman 2002: 65). My suggestion is not that we should automatically naively accept that Scandinavians in general value work, justice, equity, and community more than do other peoples. One would be hard-pressed to find any society that does not in some way place a high value on hard work, justice, equity, and community in some culturally specific form. Rather, my task here is to understand how these sentiments and their history were expressed and perceived in my field site, and specifically among independent small business owners in Aarhus with their special relationship to wage-earning Danes and big business as 'others'.

In his ethnography *Det glemte Folk* (The forgotten people) (1983), Danish ethnologist Thomas Højrup provides a detailed description of the significance of community (*fællesskab*) and work ethic (*arbejdsmoral*) specifically as these pertain to Danish self-employed fishermen and farmers.

Although Højrup did not set out to study values or morality, his detailed ethnography, conducted in the late 1970s, serves to elucidate these values among the self-employed in rural Denmark. Højrup described a community centred on the nuclear family as an economic unit, working together to maintain their way of life. However, the community of fishermen/farmers, housewives, and drivers made up an interdependent economy, in which the household unit was morally and economically embedded. The co-existence among these people required a strong moral sense of community to sustain itself. All members of the community needed to work hard not only to meet the needs of their own family, which Højrup argued, was more common for urban wage-labour-based communities; the fisher and farm families were also expected to work hard as part of the community. They were morally obliged in the sense that although they could choose not to work as hard as the other fishermen, or to produce less, the expectations from other members limited any deviation from this system of moral obligations (see also Christensen 2000). Højrup's example shows that the values I will describe have been central for the self-owning life mode that was dominant in Denmark for so long. The social organisation of this independent household enterprise life mode is not unique to rural Danes, of course. Self-employed fishers, farmers, and craftsmen exist throughout the world in small inter-dependent communities (e.g. Cohen 1999).

The most influential work on Scandinavian equality derives from the ethnographic works of Norwegian anthropologist Marianne Gullestad. Over three decades, Gullestad authored many studies of everyday life in Norway. Her influential theory of 'equality as sameness' developed from her work among working-class mothers in suburban Norway, where she found that equality translated as sameness (*likhet*) was the key determining factor by which people socialised and created a segregated and homogenized sociality (Gullestad 1984). The importance of following the codes of equality have been acknowledged as a characteristic of Scandinavian sociality that contributes to the creation of a highly segmented society where people socialize only with those who qualify as 'same', be it determined by social, economic, intellectual, ethnic, or other indices of belonging (Gullestad 2002; Larsen 2011). Judgements of sameness/equality are based on a variety of factors that can vary from the furnishings in your house to shared ideas about politics and culture (Gullestad 1984; Gullestad 2002: 47).

These ethnographies sociality gives us useful information about Scandinavian value orientations, and the similarity between the different cases across diverse Scandinavian communities provides confirmation of the importance of equality values generally. Orientations around equity, community, and work ethic are continuously confirmed and reproduced as ideologies of Scandinavian identity; they appear in the popular discourse as well as in social science and history (e.g. Gundelach 2004a; Jenkins 2011; Linnet 2011; Kastrup 2013). Although there is little doubt that the imagined sameness in Scandinavian communities is socially and culturally constructed, the fact of growing up and living in a society where these imaginaries are constantly reproduced and articulated has a profound impact on how people think and act. On the path to understanding the value of these values in Scandinavian societies we shall now review some regional ethnographic accounts of the concepts of work, sameness/equality and hygge. Can these accounts give us insights into and help us understand the Aarhus business owners' perspectives on work, sameness, and *hygge*? Can we draw generalized conclusions from these accounts?

## The Meaning of Work

*Gyldendal Store Danske* dictionary suggests that we understand the Danish word for work (*arbejde*) as an activity that demands effort. Work always stands in relation to a person's needs and desires. The definition of work emphasises that effort (*indsats*) is always necessary in order for the person to satisfy their desires, and that work should be understood as this effort (Schnack 2016). The definition goes on to state that poverty is a problem with people having limited access to fulfil their needs, but that with effort, this can be changed (ibid.).[39]

The perspective on work presented in this gives us a generous hint about the Danish perspective on work. The dictionary statements indicate an attitude towards work as something that requires engagement from the individual. As long as one puts effort into something, they can better their situation. Work is thus presented as a choice people make to meet their needs and desires. In this logic, hard work reflects a valuation of fulfilling one's needs through effort, such that those who do not fulfil their needs have simply chosen not to work hard.

One of the central themes that concerned the small business owners featured in this study was their common commitment to hard work (*arbejdsmoral*; work ethic), a work ethic that operated not only for the benefit of themselves but for the community and society. They all shared some version of a work ethic that asserted a moral value of hard work as a community-based work ethic (*arbejdsmoral*). *Arbejdsmoral* thus refers to the expectations people have towards the amount of effort, engagement, and

---

[39] This sentiment is also visible in proverbs such as '*Der er ingen ting, der kommer af sig selv, andet end lus*' (You get nothing without effort, except lice) and '*Den som vil have noget, skal arbejde for det*' (Those who desire something must work for it).

prudence a person places on their work tasks. These expectations vary across groups, workplace, generations, and between individuals.

What do Scandinavian ethnographies tell us about the work ethic, and what can history tell us about the background for such sentiments? Anthropologists have highlighted the strong Lutheran and pietistic tradition in the Scandinavian countries (Jonassen 1947; Larsen 2011). When reviewing Scandinavian ethnography with reference to the ennobling valuation of hard work, it is thus necessary to acknowledge the influence of Max Weber's (1904) hypothesis of the correlation between a Protestant work ethic and the development of Western capitalism (see e.g. Borre 2004).

Work ethic, or concern for the moral value of hard work, has been exemplified with narrative stories of women perfecting their household skills and the practical benefits of learning them, intertwined with the teaching of moral values (Gullestad 1997: 206). The idea of 'being of use', Gullestad argued, derived from a Protestant work ethic emphasising responsibility and a high valuation of hard work, together with moderate consumption habits (Gullestad 1997: 206). Similar narratives have been described about Scandinavian society (Hastrup and Löfgren 1992). These ethnographies have in common that they deal with older generations and their upbringing in a society where practical labour was present in people's lives to an extent incomparable with our modern digital realities today. Since the 1950s, there has been a massive growth in welfare, improved economic stability, and higher living standards (Gullestad 1996, 1997; Bejder and Kristensen 2016). In the older generations, the centrality of the concept of *dannelse* (proper upbringing) implied practical work in the home and at one's local workplace (Winther-Jensen 2017). Children were brought up with the notion that they should contribute, they should 'be of use' (i.e. work hard). Even in middle-class families, all members of the household were expected to contribute to the household's pursuit by doing tasks such as laundry, caring for younger siblings, or assisting in their parents' farm work (Winther-Jensen 2017). This tradition goes back centuries, as illustrated in the painting by Carl Ludvig Petersen from 1879.

Plate 2. Dannelse. This painting by Carl Ludvig Petersen (1879) illustrates the implications of Dannelse. The painting was used in the education of children up to the first decade of this century.

Despite increased value placed on individual self-realization, the strong emphasis on work discipline remains important in Scandinavian sociality. In her ethnography from a Danish neighbourhood, Birgitte Romme Larsen (2011) argued that 'working discipline and moral respectability are strongly interwoven' and that having too much free time indicates immorality in the Scandinavian society (Larsen 2011: 151–2).[40] Larsen showed that because domestic work was mostly invisible, spheres where the results of one's hard work could be seen – such as in the garden – mattered more as an arena for 'mutual moral negotiation and confirmation' (Larsen 2011: 152). These kinds of sentiments continue a long tradition for valuation of work in Danish public discourse (TNS Gallup 1960) and are visible in public debates through dramatic headlines such as, 'Psychologist Warns: Danes Are Dying from Bad Management and Too Good Work Ethic' (*Psykolog advarer:*

---

[40] See also Melhuus and Borchgrevink (1984).

*Danskerne dør af dårlig ledelse og for høj arbejdsmoral*) (Bræmer 2017) and, 'Work, Work!' (*Arbejd, arbejd!*) (Dam and Erhardtsen 2013).[41]

G. Prakash Reddy, an Indian anthropologist who carried out four months of fieldwork in the village of Hvilsager, near Aarhus, commented on Danes' propensity to work not only at the workplace, but also in and on their homes (Reddy 1993).[42]

Emphasis on work and having full-time employment became a vital element in the welfare state. One of the aims of the Scandinavian welfare states was to secure workforce participation for as many people as possible. In order for this goal to be achieved, the state was dependent on a population that was willing to take wage work or start their own firm (Stenius 2010; Bendixen, Bringslid, and Vike 2018b). The constant reproduction of hard work as a desired quality in Danish citizens (you are what you do) is thus a political goal as well as it is a socially accepted value. And the maintenance of this work ethic is confirmed repeatedly in European Value Surveys and other data showing that Danes *do* place significant value on work, and on employers' confidence that their workers will work hard even when left to their own devices ('The Values of Europeans' 2012: 16, 38). Hence, the Danish relaxed management style relies much more on employees' own self-discipline rather than continuing surveillance. Later in Chapter 5, we shall see how the emphasis on hard work is related to a general misbelief in wage-labourers' ability to fulfil the business owners' expectations of hard work.

When we have established the degree to which the work ethic, *arbejdsmoral*, plays a role in the value orientations ascribed to Danish citizens, this should mean that a concern for hard work is unique to Scandinavia or Denmark. However, in my previous fieldwork among Orang Rimba, a group of nomadic forest dwellers in Sumatra, Indonesia, I found that hard work played a much more central role in people's lives than I would say about the Danes I know. For Orang Rimba, ability to undertake hard work was the number one factor by which a spouse was chosen. The most common reason for divorce was unsatisfying work performance by the husband (Berta 2014b). Among Orang Rimba, men should expect to work up to a year to demonstrate his worth as provider to his prospective future in-laws. If his marriage proposal was accepted by the bride's family, the man must continue to work hard throughout his life to prove his worth for his affines and his wife. Making reference to hard work and drudgery was

---

[41] Note that we may recognize these sentiments also as capitalist sentiments introduced with industrial society.

[42] Although it is reasonable to speculate whether Reddy's book tells us more about his own views of Danes, his observations are useful for understanding how Danes may appear to someone completely unaware of Danish norms and culture.

central to Orang Rimba in everyday conversation, and laziness or a poor work ethic could lead to fatal social exclusion, an outcome that hardly relates to any Danish context (Berta 2014a).[43] What is important here, therefore, is not the number of hours spent at the work place, or an actual measurement of Danes' work efficiency (which according to all indices is very high). Rather it is the ethos of hard work, which is important, for it is this ethos that constitutes and is articulated as a desirable Danish cultural trait, a trait that indeed serves to distinguish 'us' from 'them', however defined (hence, the typical critique of immigrants and welfare recipients is that they 'do not want to work', and the political debates over unemployment benefits that are considered too high, such that 'it doesn't pay to work').

## Justice

Historian Hans Fredrik Dahl (1986) claims that the success of social democracy in Denmark was built upon what we might refer to, with E.P. Thompson's British working class in mind, as a peasant 'moral economy'. A 'moral economy' including ideas of equity (*lighed*), community (*fællesskab*), justice (*retfærd*), trust (*tillid*), and the value of hard work (*arbejdsmoral*), was later adopted by church and government. While these ideals might be considered an expression of a simple romanticism, there is no doubt that they were sustained by political and religious reforms. Through fairy tales, popular music, arts, and crafts, the Nordic ideals of justice and fairness (*retfærdighedsidealer*) continued to penetrate the minds of the population. Children, up until present day, have grown up with stories and music promoting values that build on and continue these incentives (Dahl 1986: 105–106). The families whom I got to know in Aarhus, together with the Danish schools, repeated these fairy tales, stories, and songs, promoting ideals of justice, modesty, and a desirable homogeneity (in the sense of not standing out, as in the infamous 'Jante' law, see below). Also, these sentiments became apparent in the business owner's narrative. Sally, the toy shop owner, justified her high prices with reference to distinguished quality. She was concerned with offering just prices to her customers, and morally judged 'the others' (large corporate firms) for offering cheap, poor quality goods that 'didn't last'. Her sense of fairness (*retfærdighedsidealer*) made her feel the need to justify why her goods were sold at a higher price than similar, but poorer quality, goods in competing shops.

---

[43] Although it is reasonable to speculate whether Reddy's book tells us more about his own views of Danes, his observations are useful for understanding how Danes may appear to someone completely unaware of Danish norms and culture.

Hans Christian Andersen, a cherished storyteller in Denmark, is known for among other stories, 'The Emperor's New Clothes', which carries a moralistic message against the upper layers of society. The story is a universal critique of vanity, self-indulgence, and pride; it exposes an unequal, pretentious, sycophant society laid bare by the straight-talking child who blurts out what others refuse to say, that the emperor has no clothes on.

Whereas the German concept of *Volk* had its origin in the upper classes and was used to legitimize aggression towards other peoples and nations, the Scandinavian meaning of folk has its roots in a discourse of democracy and equality with *Janteloven* ('The Law of Jante') as a metaphor of the Nordic small-scale, homogenous societies (Dahl 1986). The 'law' was first outlined in a book from 1933 by the Danish-Norwegian author Aksel Sandemose.

Sandemose stands as one of the central 'storytellers' promoting the ideals of equality and justice. In his essential work *En flygtning krydser sit spor* ('A fugitive crosses his tracks'), Sandemose formulated the 'Law of Jante' (*Janteloven*), which is still obligatory reading in every Danish school curriculum. *Janteloven* describes the insistence on equity, reinforced by envy, jealousy, and extreme degrees of levelling and social control. Sandemose wrote his influential *Jantelov*, composed of ten 'commandments', in a 'Thou shalt not…' fashion, as a critique of these sentiments, depicting a man who returns from the city to his remote small town of origin.

The Danish small-town society that Sandemose vividly depicts a sociality that is still relevant to contemporary Danes (see Jenkins 2011). In fact, the Law of Jante is argued to originate from a Nordic idea of caution (*forsigtighed*) in trumpeting one's own or others' good fortune (Rømhild and Schack 2018). The most important of the ten commandments that comprise the Law of Jante is a warning that one should never view oneself as special: 'You should not think that you are somebody' ('D*u skal ikke tro, du* er *noget*'). This speaks directly to the much older proverb 'Pride comes before a fall' ('*Hovmod står for fald*') (ibid.).[44] What's more, The Law of Jante still has a place in public debates when it is regularly critiqued and debated both as positive levelling mechanism against those who are too pretentious, and an impediment to individual initiative and innovation (fear of standing out, jealousy by others that one is talented). As such, *Janteloven* is often invoked in opposition to American consumerism and showing off but also in comparison to a praised American-style individualism, risk-taking and

---

[44] *Hovmod står for fald* (Arrogance brings you down) can relate both to the biblical cardinal sin, pride (latin *superbia*), and the German concept of *Schadenfreude,* which involves enjoyment in observing the misfortune of others (cognate to the Danish word *skadefryd*).

innovation (Ibsen 2012: 20). Such sentiments were repeatedly reconfirmed by the Aarhus business owners who spent a lot of time convincing me that they were sensible consumers, that they disliked people who 'showed off' their wealth, or they reminded me that they did not buy new clothes until they were worn out (because buying things you do not need is 'to waste' [*sløseri*]).

The Law of Jante has thus played an important role in the limitation of pluralism and the reproduction of homogeneity, and it is a common reference (or excuse) for Danish social conflicts or personal failures (Dahl 1986: 108–9). In this sense, justice (*retfærd*) should be understood as a set of sentiments directed at keeping individuals from standing out and maintaining sameness (*lighed*) within their social group through the limitation of injustice (*uretfærdighe*d). The social democratic appeals for Danes to show 'solidarity' (*solidaritet*), lately reincarnated as ensuring 'social cohesion' (*sammenhængskraft*)     and     appealing     for     'social-mindedness' (*samfundssind*)[45], all overlap with the stress on justice, homogeneity and sameness expressed in the *Jantelov.*

## Community, Equity, and Sameness

Many of the Scandinavian ethnographers depict Scandinavia as a region that is seemingly obsessed with equality, understood as avoidance of differences, or even refusal to acknowledge or accept differences. Sameness, homogeneity, and equality are three concepts that have made their mark on Scandinavian ethnography ever since Gullestad paved the way with her theory of 'equality as sameness' in the 1980s. On various occasions, Gullestad has provided evidence that Scandinavian individualism contains an element of conformity that favours equality in the sense of sameness. She argued that Scandinavians avoid focussing on dissimilarities and that they tend to avoid socialising with those who are different from themselves in terms of social class, economy, and moral values (Gullestad 1984).[46] Similarly – and with support from amongst others Graubard (1986) and Dahl (1986) – Gullestad argued that the Scandinavian passion for equality (as sameness) contributes to a homogeneity and denial of differences (Gullestad 1984: 1992), if not outright rejection in the form of petty racism or provincialism. What is special about the Scandinavian form of equality is

---

[45] Chosen as 'word of the year' in 2020 by the Danish Language Council.

[46] A common complaint of most foreigners who settle in Denmark for shorter or longer periods is that it is very difficult to make friends with Danes, to be invited home, or to enter Danish social circles; Danes themselves also comment on the friendliness of foreigners when they travel abroad as distinct from the more closed society from which they come.

that it does not stand in opposition to individualism. The kind of equality Gullestad suggests is dominant in Norway involves independence, self-sufficiency, and self-control, all characteristics that Richard Jenkins, in his study of Denmark, associates with Danish identity (Gullestad 1989: 85; Jenkins 2011: 55).[47]

Apart from *hygge,* high taxes, and being assessed as the happiest people in the world,[48] Denmark is perhaps most known internationally for its high levels of social equality (Bendixen, Bringslid and Vike 2018b: 2). Denmark scores high on numerous equity scales and as a nation, Denmark has for long taken on a self-representation of equity, or *lighed* better translated as sameness (Bruun, Jakobsen and Krøijer 2011).[49] What's more, equity and community (*lighed, fællesskab*) are qualities that are highlighted as explanations for why Danes continue to score high on happiness surveys, whereas economic stability and wealth are downplayed (Anderson 2016; Helliwell, Layard and Sachs 2016; Hetter 2016). The reoccurrence of reports presenting Denmark as a happy and *hyggeligt* country – due to its high level of social equality, trust, mutual respect, tolerance, and a unique sense of community spirit – is essential to the reproduction of these imaginaries. Danes are regularly exposed to media reports that confirm these ideals and encourage the belief in their veracity.[50]

Hence, our analysis obtains more nuance by supplementing the concept of equity (*lighed*) with the concept of conformity. Numerous studies, and my own field experience, suggest that Danes are more conformist than they are equal. People conform to the norms and regulations of the welfare state, showing high levels of trust in the authority of the state (Schultz-Jørgensen and Christensen 2011). If we consider the fact that most Danish parents will place their children in day-care institutions before or soon after they celebrate their first birthday, we should think that the future would be even more conformist. Principles of conformity articulated as learning 'social skills' (*sociale færdigheder*) or learning to 'cooperate' ('*samarbejde*') characterise the day-care institutions. As an incentive to minimize social differences, the day-care institutions aim to offer *equal* opportunities for all children. In the teaching plan (*pædagogisk læreplan*) for Danish schools and day-care institutions, three key concepts are central:

---

[47] It also involves home-centeredness, desire for peace and quiet, appreciation of nature, and stability (Gullestad 1989: 85).

[48] See Helliwell, Layard, and Sachs (2016).

[49] The word '*lige*' in Danish can mean either 'equal', 'alike', or 'the same'; *lighed* can mean 'likeness' as well as 'equality' or 'equity'.

[50] See for example A. M. Jakobsen 2000; Drachmann 2005; Falbe 2011; Ritzau 2015; Svansø and Larsen 2017).

individuality (*individualitet*), community (*fællesskab*), and equity (*lighed*) (see Børne- og undervisningsministeriet [Ministry of Children and Education] 2018). These principles specify the importance of individual needs, simultaneously stating the high importance of social competence, which can only be achieved through participation in the community (*fællesskabet*). The teaching plans highlight the importance of cooperation and that children learn to become a part of and stay in the group. The teaching plan states that it is only through membership in the community that the children can experience strength (*styrke*), meaning (*betydning*), and social recognition (*anerkendelse*). The plan further states that it is only through daily repetition of re-creating this community that children can become socially competent. Little wonder that attempts to measure children's aptitudes using various tests, which would serve to distinguish talented from less talented children, are bitterly opposed by the pedagogues as antithetical to community and solidarity.

The consequence of a well-functioning welfare state focusing on dual earner families, increased pension age, and early institutionalisation of children, is a system where the state takes growing responsibility for children's upbringing, thus ensuring and enhancing the level of conformity to the group. The frequent reminders of how equal, just, communal, and hardworking 'we Danes' (*os Danskere*) are, produces a feeling of moral commitment to live up to these values (and shaming of those who do not; for example, Danes who took vacations to Dubai during the winter of 2020–21 while citizens had been instructed not to undertake foreign travel). They also inspire aspirations toward their Danish national identity (Jenkins 2006: 385). The cultural construction of community and equality, therefore, does not 'occur in a void'. Achieving these values requires 'human action in the present' and in the Nordic nations, equality and freedom of individuality have been combined in a 'freedom of equality' (Stråth 2018: 47).

Moreover, the creation of a unique 'Danishness' with shared social democratic values is an important governmental objective, intended to ensure that the population remains loyal to the political system (Melhuus 1999: 71; Fridberg 2004; Hall and Campbell 2017). The social democratic welfare state is dependent on the population's willingness to contribute to the collective (paying taxes, taking full-time work instead of relying on welfare benefits). The government has succeeded in creating a sense of the population's ownership of the welfare state. Individual Danes express the view that the welfare state is theirs, and by cheating and betraying the welfare system, you betray yourself (Gundelach 2004b: 271). This moral conviction forms an important part of Scandinavian conformity that brings the individual into a binding community (Stenius 1997). The Aarhus business owners revealed their belief in this moral conformity when they claimed that they were happy to pay taxes.

Nordic and Danish citizens are confronted with a presentation of their own country, society, state, and selves as agents of these sentiments in their everyday lives, through the constant reproduction of such self-proclamations. In order to understand the realities of the Danes who are described in this book, it is thus important to keep in mind the amount of exposure they have to such promotion about themselves and their societies as communicated through various institutions, education and media channels. Another social construction is the concept of *hygge*.

## A Note on the Concept of Hygge

No ethnography on Denmark can escape *hygge* (pronounced HEU-geh). It deserves an explanation just because during the months I spent in Denmark, we were constantly having conversations about and performing *hygge*. The phrase, 'We are having a *hyggelig* time' (*'Nei, hvor vi hygger os'*), which is the common response to 'What are you doing?' (*'Hvad laver I?'*), is well known to any Dane, or person who has spent more than – I dare say – a few hours with a group of Danes in any informal setting. *Hygge* is important for many reasons, but I discuss it here because it plays a key role in the everyday life of the people with whom I did fieldwork. *Hygge* is an emic, Danish term that can refer to a specific object, person, place, situation, mood, or atmosphere, which generates a feeling of well-being in the individuals who are experiencing it. It is a concept that many ethnographers working in Denmark and Scandinavia have described and analysed,[51] and it is recognised as an important cultural trait (see for example Hansen 1980; Gullestad 1984; Borish 1991; Bruun 2011; Bruun, Jakobsen and Krøijer 2011). In recent years, the concept of *hygge* has become popularized to an extent that *hygge* has been recognised as an iconic Danish concept, if not a brand. Its international popularity peaked in 2017 when it gained official status as an English word and made its way into the *Oxford English Dictionary*. The English translation describes *hygge* as: 'A quality of cosiness and comfortable conviviality that engenders a feeling of contentment or well-being (regarded as a defining characteristic of Danish culture)' (see Oxford Dictionary n.d.). However, the Danish use of the term *hygge* gives it both much more specific and much broader connotations at the same time. According to anthropologist and '*hygge* expert' Jeppe Trolle Linnet, *hygge* is:

---

[51] The Swedish equivalent is *mysigt*, and in Norwegian *koselig*.

an emic Danish term for a certain quality of sociality, its etymological origin lying in the Norwegian language (and further back to Old Norse). References to its meaning in eighteenth-century Norwegian centre on such connotations as the safe habitat; the experience of comfort and joy, especially in one's home and family; a caring orientation, for example toward children; a civilized mode of behaviour that other people find easy to get along with, one that soothes them and builds their trust; a house that, while not splendid or overly stylish, is respectably clean and well-kept (Linnet 2011: 22–23).

*Hygge* is a concept that is important to Danes, at the individual up to the political level (see Linnet 2011; 2012a; 2012b). Contrary to the inherent meaning of the term, *hygge* has become an export item. True *hygge* enthusiasts would refuse to admit that *hygge* has grown to become a marketing ploy. Nevertheless, *hygge* can be purchased in the form of a *hyggelig* sofa or the *hyggelig* atmosphere in a café. Everything can be *hyggeligt*, and the consequence is an *uhyggelig* (un-*hyggelig*) reaction for those who insist on the genius of the concept. *Hygge* is popularly understood in relation to the other Danish values of modesty, simplicity, trust, and non-material well-being (Bennike 2016).

While carrying out fieldwork in Aarhus, I experienced 'genuine *hygge*' when my host family and I shared a bowl of our favourite sweets (*slik*) in front of the TV on Friday nights. We created *hygge* when we brought tea candles to a summer cottage, even as we worried that our rented cottage would not have any candle plate to put them on, possibly taking away an important element of *hygge*. We were having *hygge* when we rolled the *kransekage stængler* (marzipan logs), together in the bakery, and we met *hyggelige* people who chatted with us when they served us our coffee at the café. It was *hyggelig* with snow in December, and we noticed that some people found it *uhyggeligt* (uncomfortable, disconcerting) when they saw an immigrant woman wearing a burqa. If I were to list how many times I heard reference to *hygge* in one day, as a verb, adjective, or noun, to describe a situation, an activity, a person, or an atmosphere, I would be an anthropologist of *hygge,* too. My point is that *hygge*, whether it is a cultural construct used to mask hierarchy, cover differences, or deal with otherwise boring work tasks and uncomfortable situations, it is an important part of people's everyday lives.

## Conclusion

The Aarhus business owners enact a dominant moral imaginary. This chapter has dealt with the analytical concepts of values and morality. It has discussed different analytical as well as methodological approaches to these concepts. To draw out what I suggest are the components of a dominant morality in the world of the Aarhusian business owners, I have identified some central values and their expression in history, public discourse, and in the ethnographic studies of Scandinavian communities. These values involve the concepts of work ethic, equality understood as sameness, ideals of justice, and community.

Common for the concepts of work ethic, justice, equality, and community (*arbejdsmoral, retfærd, lighed,* and *fællesskab*) are that they are all value orientations built on perceptions about what is right and wrong (*rigtigt og forkert*). In the enactment of the local perception of morality (*moral*), I witnessed that these four value concepts were central elements in the social construct of a 'Danish' morality. When the local morality (*moral*) is expressed in the following chapters, the meanings ascribed to *moral* will vary, and I will deal with these meanings when they occur. However, we may fruitfully translate the Danish concept of *moral* into the English equivalent of morality without requiring further explanation.

As an analytical tool, morality refers to the sentimental judgements people make in their everyday lives. It refers to everyday moral judgements of right and wrong. The local concept *moral* represents the container of what is perceived by the majority of local society to be proper and improper behaviour, attitudes, and sentiments. Highly simplified; *moral* is the overall term used to refer to values of right and wrong. Ideas and incentives that promote work ethic, community, sameness, and justice are inherent in Danish social, political and social science discourses. *Hygge* proves to be a crucial factor in constituting or expressing the desired behaviour.

Although the meaning prescribed to social values differs among groups, individuals, temporalities, and social situations, there exists a general perception among the Aarhusian business owners, as with any human community, that their values and morality are shared and mutually understood by all members of society and the given group. These values and moral precepts are viewed as implicit in society, as natural, as 'the way we do things'. Because they are implicit and taken to be general, *moral* is always a potential source of conflict (Heintz 2008). Morality and values are not stable, of course. They evolve and change over time, between generations, depending on situations, and in different social relationships.

While Danish politicians strive to maintain an equity-ideal, this does not mean that Scandinavia, Denmark, or the business owners in Aarhus are egalitarian societies. Their emphasis on equality (as sameness), however, creates a society divided into different, homogeneous groups, all of which are at work trying to maintain sameness within their own exclusive community or enclave. These social enclaves can be centred around the neighbourhood, the workplace, the family, or a business zone somewhere in the city.

Throughout this study, therefore, we will endeavour to show how business owners, employees, and family members, through various strategies, try to maintain equality, understood as sameness, within their own group. More importantly, we shall see how what I refer to as moralities, including work ethics and values of community, sameness and justice, are not only vital to the success of these self-employed business owners, but operate as moral control mechanisms that are essential to the financial success of their firms. Morality and petty capitalism go hand in hand.

*Chapter 4*
# Ikan: A Family Firm as an Economic and Moral Unit

What exactly is a 'family firm', and how does it differ from an ordinary capitalist enterprise? This chapter seeks to answer this question by giving a detailed description of one particular family firm, a fish wholesaler and retailer which I call 'Ikan'. Like any social unit, Ikan has its own history and dynamics. Hence, we begin by describing the origins of Ikan as a family firm and the varying socio-political circumstances in which the firm has evolved. What were the terms of Ikan's fish business, and how have they changed over time? How has the market changed from the late nineteenth to the twenty-first century? What did the husband-and-wife team who founded Ikan do to succeed in business? What were, and are, the roles of family members in this particular social unit called the 'family firm'? This chapter uses the developments within Ikan to highlight the challenges facing other similar small, independent enterprises as they try to cope with the dynamics of today's neoliberal market capitalism.

Family firms are never stable. Hence, in the second part of this chapter, we describe the major changes in management which led to a conflict between Karl, the current owner, and the firm's apparent successor, his son-in-law, Poul. While this conflict was ostensibly centred on changing styles of management, there was also a deeper conflict over a set of moral values as to how a family business should be run. This interaction between family economy and family morality is the theme of this chapter.

The term 'moral values' is ambiguous. However, I use it to emphasize that this study deals with business owners who, as independent small business people, oppose large-scale corporate capitalism. These small business owners operate with a value set which encourage a combination of modest consumption and hard, independent work, symbolized by long hours of labour at the workplace, and motivated by a will to contribute to the community rather than simply accumulating personal wealth. This particular set of small business values, together with the fact that they all pursue their dreams of doing something they personally enjoy, either by making a living out of their hobbies or by creating something new, is a vital foundation to their commitment to their firm and to the firm's very existence. This kind of value set can be threatened. It can be threatened when the firm undergoes shocks from outside, changes from within, or even what may be a routine generation transfer from older owner to younger family member who might have a more management-centred style. Ikan was affected by these kinds of tensions. By examining a rupture in this family firm and the possible factors behind it, I will show how the invocation and sticking to the moral code – understood as the values listed above – is of vital importance to the firm's reproduction. It is important because morality operates at two levels: it enables the firm to survive and prosper, and it fulfils the kinds of family obligations which ultimately form the backbone of most family firms. I present the family from three perspectives: narrative, archival, and historical. With the narrative perspective, we obtain insight into family members' sentiments as they were expressed to me during my fieldwork as anthropologist, family friend, work colleague, and household member. Through the many roles I played in data collection, the various stories I heard about the Ikan firm varied in length, detail, focus, and content, depending on who was narrating and the context of the story-telling. The informants' narrative perspective was always limited to the information the narrator wanted me to have. However, the narrative accounts provide valuable insights into the moral and social values of the narrators. The stories they choose to share and how they frame these stories can help us understand who they are and what kind of firm they think Ikan is and should be. To fill as many gaps as possible, I complement the story with archival material and historical accounts. I will begin with the story of Ikan, as it is presented in historical and archival accounts.

## Genealogies of a Firm: A History of Patriarchy

In the late nineteenth century, Sunday school teacher 'Niels Ikan' (a pseudonym) decided to transform his private fishing boat into a retail counter for fresh fish. His role as a Sunday school teacher hints to Niels' prominent position in the community. When he established his firm, around 1890 Christianity still had a strong presence in local Danish society, and clergy of the Evangelical Lutheran church (which is also the Danish state church) were much respected. Niels was off to a good start: he already had the boat, and his initial capital most likely came from his own savings. There was considerable overlap between his household- and his business economy, as was typical for small family firms at the time and was certainly not as marked as today's contemporary limited liability company (Danish A/S, German GmbH) business structure. With industrialisation and urbanisation, the need for new capital investments also increased the need for credit. This led to the gradual separation of the firm's economy from the household's economy (Weber 1999). Hence, instead of placing the debt upon the entire family, aspiring Danish small business owners gradually separated the finances of their household from those of the firm (Weber 1999: 81–2). This was also the case with Niels Ikan's fishmongering firm (cf. Løkke and Faye Jacobsen 1997).

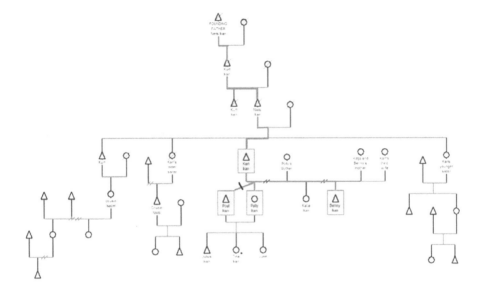

Figure 1. The Ikan family.

In the late nineteenth century, the Aarhus dock was alive with fishing boats and shops. The harbour had expanded heavily between 1840 and 1860, allowing long distance trade to an extent that rapidly made Aarhus into Denmark's second largest city, flourishing with businesses (Jessen 2016). When the city's inhabitants wanted fresh fish, the dock was the place to buy it, and Niels' business was headquartered there. In the early hours of the morning, the catch of the night arrived with the many fishing vessels, and the fishermen immediately sold off their catch in auctions on the dock. Like the other fishmongers, Niels would bid on the different fish and take it back to his boat, where he would rinse and prepare the fish for his customers. In the first years after Niels started his business, the population of Aarhus expanded from 15,000 in 1870 to more than 50,000 in 1900, and Niels and other entrepreneurs also saw their businesses grow (see also Jessen 2016).

Forty years later, in the 1930s, when Niels's son Kurt had taken over his father's firm, the market was still vibrant. The family narratives describe Kurt as an innovative person who, like his father, was engaged in the local community. Business went well, and Kurt wanted to try something different. Soon he started a wholesale section of his fishmongering, alongside the retail trade, and he continued his success on the dock. With the exception of the financial crisis of the 1930s and the German occupation between 1940 and 1945, the Ikan fishmongering firm grew steadily (Kold 2015). In the decades after the Second World War, Aarhus also continued to grow as an urban economic centre for Jutland and for foreign markets. The city acquired high-rise apartment buildings, row-house developments and modernist architecture similar to that of other growing European cities (Jessen 2016). The dominant industries consisted of two main corporations: one manufacturing dairy and other farm products from the surrounding agricultural hinterland, and one in fish processing. All industry was located in the harbour area, and although Aarhus has developed far beyond the harbour, the Aarhus dock still stands as an iconic image representing the city's industry, innovation, education, economic development and connection with the outside world.

Seventy years after Niels started to deal fish from his pram on the dock, it was time for the third generation to take over. It was the mid-1900s, and Ikan now consisted of a wholesale depot on the dock and a retail shop in the city centre. After 40 years of ownership, Kurt divided the business between his two sons. The oldest, also named Kurt, took over the retail section, and second son Niels continued the wholesale section (see figure 1). Like his father and his father before him, Niels involved his own sons in the firm from an early age. He expected the children to work in the firm when they were not in school. Only a few years after Niels and Kurt had taken over the two shops from their father in the 1960s, Kurt senior died unexpectedly. Niels decided to take his youngest son Karl, still a teenager, out of school. Since Kurt junior had no heirs, Karl took over his retail shop. Karl never returned to school, but he proved to be an able worker and manager, despite his young age.

After ten years of managing the retail shop uptown, in Aarhus centre, Karl took over the wholesale unit from his father. He tried to manage both shops, but changes in the market made it difficult to run two businesses located in different parts of the city. Karl therefore decided to merge his retail shop with the wholesale premises on the dock. The reason Karl gave me for closing the retail shop in the centre of town, which, according to newspaper archives, had a good reputation and was popular among customers, was that the fish auctions did not yield enough surplus fish to be sold in the shop. Karl's older brother had also opened his own retail business uptown, but he closed it before he could pass it on to his children. Unlike Karl, he did not have success in the fishmonger business. The family's official reason was that times were bad and that he did not scale down in time, like Karl did.

Many factors can have compelled Karl to merge his two businesses. In the 1970s, the Aarhus basin, exhausted from overfishing, was indeed producing less fish. The oil crisis, followed by a significant rise in oil prices in the late 1970s and 1980s also affected consumption of fresh fish (Jensen et al. 2011: 6; Rerup 2017). This changed the entire seaside area from being a part of the city that had flourished with fishing cutters, auctions, fishmongers, fish processing plants and cafeterias, to an empty dock, soon to be populated by private yachts. For Karl, the dock area became a place where there was nothing going on: 'no culture' (*ingen kultur*), referring to the absence of small, local businesses and fishing vessels.

In 2015, fishing in the Aarhus area was limited to individuals fishing for their own private consumption. Ikan purchased most of its fish at fish auctions far from Aarhus, on the north-western (North Sea) coast of Denmark. The fish market had been globalized, like the rest of the market, and along with fish originating in Danish waters, Ikan traded fish from Norwegian fish farms, the North Sea, the Mediterranean, the Atlantic Ocean, Barents Sea, the Greenland coast, and even some exotic fish from New Zealand.

According to the narratives told by various members of the Ikan family, it was with Karl that the story of Ikan really began (or was remembered). Karl described how he looked up to his father and listened carefully, learning as much as possible from the successful fishmonger. Ikan being a link in the global fish supply chain, Karl expanded the firm, developing the wholesale section into a competitive business that provided fish to numerous restaurants and public institutions, with customers far beyond Aarhus' city limits. Every day, six to eight vans loaded with fish set out to deliver Ikan fish to restaurants, public canteens, hospitals, nursing homes, the surrounding areas, and across Jutland. Despite the changes in the fish market in the 1970s and 1980s, and in contrast to numerous other fishmongers who disappeared along with the local fishermen, Karl's success continued. Ikan became a well-established firm in the food wholesale sector.

During Karl's lifetime as a fishmonger, the fishing industry in Denmark underwent substantial changes: the local small-holder fishing cooperatives gave way to large corporations with monstrous trawlers (Højrup and Schriewer 2012). While competition among independent fishmongers decreased as their numbers became fewer, supermarkets started to offer fresh fish over the counter. Overall fish consumption decreased with various financial crises in the 1980s, and the market for wholesale and retail fish became more competitive. In addition, the market was accompanied by stricter government regulation of fish quota catches and fish quality. Archival documents present us with a history of Ikan passing through a series of success stories, followed by hardships and re-orientations with the political and economic conjunctures.

Under these changing conditions over the decades, there is little doubt that Karl's business acumen and timing has played a significant role in his success. Not only did his business survive economic downturns and other hardships, it thrived. This success was not without costs, however. Karl paid careful attention to market developments and made the necessary cutbacks during challenging times. As Karl explained to me, 'Through the years, I've had to fire many employees'.[52] In the 1980s, Denmark, like most Western economies, suffered from rampant inflation, and interest rates on loans went up drastically. Karl had made prudent investments and did not suffer significantly, 'Things didn't go really wrong back then'. Karl had a frugal business strategy, and Ikan continued to grow. On several occasions, when sales slumped or money was tight, he made compromises to keep the business going. Karl's decision to close his retail shop in the shopping district proved wise, as it freed up resources for his merged wholesaling and retail business on the dock. He made some compromises in the quality of products, but never more than what could 'pass' without the customer noticing. Karl knew that to be successful, it was important to 'work hard' and 'know the business'. Newspaper articles describe Karl's retail shop as famous for being 'a wonderful, clean, and appealing shop where it never smelled of old fish' (quote from newspaper archives).[53]

Although Ikan expanded, Karl never stopped working on the shop floor with his employees. He emphasized the importance of knowing what was going in all parts of the firm and not losing touch with any of its many components. All this was contained in his characteristic phrase, 'You have to cut [the fish] yourself!'[54] A mantra I heard him repeat numerous times.[55]

---

[52] Original quote in Danish: 'Gennem årene har jeg været nødt til at fyre mange medarbejdere.'

[53] Source is not included for reasons of anonymity. For the same reason, I only include my English translation. This applies to all future citations taken from public archives.

[54] Original quote in Danish: 'Du skal selv ned og skære.'

[55] *Skære* is the Danish word for 'to cut' and was commonly used to refer to the preparation of whole fish, involving rinsing, filleting, removing heads, bones, mincing, and portioning. In this context, *skære* refers to the entire process, from unpacking newly landed fish to sorting different 'cut' products.

Karl admits that when he merged the retail and the wholesale sections of this business, he had great plans to expand. His grandfather had purchased the land on which the combined wholesale and retail firm was now located, and Karl wanted to enlarge the building. After several years of insistently reapplying to the municipality to obtain the building permit, Karl was finally granted permission. Soon he had realized his plans of a large retail shop, storage facilities, offices, and a processing section; all at one location, on land that he legally owned. One of his cousins vividly recounts how Karl's father, who was still alive when the construction took place, proudly watched his son develop the family firm. However, Karl did not invest all the capital he accumulated over the years back into the firm. He bought property and stock as well. In 2015, he owned a large house in one of the wealthy Aarhus suburbs and he had two other apartments that he rented out. He also invested some of his money in stocks. In this manner, Karl was the most overtly capitalist of all the business owners with whom I did fieldwork.

In the early 2000s, Karl contracted a severe medical condition, and he found himself forced to transfer day-to-day management of Ikan to the next generation. Fortunately for Karl, his oldest daughter Polly and son-in-law Poul were both working in the firm at the time. They were also willing to take over immediately. After a period of successful management, Polly and Poul established a limited liability company (*anpartsselskab/ApS*).[56] They rented the premises from Karl, with all its stock and facilities. Karl was thus still the legal owner of the property, and he had his own company (a Danish *aktieselskab, written A/S*, a corporation with a higher degree of capitalization than an ApS). Hence, although Polly and Poul, with their 'Ikan Fresh ApS' 'took over' the Ikan business activity the firm, Ikan remained in Karl's possession. Karl's firm, Ikan A/S received monthly lease payments paid by Polly and Poul's firm, Ikan Fresh ApS. For customers, the public, and anyone who asked, Ikan had simply been 'passed on' from Karl to the next generation. Polly and Poul, who at the time were in their late twenties, played along. They made no changes to Ikan's exterior façade. It was the same old Ikan. Formally, however, Karl still owned the property, the rights to the family firm name, and he remained director of Ikan A/S, owning 100 per cent of the shares. Poul and a cousin, Niels, were members of the board Ikan A/S (see figure 2 and 3).

As Karl's oldest daughter, Polly had been involved in the firm her entire life. While growing up, her favourite activity had been to join her father at work, and she never missed an opportunity to assist him in the

---

[56] An ApS, a form of Danish limited liability company, requires a start capital of minimum DKK 50,000. A Danish corporation called A/S, requires larger capitalization and can issue shares.

business. Polly often told me how 'it was my favourite thing when I was little, to go with dad to the shop and to the fish auctions'.[57] Poul, Polly's husband, had an enormous interest for fish since childhood, and he had worked for another fishmonger at the young age of thirteen, cutting fish every day after school. A few years later, Poul started working at Ikan. When Polly and Poul took over management, Polly's two younger siblings were still in primary school.

Although Polly and Poul took over the firm prematurely because of Karl's unexpected medical condition, they could also be seen as the natural successors. They had expected to take over the firm at some later point, and they had started to prepare for it. They had developed clear ideas of how to run the firm. In a newspaper article, Poul was asked about the year's scarcity of codfish, which is the traditional meal prepared for the Danish New Year's Eve's dinners. The weather, combined with several public holidays when the fishermen did not work, had limited the cod supply, and demand was much higher than supply. Poul was quoted in the article as saying that the prices in their shop, in contrast to other fishmongers across the country, would remain 'close to normal' because he had foreseen the low supply. He explained that Ikan had started stocking up on cod in the beginning of December:

> Then we cleaned them and vacuum-packed them and froze them, so they will be ready for New Year's Eve. This enables us to sell them for close to normal price. We would rather make a little less per kilo and sell a lot, than sell at high price and risk that we will have many leftover fish because it was too expensive for our customers.

Poul also made a comment about Ikan being an old firm and that he therefore knew what to do in situations like this, 'We have some experience to draw upon', he assured me.

Polly had the same passion for the fish industry as her father, and Poul had entered many competitions involving fish (such as filleting, various ways of preparing fish, cutting, and so on) and he had won several national and international championships. At the time when Polly and Poul took over, in the early 2000s, the business was going well. Their first real challenge, however, would come soon afterwards, with the 2008 financial crisis and the collapse of the housing market. Consumption declined drastically, including consumption of fresh fish (which is relatively high-priced), and many Danes fell deeply into debt.

Despite the fall in consumption, Polly and Poul managed to keep the business afloat. Poul admitted that 'a challenging period started around that

---

[57] Original quote in Danish: 'Det var det bedste jeg vidste, da jeg var lille; at tage med far i butikken og på fiskeauktioner'.

time, but it will turn [better] again very soon'.[58] Poul, who assumed the title of director of Ikan, had followed technological developments in commerce and had established a 'presence' for Ikan on social media with a website and a Facebook account. In an interview with the local newspaper, Poul explained, 'You know, you need a digital business card these days, and that's why we're on Facebook.' Ikan also operated several truck vendors in addition to its main premises on the dock, and they continued to organize social and educational events, as Karl had done when he was in charge. After a few years, by 2015, Karl had recovered from his medical condition, but he remained retired from day-to-day management of his firm. Polly and Poul held a ten-year leasing contract for the premises, which was to be renewed in January 2017. According to the financial accounts, and what Polly and Poul have reported, the couple managed to continue Ikan's profitability through this first challenging period, about five years.

## Overcoming New Challenges

In the development of Aarhus city, the docklands area, which had formerly been dominated by industry, factories, parking lots, and shipping containers, became the site of architecturally impressive skyscrapers and apartments. By 2015, this construction boom began to impact Ikan. Although the Ikan family owned the actual land, they could not control the physical accessibility of the dock, and the construction began to impede access to the dock significantly. Roads were closed, and the entire area was transformed into a construction site. Although the city planners had constructed an alternative entrance route for cars, it entailed a two km detour in an area known by the city's inhabitants always to be clogged with traffic. For more than three years, Ikan found itself in the middle of a construction area with only one unsatisfactory access route. Poul and Polly made many efforts to attract people to the dock, and they filed numerous complaints with the municipality. They sought to attract customers with wholesale prices, offered free home delivery to addresses throughout the city, advertised catering services, and so forth. 'We extended delivery to include home delivery to private individuals, because it was impossible for them to get to the store', Poul explained. Retail trade (especially in fresh fish) requires 'traffic' (fish, unlike other items, cannot just sit for days on the shelf), and the construction had caused a major disruption of traffic to Ikan's storefront.

On the bright side, Ikan was able to avoid being evicted entirely. They owned the land and could remain, if they so desired. It was Karl who

---

[58] Original quote in Danish: 'Der startede en periode med modgang, ja men der går nok snart godt igen'.

declared to me that 'They cannot throw us out because we own the land.' Ikan also had another 'weapon' in its fight against eviction: namely, their old family history. The fact that Ikan was among Denmark's oldest shops, several generations old in fact, became a convincing argument when the municipality tried to compel the firm to sell or move. Although Polly and Poul were the official owners of the business (subcontracting it from Karl under their own ApS), the physical premises was still under Karl's ownership. Although Karl's daughter and her husband were engaged in the firm, Karl also fought for years, despite constant pressure, not to give up the property and succumb to urban re-development.

Karl had long and broad experience in dealing with municipal officials, both as an engaged citizen and as a *fiskemand* (fishmonger). When Ikan was threatened, Karl thus played what might be called 'the heritage card': he engaged the historic preservation office, who supported his cause, and together they managed to convince the municipality to grant the location of his shop status as a 'historic preservation site' and part of an 'open-air museum'. Ikan would be part of the Aarhus 'Old City' museum, (*Den gamle by*) an open-air museum located on the other side of the city, consisting of old buildings representing different period in Aarhus' history. The street where Ikan was located fit into the museum framework, representing the old fishery street (*fiskerigade*). Of the entire dock area, the single street where Ikan was located was thus spared because of its historic value. Together with the local historic preservation office, Ikan and Karl had thus helped preserve an important part of Aarhus's history. Ikan was not just a business. It was part of Aarhus' cultural heritage.

According to Karl, he was not primarily motivated by financial returns, although saving the business was undoubtedly an important motivation for his engagement. If he had not managed to maintain his location at the dock, Karl, together with his daughter and son-in-law, would certainly have been able to reopen their business elsewhere, Karl assured me. He was not ready to give up his family legacy that easily.

Karl was not just a businessman, however. He was an engaged citizen and a protector of his family's legacy. He was a person who could get things done. Throughout his life, he had founded, led and directed numerous fish-related organisations and campaigns, helping to sustain the always volatile fishing industry and the livelihood of the independent fishmongers. His legacy provided him with pride and sentiments of responsibility, not only to preserve his business and his family's history but also that of the fishing industry's anglers and fishmongers nation-wide. A newspaper article from the 2000s, referred to Karl and Ikan in the following words:

Everyone knew [Karl Ikan]. He was quite famous, and he was elected director of the Danish Fishmongers Association. People also know [Ikan's] story because it is not just a business. It is a family business and an old one, too. There are not many of those.

Customers also confirmed a sense of 'belonging' to the firm through statements such as 'My family has shopped at [Ikan] for 50 years, and although we make a deviation from time to time, we always come back.' Karl has also been active in the national campaign to get Danes to eat more fish, preferably twice a week for dinner, as a health incentive; hence the campaign was known as the 'Twice a week' campaign (*'to gange om ugen'*). Karl's engagement is evident in the many logos on the Ikan work uniforms, showing various fish-related associations and slogans (see Plate 3).

Plate 3. Ikan firm work clothes showing three of the campaigns/organizations in which Ikan and Karl were actively involved.

Although Karl has been a successful businessman, he has had to endure the entry of modern, American-inspired supermarkets in the 1960s, followed by the giant hypermarkets offering a growing variety of products under one roof. These mass retailing industries now offer consumers every possible product, from shoes and electronics to fresh bread and now, fresh fish, and they have threatened and even eliminated independent shops and businesses in several sectors (Lundkvist 2009a). The reality in which Karl and his daughter operate is now radically different than decades ago, when Karl's great-grandfather started selling fish from the quay. Supermarkets now have fresh meat and bread, with their own butchers and bakeries, and have recently begun to sell fresh fish as well.

The Danish food sector has changed from the predominantly small and medium-sized independent merchants to a domination of a few giant corporate chains. In Denmark, most of the food retailers are owned and operated by one successful family, the Salling family, who started their first American-inspired supermarket, Føtex, in Aarhus in 1960 (their first retail shop opened in 1906). In 2017, the corporation Dansk Supermarked Group owned most of the Danish supermarkets and shopping malls, and 81 per cent of the shares of Dansk Supermarked are owned by the Salling family.[59] The other Danish supermarket group, Coop Nordic, started as a cooperative of small merchants in 1844 and has since expanded into a large conglomerate consisting of several supermarket chains in Denmark and Sweden. Other dominating supermarket corporations operating in Denmark are the 'discount' supermarkets German Lidl, Norwegian Rema 1000, and the upscale Meny (Norgesgruppen).

The more upscale supermarkets, such as Føtex and Meny, have developed more specialized bakery, vegetables, meat, and fish sections, offering fresh products with the same quality as independent butchers, bakeries, and fishmongers. Obviously, this development toward specialized boutiques within giant supermarkets, generally open for longer hours and even on Sundays, constitutes a major threat to independent niche merchants who have built up their businesses on the same values of having fresh, quality, retail expertise and personalized service to a loyal customer base. The small shops had had a niche because they had specialized product availability previously lacking even in the large supermarkets that focused on competitive prices and broad selection. In an article published by the Danish Broadcast Service (DR), statistics documenting the decline of independent Danish fishmongers were explained in terms of changes in consumption patterns. Danes ate less fresh fish and instead purchased more

---

[59] This includes 1400 stores in Denmark, Sweden, Germany, and The United Kingdom, with the supermarket brands Føtex, Bilka, Netto, and Salling (www.dansksupermarked.com).

frozen fish in the supermarkets. A fishmonger was quoted saying that 'Danes have become worse at eating fish' (Olesen 2013). With constant improvement of supermarkets and department stores offering 'everything you need in one place', the small niche shops must compete even harder. They must offer a product, or a service, that people will go out of their way for, and perhaps even pay more for.

Karl, who was still a firm believer in Ikan, refused to back down from the corporate competition. When his children brought up the growing challenges of a corporate, global economy, cheaper products being offered at central locations in 'all at one place' stores, Karl's response was that it only meant that you had to work even harder. With the phrase 'You have to cut with your own hands', Karl invoked the need for the owner himself to get down on the shop floor and do the manual work. His phrase 'a fishmonger is a worker', implies direct connotations to a hardworking, manual labourer. A fishmonger needs to perform manual labour to save money, ensure top quality, and maintain an intimate relationship with customers. Karl refused to believe that there was no future markct for his niche. In conversation with me, he insisted that people would continue to understand and appreciate the difference between local, expert specialists and that 'people will continue to appreciate quality and good craftsmanship'. Karl's sentiments around these issues have been documented in many newspaper interviews over the past few decades. In conversation, he claimed that the reason why his firm has survived, unlike the 35 other fishmongers in the Aarhus area, who have disappeared over just a few years, was because 'I am engaged in my craft'. He also stressed the importance of the five remaining fishmongers sticking together and collaborating, precisely because there were so few of them left. 'We are stronger together', Karl emphasized. The emphasis on a close relationship with customers, the owners' direct involvement in manual labour, and attention to detail, quality and freshness, were repeated conversational topics whenever I talked with Karl. These values were visible in his continuing engagement in various fish-related associations, both local and national. Customer statements such as '[Ikan] is an awesome place with fun people who give out hugs, and they have the best fish in town!' also confirmed the emphasis on the owners' involvement and focus on quality and expertise. Other accounts described more personal encounters. One customer stated, 'I had the best experience together with my daughter, who is paralysed and connected to a respirator machine. The sweet person who helped me talked to her, taught her about the fish, and teased her. We really enjoyed the fish and the experience'.[60]

---

[60] The quote has been slightly modified to anonymize. Author's translation from the Danish.

The story of the Ikan family is not just a business narrative. It is also the story of engaged individuals who dedicate their lives to their passion, which lies in their inherited profession. A search through the archives of the local newspaper provides us with numerous articles and interviews with and about Ikan and their owners. It tells the story of a family who is dedicated to fish on multiple levels, highlighting their commitment to their occupation and to their local community. These stories keep alive Ikan's long history and reputation, as owners who are 'real people', 'cutting the fish themselves' and representing the firm and the industry. The local newspaper regularly visits the shop to update its readers on the current state of this local 'beloved' firm, giving Ikan and its owners a place in the history of Aarhus. They are the iconic family firm.

## Polly and Poul

Poul was in his early forties and had been owner of Ikan LLC (Ikan ApS) for nine years when I met him for the first time. Poul had a personal interest in fish and a great fascination for marine species. He told me his story while we drove through the neighbourhood where he grew up, living in an apartment building with his parents and younger brother. 'I spent more time teaching myself about sea life than paying attention at school'. His father worked in the agricultural division of the municipality, and his mother worked part-time at a day-care centre. Neither of his parents had a higher education, and his life circumstances could be described as modest.

Although Poul's father held a position that may be described as working class in a Danish sense, he cultivated the typical self-employed values of modesty, frugality, hard physical work, and 'managing on your own' (*klare sig selv*) (Hastrup and Löfgren 1992). Another important marker of Polly's 'managing on your own'-mind-set, is how Poul's parents expected for him and his brother to manage financially. Their parents gave their children all the basic necessities of life but reserved other treats for special occasions. These circumstances encouraged Poul to take up part-time work from age 13. He started working for a fishmonger in his neighbourhood, cutting fish early in the morning before school. It was at about this time that he met Polly.

Polly grew up in middle-class circumstances, but like Poul, she also acquired the self-employed ethic of having to work for her own fortune. Polly's parents separated when she was only a few years old, and while she enjoyed working in her father's fish business, she lived with her mother, who never remarried. Karl, meanwhile, remarried and had two children with his new wife. Polly was not comfortable living with Karl's new family. Unlike her father Karl, who owned a profitable firm, Polly's mother was employed in various service businesses and struggled to make ends meet as a single mother. Polly had to pay rent to her mother from age 15, a practice not uncommon in Denmark.

Being the daughter of a successful business owner did not benefit Polly materially. However, Karl chose Polly to be his successor. He taught her from a young age how to manage on her own and treated her as his successor when he taught her about fish and how the firm worked. Although she continued to live with her mother, Polly spent as much time as she could helping her father in his firm. In order to succeed, Karl imprinted on Polly the importance of 'standing on your own two feet'. Although Karl could hardly be described as working class in financial terms, his attachment to the physical work of running the fish business made him strongly identify as a worker. He referred to himself and his ancestors as workers (*arbejdere*).

I suggest that we understand Karl's invoking these qualities as signs of being self-employed (selvstændig erhvervsdrivende), rather than working class. The self-employed have quite different values than working-class people regarding work, salary, frcc time, self-realization, and so forth. (see Højrup 1983). For workers, work is a means to an end, the end is realized in free time. For the self-employed, work is both end and means: Work is their life. I will discuss this further in Chapter 5. Although Karl's own style was to emphasize the hard physical work and long hours spent on the floor. These self-employed life mode characteristics are described by Joseph Schumpeter (1943: 132) in the following way 'getting things done' and 'you are the creator of your own happiness'. These, features have also been identified in Scandinavian peasant society (Hastrup and Löfgren 1992) and among Scandinavian self-employed fishers and craftsmen generally (Højrup 1983).

Polly and Poul grew up at a time when the Danish welfare state was developing, but when women's rights and the structural adjustments for women's employment, were not fully developed with maternal leave, universal day-care, and other social benefits that enable women to work, give birth and take care of children. Women had entered the workforce on a large scale. Polly and Poul's mothers, therefore, knew the burdens of taking care of household while having to make money independently, and they placed great importance on transferring the values of 'managing for oneself' onto their children (Gullestad 1997).

These details about Polly and Poul's upbringing as children of workers (*arbejdere*), are important to understand when we review the choices and actions, they made in running the fish business and in their personal lives. Their working-class backgrounds (but with unique access to the life chances offered by entering a small business) became an important source of influence for the development of their social values.

When Polly and Poul became a couple, they shared the enthusiasm for fish, and Poul quickly entered his father-in-law's firm. Initially, Polly went to school to become a care worker and was only involved in the firm part-time. By her mid-twenties, however, she was working full-time in the firm. She was employed as a bookkeeper, but she (still) described herself as a 'potato' (*kartoffel*), meaning that her work involved various tasks. Before taking over management, the couple had rented a flat downtown, close to the shop, and Poul immersed himself completely in the firm. He rarely had time off and justified this by their being so close to the firm. 'It was hard to stay away from the business when it was just a quick jog away', Poul explained, laughing and shaking his head.

Poul gradually received more responsibilities in the firm, as his father in-law prepared him and Polly to take over management someday. When Karl suddenly fell severely ill and Poul stepped in as manager, the medical reports concluded that Karl would never fully recover. As a result, Polly and Poul formally took over management through the establishment of their own firm, 'Ikan Fresh ApS'. As described above, Polly and Poul had a leasing agreement with Karl's 'Ikan'. At the time, the couple had a toddler and a new baby on the way. Polly worked fewer hours than Poul, using the day-care offerings available during normal working hours. Polly returned to work when their first-born was seven months old, placing him in day-care. Soon after the transfer of Ikan to their hands, Polly and Poul decided to move further away from the business, ostensibly to 'get some distance from the firm', as Poul explained. and realize their dream of having their own home in a village. They did that by purchasing a small farm with two houses, together with Poul's parents.

These details about Polly and Poul's life give some indication about their priorities and their ambitions. They tell us about their relationship with kin and offer information about how their daily lives are organized. Polly and Poul wanted a comfortable home for themselves and for their family. They wanted their children to grow up outside the city, in contrast to their own urban upbringing: 'Here the children can play outside and run over to their [paternal] grandparents any time, and we [Polly and Poul] will not be running down to the shop all the time'.[61] Their choice to move away from the city and have a house in the countryside was not just a typical middle-class dream. It was a strategy to separate the private sphere from that of the

---

[61] In Danish: 'Her kan ungerne løbe frit ude, og de kan løbe over til farmor og farfar hvornår som helst, og vi kan ikke løbe ned i butikken hele tiden'.

firm and a means of ensuring that they would spend more time together as a family.

The big house and mortgage came with financial obligations.[62] Not only did it encourage Poul to work hard to pay the mortgage payments, but the couple's indebtedness now necessitated that the business went well. Otherwise, they risked losing the house, as so many Danes did during the 2009 financial crisis. Under these conditions, Poul began to reassess his engagement in the business: from a simple passion for fish to a more profit-oriented motivation.

When Polly and Poul took over the firm, Poul wanted the business to grow. He therefore engaged a professional salesperson to travel around to recruit new wholesale customers and maintain a good relationship with existing customers. As part of expanding retail sales, Ikan bought and managed several street vendor trucks that operated in designated spots around the city. Poul was trying to turn Ikan from a simple self-employed shop to a capitalist enterprise.

In time, Poul allowed himself to step back from the fish processing and employed people to manage the manual labour, allowing him more office time. Although the hours spent on the premises did not change much, his roles and tasks changed drastically over the ten-year period after he took over management. Poul went from spending most of his time on the floor, cutting fish, to focusing on administrative tasks in the office, buying, selling, negotiating and filling orders. With Polly by his side, Poul managed the firm with success, even after the global financial breakdown in the late 2000s (see Hall and Campbell 2017). In 2009, Ikan won a prize for 'most successful business of the year' in a local contest. A few years later, however, Ikan began to encounter difficulties. There were a variety of factors involved: a slow reaction to the crash in the market, poor management decisions, the impact of the reconstruction of the dock, and other factors as well. Ikan's business difficulties led to a rupture within the family.

---

[62] Danish mortgages at the time required a five per cent down payment from the buyer's own savings, with the remainder in the form of 15 per cent bank loan and the remaining 80 per cent as a much cheaper 30-year mortgage. Banks can approve lenders to pay either variable or fixed mortgage interest, and borrowers can also be approved to pay interest-only for up to ten years with a low monthly payment, with part of the interest being tax deductible. The obstacle facing first-time buyers, besides bank approval, is having the saved-up cash for five per cent deposit and for the 15 per cent more expensive bank loan. Polly and Pouls mortgage, however, was a much cheaper mortgage loan, in which the house is put up as collateral.

## Rupture

Having left Aarhus in February of 2016, I returned five months later, in the summer of 2016. Although I focused my research on firms other than Ikan, I stopped by the shop from time to time and also visited Polly and Poul in their home. Something was amiss, but I could not figure out what. Every time I went to visit Ikan, something had changed in the shop. The upstairs office had been painted, Poul was not there during normal business hours, the store was differently arranged, and every time I went, I met only Polly's younger (half-)brother, Benny, who was cutting and preparing fish. When I asked about Polly or Poul, the employees seemed distressed and told me they had gone home for the day. When I sometimes found Poul in the premises, he was not in his office dealing with orders as usual; he was now back on the cutting floor, preparing fish. When I asked why he was down cutting so much lately, I never got a clear answer; he just mumbled something about changing times. I never met Karl in the shop during this time.

I also learned that Frode, one of their most enduring employees and close personal friend, and described as 'Poul's right hand', had resigned. I now understood that something was not right. Frode would not have left Ikan unless something was seriously wrong. Frode never provided me with any details about his departure, but he told me that if he were to work for Ikan, it would be for no one else than Polly and Poul. Another employee confirmed my suspicion. It turned out that Karl had decided not to renew the leasing agreement that allowed Polly and Poul to run the business with the family name. The lease would expire in six months. After ten years of running and managing Ikan, effectively 'performing' as owners, Poul would be replaced by Polly's younger brother Benny. Benny was in his early twenties and had never before had a full-time job or expressed much interest in taking over the firm. Yet, he had now taken over management functions from Poul, while Polly, I would later discover, had remained as bookkeeper. Effectively, Polly lost the benefits she had had as a co-owner together with her husband, but Polly's formal role did not change. She remained the bookkeeper, but the influence she had had in practice, as a co-decision maker in the firm, disappeared with Poul's formal lease. She was now reduced to 'just' a bookkeeper.

I had obtained the news about Benny's 'takeover' of Ikan from the employees. I wanted to talk to Polly and Poul about what had happened and get the full story. However, I quickly understood that the topic was extremely sensitive. I had spent six months living with Polly and Poul in their home. I knew them as the proud owners of a fifth-generation family firm. Poul had shared with me his plans and dreams for the future, and he had never given me any hint that he wanted to do anything else than run and develop Ikan. Polly and Poul were my friends and while in Aarhus, they were my family. I felt that I knew them very well, and I knew that Poul took great pride in being the owner-operator of Ikan, even though it was technically speaking a leasing arrangement with his father-in-law. Why had they not told me about this? I always asked about the business whenever I went to their house, and on each occasion, they assured me that everything was normal, 'No news' ('*intet nyt*') was their usual reply. However, a change was now visible, also in their home.

When my family and I went to visit Polly and Poul for dinner one afternoon, Poul took me up to the room I used to sleep in, to show me a collection of clothes he had purchased from a liquidation sale. He wanted to know if I was interested in buying any of these outfits. The confident, generous Poul I knew, the one managing a growing fish business, had been replaced by a nervous salesman who desperately tried to push me into buying clothes that I was clearly not interested in. The situation was awkward. His behaviour was strange. But when I hinted about changes in the firm, he refused to talk. It was only after I finished all my fieldwork, and their family came to visit me at my home in Norway, in February 2017, that they were finally ready to talk.

Their lease on Ikan had now expired. 'We were not prepared', Poul lamented. They simply had not foreseen that Karl would not renew their lease and replace them with Benny. They insisted, moreover, that they did not know why this had happened. Poul was, as usual, more diplomatic than Polly, who spoke more freely. Business had not been good, they admitted, but the circumstances had been extraordinary with the reconstruction of the dock. They felt they had done everything they could.

Karl had simply taken the firm back by not renewing Polly and Poul's lease after ten years. According to Polly and Poul, Karl had not discussed with them his plans to put Benny in management. According to them, Karl had told them nothing until he told them everything, and it was clear that he was not going to renew their lease, just a few months before it expired. While Polly continued her job as the bookkeeper, Poul moved back down on the floor to cut fish, a job his health had not allowed him the past few years. How long could he endure? When the family came to see me in February 2017, neither of them had received any salary yet, Poul told me shaking his head in frustration (two months had passed without any income). 'We don't know how much we are getting in salary because we haven't received any salary'. At least they had not been fired, was their conclusion. The couple did not hide their frustration, nor their profound disappointment. 'Fish is our life, you know', Poul said raising his eyebrows, 'We know no other life than Ikan'. Although Polly had occasionally expressed the idea that it would have been fun to open her own, completely different business someday, fish *was* indeed their life. Karl had thrown a wrench into the motor.

| Registered Firms in the Ikan family 2015 | | | | |
|---|---|---|---|---|
| Name of firm | Ikan A/S | Ikan Fresh ApS | Poul holding ApS | Karl Ikan holding ApS |
| Established | 2000 | 2007 | 2007 | 2002 |
| Share holders | Karl Ikan holding 100% | Poul holding 100 % | Poul 100 % | Karl 100 % |
| Board members | Katja (Polly's sister), Karl, Polly | Poul, Karl, Niels (cousin) | - | - |
| Director | Karl | Poul | Poul | Karl |
| Function | Leasing premises | Wholesale and retail | Wholesale and retail | Non-financial holding company |
| Equity € | 67.115 | -114.100 | 17.543 | 17.543 |
| Gross profit € | 8000 | 604.000 | 1300 | -18.792 |
| Net income € | -20.134 | -53.692 | -106 | -18.792 |
| Results € | 67.115 | -53.692 | -83 | 18.792 |
| Assets € | 698.000 | 402.693 | 26.846 | 147.654 |
| Number of registered employees | 1 | 5-9 | - | - |
| Status | Active | Active | Active | Active |

Figure 2. Registered firms in the Ikan family 2015. (Source: virk.dk and Ikan's annual financial statements).[63]

He had finally convinced his only son, who had not had a job since he finished secondary school three years previously, to come into the firm. Instead of leasing the premises to Benny, as he had done with Polly and Poul who had their own firm Ikan Fresh ApS, Karl came back in and made Benny managing director of Ikan, with Karl as board chairman. At least that was the official story reported in the local news media and which was widely

---

[63] Virk.dk is a website which provides data about all Danish companies based on their company registration (CVR); this information includes financial statements, ownership records, location, etc.

discussed on other forums. A particularly important detail, unmentioned in all official statements, was that Benny had no formal power in the firm. Publicly, it was stated that Poul had withdrawn from Ikan as director due to health reasons and been replaced as managing director by Benny. The mention of Poul in public media coverage slowly faded, and in 2018, Poul's name vanished from any public statements about Ikan. Benny was presented as the youngest generation in the line of Ikan fishmongers. Media channels and social media profiles representing the firm simply erased the era of Polly and Poul from the history of the firm. Nevertheless, their roles and existence in the firm remained in the hard copies of numerous published books on Aarhus cultural and business heritage, showing the couple in their shop, and describing them as the owners and managers of Ikan.

In order to obtain a clearer picture of the changes in firm-family arrangements, I have produced two tables listing all the different firms owned by members of the Ikan family from 2015 (see Figure 2) through the changes in 2017. These charts reflect the firm's financial statements and the formal roles of family members. The official narrative was that Benny was now both the owner and CEO, as well as the public 'face' of Ikan. Benny was active in promoting the firm and was regularly seen in public and on social media advertising new campaigns, fish-marketing competitions, events or contributing to public debates about fish and fish consumption. If we examine the firm records, however, Benny had in fact very little formal power or responsibility in the firm. The power lays with his father Karl. Viewed in more cynical fashion, Benny was but a figurehead.

| Registered firms in the Ikan family 2017 | | | | |
|---|---|---|---|---|
| Name of firm | Ikan A/S | Ikan Fresh ApS | Poul holding ApS | Karl Ikan holding ApS | Ikan Ny A/S |
| Established | 2000 | 2007 | 2007 | 2002 | 2016 |
| Share holders | Karl Ikan holding 100 % | Poul is removed as 100% share holder. | Poul 100 % | Karl 100 % | Karl Ikan holding 100 % |
| Board members | Karl, Benny, Polly | Poul, Niels and Karl exit as board members. | - | - | Karl (100 % voters share), Benny, Polly |
| Director | Karl | Poul is removed as director | Poul | Karl | Karl |
| Function | Retail | - | Retail | Non-financial holding company | Retail + wholesale |
| Equity € | 67.105 | - | - | 16.776 | 67.105 |
| Gross profit € | 22.815 | - | - | -10.736 | n.a. |
| Net income € | -17.447 | - | - | -11.407 | n.a. |
| Results € | -13.421 | - | - | | |
| Assets € | 738.155 | - | - | 154.341 | n.a. |
| Number of registered employess | 1 | - | - | 1 | 20-49 |
| Status | Active | Enforced liquidation 2017 | Liquidated | Active | Active |

Figure 3. Registered firms in the Ikan family 2017. (Source: virk.dk and Ikan's annual financial statements).

As Figure 3 shows, Polly and Poul's firm (Ikan Fresh ApS) was officially declared bankrupt and liquidated by the end of 2017. Karl's original firm, Ikan A/S, on the other hand, took on new board members: Benny replaced Katja, Karl's middle child, and Karl and Polly remained. Karl was still director of the firm and owned 100 per cent of the shares. Unlike Polly and Poul, Benny had not established his own firm but was instead brought on as ordinary board member of his father's firm, alongside Polly. In terms of ownership, Benny owned no share in any firm, and neither did Polly. Moreover, with the demise of Polly and Poul's firm, a new firm, 'Ikan Ny' was established in December 2016, with Benny, Karl, and Polly as board members. Karl remained founder and sole owner, while Benny had no formal ownership or real power. He was the 'front man' and public representative for this new family firm, but lacking any formal share ownership, he was in a much more precarious situation than were his predecessors. In theory, if Karl did not agree with any of Benny's operating decisions, he could always decide on his own. Karl was the director and owner of both Ikan A/S and Ikan Ny. There was no leasing partner, as had been the case with Polly and Poul. Although we can never know the full story, we can construct some reasonable hypotheses as to why Karl might have wanted to take back control of his firm.

One possible explanation is that Karl was concerned with Ikan's profitability. After all, any business owner should be concerned with making profits, and both Karl and Poul were no exceptions. What might be further examined, however, is Poul's motivation for making money and the effect this had on the business as such. Poul, as I knew him, was a man torn in two directions. Like anyone, he sought to live up to the moral values he believed in and to fulfil his own personal goals, which in some areas reflected contradictory moral values.

On the one hand, Poul presented himself as a moral person who paid ample respect to the values of modest consumption, frugality, charity, hard work, and fairness. These values were visible in the way he criticized wealthy people who he felt flouted their wealth. Poul would comment on people who wore nice, expensive clothes (walking around in suits and tie), drove expensive cars, ate in fancy restaurants, or in other ways acted in a way which reflected what Poul expressed as, 'they believe they are better than everyone else'. Poul often commented on people who behaved in this way, explaining to me that 'I probably have just as much money as him, but I don't need to show off.' Poul emphasized modesty: when he occasionally took the family out for dinner, he would prefer the cheaper restaurants. He made a point out of insisting on wearing the same, old, worn-out clothes every day, whatever the occasion, and he looked for the cheapest alternative in the supermarket. This was not simply because he was thrifty. He also expressed an aversion to wasteful consumption. 'We should not spend just for the sake of spending', was the attitude he expressed in these actions. Poul gladly spent money, but he made sure that any money spent would be on 'things that were useful'.[64] In order to allow himself material goods in line with his own values, Poul would negotiate to get the price down. This kind of bargaining behaviour and sentiments reflects the moral values shared among all the business owners with whom I did fieldwork. It is a value set that taps into the ideals of equity that have been reproduced and promoted as Danish and Scandinavian identity markers (Dahl 1986; Jenkins 2006: 385; Bendixen, Bringslid and Vike 2018).

On the other hand, Poul, like most of us, desired a materially comfortable lifestyle, which in some respects was in complete contrast to the kind of morality that he and his community promoted. While Poul stressed equity ideals by dressing casually, eating the same food as his employees, and talking in the same sociolect as his workers, he also enjoyed fast cars; and because he could afford it, he owned a sports car worth around €133,000. The conspicuous engine noise of Poul's sports car immediately revealed its prestige and high price. However, as if to compensate for this luxury item, Poul used his other small, standard vehicle for his everyday tasks. Poul could thus compensate for this deviation from the frugality ideal by putting his luxury aside. For example, Poul could buy expensive limited-edition liquor, then hide it deep inside the closet, assuring me that he did not enjoy liquor. Alternatively, he could purchase an expensive piece of clothing and then hide it away because, as he explained, 'It was too nice to wear'. Poul's luxury purchases were much more visible in the privacy of his home sphere, where he lived in a large, spacious, and always comfortably heated house, with an oversized TV screen and advanced speaker system. The success Polly and Poul experienced in their first years as business owners allowed them to develop a materially comfortable lifestyle that was much more luxurious than most of the other business owners whom I met.

At the time I began my fieldwork with Ikan (2015), the firm faced various challenges that might explain some of the choices Polly and Poul had made in running the business, but which might also have led Karl to be sceptical and decide not to renew Polly and Poul's lease. Besides facing the challenge of fewer customers after the financial crisis of 2009 and the reconstruction of the dock, there was a falling out between Poul and his traveling sales representative, who then resigned. Not only did she leave the firm, but she also took with her several major customers, causing Ikan to lose a considerable chunk of anticipated revenue.[65] In addition, the vendor trucks did not make the expected sales that Polly and Poul had calculated, and they suspected that some of the vendors were siphoning off cash from

---

[64] 'Ting der er nyttige'.

[65] Out of respect for my interlocutors, I cannot reveal more details about this case. I can only add that there were a series of unwise decisions made by Poul that led to this drama.

sales. 'It is hard to control the vendors because they are on their own, and there is no way for us to monitor what they are doing there', Polly complained to me.

These income shortfalls (and possibly other factors that remain unknown to me) meant that Poul had to make cutbacks in the operation of Ikan. He had to lay off employees and give himself and Polly lower salaries. This was one of the areas of conflict between Polly and Poul and Polly's father. Karl regularly visited the premises. He surveyed the shop several times per week and was not shy about expressing his opinion concerning Polly and Poul's business decisions. For example, Polly and Poul had a principle of never compromising on the quality of their produce. When the prices of salmon went up, Karl advised Poul to buy frozen instead of fresh salmon from a contact he had. Karl argued that the customers would not be able to know the difference, and that the frozen salmon was just as good quality as the freshly caught salmon. Poul disagreed and disregarded his father-in-law's advice. Karl then approached his daughter, thinking that she might be willing to convince her husband, but Polly and Poul were a team, and she supported her husband. On occasions like these, of which I witnessed several, Karl showed great frustration, complaining that the young generation did not understand business the way he did. His concluding comment, each time, was that a business owner 'needs to go down [on the floor] and cut fish himself', a reference to the necessity of manual labour both as an incentive to save labour costs and as a means of ensuring quality.

Poul suffered from a medical condition that prevented him from cutting and filleting fish. The static and tedious work of cutting teared on Poul's shoulders, and after several surgeries, his doctor declared him unable to carry out this particular work task. Although Karl knew this, he did not accept it, and he continued to emphasize that Poul should not hire a lot of other people to do the cutting tasks, adding that 'I never did that, and neither did my father nor grandfather'. It was clear that Karl was not satisfied with his son in-law's work ethic.

In fact, Poul shared his father in-law's high valuation of quality work; the difference lay in the content of what 'hard work' meant to Poul and to his father-in-law. For Poul, 'hard work' meant time spent in engagement with the firm, often in tasks that for Karl seemed not to be 'real work' (typically office work, accounting, marketing, sales meetings and other tasks not directly related to 'production', i.e. cutting and packing fish). Poul spent long hours at the firm, dealing fish, travelling around to customers and suppliers, negotiating and checking purchase orders, etc. However, in recent years, his work tasks had been increasingly alienated form the manual labour of *skæring*, partly due to these abstract management tasks, and also due to his medical challenges.

For Karl, Poul was not doing 'real work' or 'hard work'. Poul was doing 'paperwork' or 'office work', which in large segments of Danish society is not seen as 'real work', and at worst as 'wasted work' or 'bureaucracy'. No longer able to cut fish, Poul was assisted by Frode, who had worked at Ikan full-time (and often overtime) for ten years, and by some part-time employees. Karl disapproved of Poul's decision to delegate the fish cutting to others. However, as long as Poul was the director of the firm, and Polly and Poul owned the rights to the lease, Karl's found it difficult to influence these kinds of decisions.

When Ikan's accounting records started to show larger expenses and declining revenue, Polly and Poul had begun to become accustomed to their more comfortable lifestyle. Their socio-economic backgrounds were modest, and although Poul insisted that he frowned upon conspicuous consumption and what he described as 'slovenliness' (*sløseri*). Nevertheless, he enjoyed his expensive sports car, modern house, whatever food he felt like cooking, long, hot showers, and his well-equipped home entertainment centre. For Polly's birthday, he bought her nothing less than a new, cutting-edge double refrigerator (the one they already had was working perfectly), *and* the most expensive sewing machine available in the shop, plus a surprise lunch at a fancy restaurant for her and a party of twelve. Sewing was one of Polly's hobbies, and a new sewing machine was something she had told Poul and me that she wanted for her birthday. She had also complained, for some time, that she did not like their refrigerator and wanted a new one. It was Poul's habit to buy or arrange extraordinary birthday presents.[66] I joined Poul when he went shopping for these items, and we planned Polly's birthday breakfast and lunch together.[67] I therefore know that he spent more than €3,400 (DKK 26,000) on Polly's birthday alone. There was nothing frugal here. Such large expenditures were considered normal for Poul. When he felt like spending a lot of money on something for either himself (such as new interior in his car) or his family, he did not hesitate to do so.

Poul's unwillingness to cut back on these luxuries probably impelled him to develop alternative ways of sustaining his family's lifestyle when the fish business did not generate the income to which he had grown

---

[66] He once brought Polly's sister, who lived in the UK, a ticket home to Denmark for a weekend to surprise one of the family members on their birthday.

[67] It was customary in the family (as in many Danish families) to invite extended family members for a family breakfast on 'round' birthdays (40, 50, 60 years, etc.). Uncle, aunts, cousins, sisters, parents and grandparents would come to the house early in the morning and wake up the family member whose birthday it was by singing a birthday song.

accustomed. As is common for business owners, Poul made use of his social network whenever he wanted something for his personal consumption (Hart 2005). He had developed an extensive network of contacts, and people knew him all over town as *fiskemanden* ('the fish man'). People in all kinds of businesses knew that Poul was always ready to make a good deal. He had learned to take great advantage of a broad and extensive network of favours, trusted agreements and reciprocal gift giving, and he utilized this network to the fullest in order to sustain his lifestyle. Poul often took me with him on car rides to 'take care of stuff' (*'fixe noget'*). This usually meant meeting with someone with whom he could make a barter agreement or cut-rate discount sale in return for fish products from Ikan.

Poul's gifts and favours came in the form of products from his firm, and the transactions were often 'off the books'. When the firm did not make sufficient profit and Poul continued with a high number of unregistered transactions, it generated an imbalance between registered and unregistered transactions, typically identified through a lack of electronic VAT incoming and outgoing payments. While every business owner has a certain amount of unregistered transactions (i.e. cash, barter, third party, etc.) they must endeavour to have a sufficient balance between the registered and unregistered transactions. Otherwise, they risk having difficulties with the regulatory authorities or tax office, risking insolvency, bankruptcy, financial investigations or accusations of swindle or tax evasion. Poul's eagerness to deal off the books, even though if may have been in good faith (i.e. to help keep the business alive) may be one reason why Karl decided to intervene and end their leasing agreement. Poul was acting in a way that Karl found undesirable, and the results in the company accounts did not look promising. Ikan was in financial difficulty, and for Karl, it was the fault of Poul and Polly.

Poul's informal network was part of a community of self-employed business owners who helped each other in an endless network of reciprocal favours and gifts. They viewed their various exchanges – barter, cash, VAT-free, cut-rate deals, informal credit agreements, and so forth – as morally legitimate (see also Sampson 1985; Williams 2004a). As an example, Poul did not try to hide that he brought gifts of fresh fish to his friend, who imported vintage wines, from which Poul bought below market price. Neither did any of his neighbours view it as morally wrong that they and others benefitted from discount fish that Poul delivered to their door every now and then. To those involved in this network, these transactions were but fringe benefits of knowing a fish man (*fiskemand*). What Poul was doing – barter exchange, gifts, cash deals, cutting corners, off-the-books, special discounts – was certainly also something Karl did, and is standard practice among all self-employed business owners the world over. Moreover, such practices are largely viewed emically as 'the way to do business' rather than being seen as illegal or immoral.

Poul's gifts came solely from his formal business as manager of Ikan. He could give gifts of fish or offer special discounts to selected recipients. While some of these benefits helped his business, other benefits accrued to him privately. These fringe benefits become an important factor of risk, if they are overexploited (Sampson 1985; see for example Gershuny 1988; Hart 1997; Williams 2004b). In other words, there is a tipping point where the informal transactions, instead of helping the firm overcome a rough patch, begin to drag down the firm at its core. This may also be what happened at Ikan, leading Karl to intervene. Alternatively, Karl may have had suspicious that Poul's consumption habits were violating some kind of unwritten moral code of frugality. Karl's decision was most likely a combination of what he felt were Poul and Polly's ignoring his advice and an unsatisfactory financial bottom line at Ikan.

## Conflicting Values

Families are units of solidarity, but they are also units of unique kinds of tensions and even bitter conflict (Yanagisako 1979: 173, 181). The transfer of Ikan from Karl to the next generation could have taken place in many ways. If Karl's desire had been to bring his son Benny into the firm, he could have encouraged Benny to purchase an interest in Polly and Poul's firm, and they could have managed the business together. As far as I am aware, they never discussed this option. The time I spent with the Ikan family certainly revealed tensions between Karl and Polly and Poul. When Karl arrived to spend time in Ikan's lunchroom, he never failed to comment on Polly and Poul's management style, often in the negative. Polly explained that her father had difficulty letting go, and that he did not agree with all the new measures they had taken to improve business. 'He does not always understand the things we do to renew [Ikan]', she said. According to her, Karl was stuck in the old ways of doing business. In Karl's view, he felt that he had exited his firm prematurely. Having recovered from his illness, he now regretted that he did not have the kind of control over the firm that he wanted.

Karl was an old-fashioned man, holding on to his ways of doing business. To him, there were several key elements that were essential to how a firm should be managed. At the top of the list was a 'direct and personal relationship with the customers'. This emphasis on treating customers as individuals was a primary business strategy for Karl, as it has been for most shops and face-to-face businesses. It was important that the customers never became faceless consumers. To Karl, this meant that the owner was downstairs, on the shop floor, to show his face and share his expertise with customers and employees. Karl insisted that this was a key strategy to obtaining and keeping faithful customers. Karl has pursued this strategy by ensuring that his son would now manage the firm in a personalized manner, promoting himself as the face and character of Ikan, just as Karl did in his time. Karl also stressed that being visible was not just a customer-relations strategy. It was also a means of ensuring a 'tight ship' over employees and monitoring affairs on the shop floor.

Poul also believed in monitoring the production process and employees. But instead of being down on the floor (*nedenunder*), as Karl insisted, Poul had invested in a video surveillance system that was connected to his phone, allowing him 24-hour surveillance of any activity in all rooms of the building. Through the CCTV cameras, Poul could monitor activities in the shop and in the wholesale section. He could keep an eye on the employees and monitor the flow of customers. The system, initially installed to prevent burglary, had become an efficient way to monitor the activities in the shop. It was part of having a modern, technologically sophisticated business.

Karl saw things differently. He viewed the video monitoring as a handicap. It prevented Poul from physically immersing himself in the day-to-day work of the firm. Poul may have been putting in the hours, but for Karl, he was shirking the work ethic. Work was what you did on the floor, not up in the office. This conflict between the younger and the older generation about what was a 'good work ethic' may be one of the contributing factors that caused Karl to decide to remove Poul from his position.

There were other external challenges as well. Poul was responsible for the success of the firm during a particularly difficult period in Ikan's history. The market for fresh fish was changing. Constantly growing competition from large supermarkets and department stores had reduced the number of independent fishmongers in Aarhus from forty in Karl's time to five in 2016. Karl was very aware of these challenges and had been actively involved in the conservation of independent fishmongers through an interest organisation. Nevertheless, Karl continued to insist that Poul should make more efforts to be physically down on the floor. Whenever the question of difficult financial times was brought up, Karl was unwilling to accept Polly and Poul's response. Karl's reasoning was that he had managed the firm through several crises and had always managed to keep the business running. He showed no sympathy for Polly and Poul's struggles and continued to tell them that they did not work enough on the floor. Polly and Poul responded by claiming that Karl did not realize how much the market had changed and the severity of the challenges they were facing.

These different perceptions on how to manage a firm correctly reflect not only different business strategies. They also indicate conflicting value orientations. While both Karl and Poul valued 'hard work', the meaning they placed on 'hard work' differed. Whereas Poul valued hard work in the office as virtuous, Karl viewed only on manual labour on the floor as virtuous. The two also differed regarding perceptions about quality. Both Karl and Poul were concerned with quality, but for Karl, quality was indicated by who had cut the fish, whereas for Poul quality had to do with the origin and condition of the product (always fresh, never frozen). Karl was also concerned with the choices Polly and Poul had made in their private lives. He saw these consumption choices as indicators of how they spent the firm's capital. He criticized Polly and Poul's private consumption habits when they kept taking out salaries for themselves, even when the firm brought in less income.

The fact that Karl kept praising manual labour and presence on the floor while Poul observed the floor from surveillance cameras, prioritizing contact with wholesale customers and suppliers (instead of retail customers), is not simply a reflection of two different 'business strategies'. More was at stake. When Karl kept pointing out Poul's absence from the floor, Karl acted as if manual labour was the solution to the firm's problems. Whenever there was talk about challenges in the firm, Karl would bring up Poul's absence from the floor. Karl argued that being physically present on the shop floor was important for maintaining control and ensuring quality. On the other hand, Karl had no qualms about deviating from quality by purchasing frozen fish to sell as fresh when prices were high. Poul was unwilling to sell fish that had been frozen as fresh fish because it deviated from his idea of good quality. We see here that Karl and Poul are both concerned with quality and control, but they disagree on the definitions and practicalities of quality; they express different values, not simply different business strategies.

Another area where Poul and Karl expressed different values was their ideas about which customers to prioritize. Karl argued for staying on the floor in order to stay close to customers and nurture a close relationship with them. Poul also nurtured Ikan's relationship with customers, but not the same retail customers to whom Karl referred (those coming into the retail shop). Instead, Poul prioritized the wholesale customers and suppliers. He could spend time with them without exhausting himself physically cutting fish. Poul and Karl thus expressed conflicting ideas of where it was important to place most time and effort in the firm. This kind of value conflict is ethnographically interesting because it illuminates different perspectives on what is good, right and meaningful.

Karl seemed to believe that that all that was needed was an extra effort at manual labour, together with proximity to the customers. Not to speak of the money saved by doing more of the manual labour with your own hands. The insistence on manual labour and proximity to customers is invoked by all the small business owners in my sample. Karl resembled Marie and Ole in their bakery, Julian the goldsmith and Sally the toy shop owner in placing great value on customer contact and doing manual labour. To them, part of what had inspired them to open their own shop was the human contact and the self-fulfilment they experienced in producing something they materialized with their own hands. Perhaps one of Karl's issues with Poul was that he felt that Poul did not appreciate this task. Perhaps Karl felt that Poul was in the business for the wrong reason.

To Karl, Poul's medical problem was a poor excuse for not spending more time on the floor. There are, of course, many successful firms where the owner does not perform manual labour or spend facetime with customers. Even within the specialized shops described here, we can find firms where the owner is distanced from work on the floor.[68] Although manual labour and proximity to customers has been important in Karl's years operating the shop, his insistence suggests that it has more to do with his values than with any specific business strategy. Karl often talked about his father and grandfather, and several generations of fishmongers before him, and how they had always done the work with their own hands. They had 'been there for the [local] community' as Karl would say, by being present on the shop floor ready to offer expertise to customers and employees. The insistence and repeated invocation of manual labour and closeness to customers may be viewed as nostalgia, rooted in Karl's feeling of loss (of the firm). In any event, these issues were not a primary concern of Poul's.

Frode, who did the fish cutting for Poul, was an experienced chef who had more than twenty years' experience cutting fish. He was a close and loyal friend of the family, and he took pride in doing a good job. He had competed in the same fish cutting competitions as Poul, and he worked more than twelve-hour shifts every day. There was no doubt that he did everything he could to ensure top quality for Ikan. Similarly, Polly's cousin, who managed the retail shop, took great pride in his work and went far to exercise excellent customer service, assisting other employees to ensure that they did the same. Polly and Poul clearly had quality as one of their primary values. In fact, Karl argued that with hard labour one could undercut quality. Karl

---

[68] See for example Lush cosmetics, a global company specializing in handmade soaps and other cosmetics. Starting out as a small shop in the UK producing specialized, handmade soaps made from fresh fruits, it is now operating in 49 countries world-wide.

argued that one could look to cheaper suppliers when fish was in short supply if one ensured quality by handling the product with your own hands. Karl's reasoning goes against his own principles of always ensuring top quality, perhaps provoked by his values of hard labour. Polly and Poul operated with other strategies than Karl. Instead of cutting back on quality, they dismissed some employees during a period when Ikan had lower sales income. Polly and Poul placed greater value on offering consistently high quality of their products than being on the floor to cut the fresh fish. These were value conflicts: Poul and Karl disagreed on what was good and right in various situations. Poul did not want to lie to his customers (about the freshness of the fish). Karl meant that it was more important to be where your (retail) customers were, performing the manual labour with your own hands, thereby knowing the quality of the products.

Aside from differences in how the firm was being run, there were other conflicts connected to personal lifestyle choices or networking activities. A combination of Poul's expensive habits and the possible exhaustion of his informal reciprocal network in which the firm's surplus resources were depleted, may explain why Ikan's economic situation became more difficult. Reaching his breaking point, Karl decided to intervene.

A look through the publicly available business records reveals several statements that support Karl's concern that Poul was not managing the firm effectively. Four years previously, the public registry of businesses produced a report with the very descriptive headline '[Ikan Fresh ApS] delivers another negative result despite positive growth'. A brief note stated that the firm had a ten per cent growth rate from the previous year, but its total net result was still minus 33 per cent. The next year, the public business registry reproduced the same headline, but now the report stated that the firm had a growth of 44 per cent. Yet, its net profit was still minus 11 per cent. This was the fourth year in a row that the company was operating at a loss. Similarly, Karl's own firm, which subsisted on the profits from renting out the business premises to Polly and Poul's Ikan Fresh ApS, suffered. One can imagine Karl's feelings of powerlessness, standing on the sideline, watching his (and his father's, grandfather's, and great-grandfather's before him) life work moving closer and closer to bankruptcy.

We also need to explore the possibility that Karl wanted to pass down his firm to his son Benny, continuing the line of patrilineal decent. This option seems less likely if we review the archival material. Karl had engaged his daughter in the firm from the time she was a little girl, and he proudly showed her off to the public as the next generation fishmonger. When Benny was born more than ten years later, Karl's relationship with his daughter did not change. Polly and her husband were both involved and engaged in the firm, and Karl continued to encourage their participation in the business. When Polly and Poul married, Poul took Polly's family name, indicating his intended future role as owner and manager of Ikan. As Karl's son Benny grew up, he did not show the same interest or engagement in Ikan as his sister, and although he worked there part-time – like all other immediate family members – he did not have the same aspirations as Polly. When I first met Benny, he had just turned twenty and did not express much interest in his father's business. He was still enormously proud of his father and his family heritage, a sentiment he shared with all his other family members.

Nevertheless, Benny felt pressure from Karl to show more engagement in the business. When I told my Aarhus friends and acquaintances from other places about my work in Ikan, they would know Benny from 'around town' as the son of fishmonger Karl Ikan. Several sources reported to me that he had expressed the view that he felt pressured to 'just go and be a *fiskemand*'. This urge for the son to take over might eventually be a plausible explanation as to why Karl replaced Poul with his own son. Yanagisako, researching Italian family firms, provides examples of similar tendencies, given that blood-kin comes before cognates in kinship hierarchy (Yanagisako 2002: 56–8, 75, 158). Under such a patriarchal logic, Karl's intervention seems plausible.

We are left with a few questions, however. Why did Karl remove Poul completely from Ikan's management? Why the deceit towards Polly, not informing his daughter that he would not renew the ten-year lease? If the motives behind Karl's intervention can be related to what Karl saw as Poul's moral and economic shortcomings, which led to an exhaustion of the firm economy and an imbalance between informal and formal economic transactions, combined with conflicting ideas about the meaning of hard work, we could easily conclude that the intervention was grounded in a value conflict. And where there are such conflicts, the natural response would be to exclude Poul from the firm. If we take the shared value orientations shared between the business owners in my sample, Poul seems to be an exception, if not a deviant case. Although Poul's own representation of himself was that of someone who lived according to modest consumption virtues, highly concerned with equality and hard work – categories that fit well with the shared values among Aarhusian business owners – many of Poul's actions and habits represented something different, even as he tried to suppress the existence of such desires. Unlike the other small, niche firms, Poul did not work (much) on the floor, he did not have the kind of intimacy with the retail customers that all the other niche business owners had. The main reason why Karl decided to replace Poul with Benny was because he was disappointed that Poul did not seem to share his valuation of manual labour and presence on the floor. When Benny entered the firm, he ran it the way his father had wanted. Benny was on the floor, he cut the fish himself, and he represented the company from the shop floor.

Although, the market did indeed change under Poul's management, and although Ikan did indeed experience external challenges that would be hard for any business owner to deal with, regardless of the kind of values they articulated, Poul's subsequent choices and actions certainly did influence the course of the firm. His choices may have aggravated Ikan's economic situation, making it worse than what it was. However, the conflicting value orientations between Poul and his father-in-law grew to a level that eventually led to the end of his career as a 'fish man'. After all, it was Poul who was removed from the firm and all boards, while Polly kept her job as bookkeeper and board member in Karl's firm(s). Poul was deprived of the chance to turn the firm around. Before he had the chance, Karl took the firm back and gave Benny a chance. We can conclude here that business owners valuing manual labour and intimacy with customers provide benefits to a firm in two ways: they contribute to the financial success of a firm, and they 'perform' the moral obligations towards kin, customers, and suppliers. A family business operates with a morality that ramifies in both the firm's operations and in the family's lifestyle. This is the very nature of the self-employed family business. It is family and business, business and family, and therefore operates with a single moral value set. Its business strategy is also family morality.

Interviews revealed that customers chose to shop at Ikan for three main reasons. First, Ikan was a firm they had known since they were children. The customers felt that they 'knew' the firm and the people behind it. Statements such as 'This is my fishmonger' and 'I have grown up with [Ikan]', bear witness to people's intimate relationship with the firm. The second reason mentioned by the customers was the intimate (*hyggelig*) family relationship with the fish sellers behind the counter. Ikan employees always met customers with a smile and a joke to make them feel welcome. Finally, customers stated that they knew that when they bought fish from Ikan, they got top-quality products, sales expertise and the freshest products. Most customers would include a phrase such as 'although it is more expensive than supermarkets...' indicating that they were willing to pay more for quality, *hygge* and expertise. Those of my Aarhus friends who purchased their fish somewhere else can be grouped into those who did so because they felt a similar loyalty towards one of the other small, independent fishmongers in the city, or those who did not have the time or money to make the extra trip down to the dock to buy fish. Many, but far from all, Ikan customers felt that they had a personal relationship with the firm and therefore remained loyal. Karl claimed that this was a vital aspect of business: to be physically present when your customers walk into the shop. No matter how well business goes, it is important to 'remain down to earth'.

Karl's younger son Benny was more inexperienced and perhaps easier to influence than his daughter and son in-law. When Karl tried to give Polly and Poul advice, he found them to be uninterested in his opinions. Benny, on the other hand, was more like his father in the way he thought and acted. Where Poul was introvert, Benny was extrovert. Benny was proud of his father and the work he had done with the firm. However, Benny repeatedly told me that he was not interested in becoming a *fiskemand* (fish man). Benny lived with his father, and his life choices were undoubtedly influenced by him. However, when he took over management of Ikan – or rather when he took on the role as the face of Ikan – he did so in his own character. The firm quickly developed a more aggressive social media profile, with daily video posts in which Benny, with plenty of energy, advertised various fish products.

It is probable that Karl's influence over Benny was greater than over Polly, given that Benny had lived his entire life under the same roof as his father, and still did when he entered the business. Moreover, due to the formal arrangements of the firm, Benny did not have the same managerial power that Polly and Poul had. Although both Benny and Polly, in 2017, were on the board of the existing Ikan firm, the firm's charter stated that votes were divided among the *owners*; since Ikan Ny had only one owner, Karl himself, Karl held 100 per cent of the shares and therefore, all the votes.

With Karl holding all the shares and Benny holding no formal power position, Benny became the figurehead of the firm. He was the new young face of Ikan that was presented to the public. He was the actual son of Karl; living proof that the next generation of Ikan sons had stepped in to lead the firm. Although Benny certainly had some input in the changes that Ikan had undergone since he took over 'management', this could be executed only if Karl agreed with them. This arrangement allowed Benny to prove his worth without Karl losing formal power. If Benny proved incapable of running the firm, Karl could simply step in.

## Conclusion

In this chapter, I have shown that different values and family conflicts can create problems for both businesses and individuals in generational firms. Karl's replacement of Poul and Polly after a period where they did not manage the business in the way their father had wanted illustrates the importance of the younger generation obeying the kind of moral standard set by the older generation. Karl was not content with the way Polly and Poul managed his family's firm. Although the couple managed the firm with profits for several years, Karl's dissatisfaction increased in the years leading up to the expiration of their lease. In Karl's view, Polly and especially Poul were not just poor managers, they also had moral shortcomings. Acting according to the proper moral values was important for reasons beyond the profitability of the business.

In the case of Ikan, we have seen how blood-kin take priority over affines in the family firm matters. Karl's youngest son had grown up and was now a young adult. Although unemployed and not having shown much interest in the firm, he was nevertheless preferred over an enthusiastic son-in-law, who despite his faults and penchant for luxury goods, wanted to make Ikan a success. When Polly and Poul refused to take Karl's advice on how to manage the firm according to his standards, Karl found sufficient reason not to renew their lease and to regain control of the firm. By involving his younger son and presenting him to the public as the new owner, without granting him any formal power, Karl allowed the next generation to try to renew and reform the firm in such a way that it would be profitable again, but without Karl losing control, thus giving him the possibility to intervene if his son failed. Unlike Poul, Polly was not removed from the firm but kept her position as bookkeeper and was involved in the board of the new firms. It is hard to distinguish exactly what caused Ikan to come into financial difficulty; as is often the case, economic problems in a small firm are often due to a combination of many factors, some of which they cannot control. These factors have been described above.

Regardless of the economic challenges, however, moral obligations towards the family firm remain of vital importance. We see an emphasis on manual labour as the only 'real' work; we see the emphasis on frugality, saving money by having fewer employees and doing the work yourself; and we see the emphasis on ensuring quality as part of business ethics. We see the emphasis on not taking more out of the firm than what comes in. The importance of familiarity with customers is emphasized when Benny as new manager is placed on the floor with his face showing up regularly in public and on social media, depicting him performing manual labour and talking directly with customers. Such harmonious imagery hides the very real tensions, conflicts, and conflicting self-interests that are inherent in family firms, and in families in general (see also Kousholt 2011). It shows that the values articulated by Karl's emphasis on hard physical labour, frugality, and personal engagement with the firm, and the value placed on customer contact as an important business strategy that is shared among a wide group of small, independent, niche firms. For example, Sally's mother, the toy shop owner, did not want to manage two shops because she felt that she would be unable to control everything that happened in the shops. In addition, for a business to run well, it was vital that it be managed according to her moral values (*moral*). Similarly, Marie and Ole spent nearly all their waking hours in their bakery because this was the only way they could ensure that it would be managed according to their principles.

Freya, a handicraft shop owner, had just expanded her business and clearly expressed that this was as big as it would ever get because it was as much as she could handle. According to these business owners, the main explanation for why a business succeeds is that the business is managed according to the (moral) values set by the owner. When Karl witnessed Poul deviating from what he considered to be the morally correct way to do business, and when saw evidence of this deviation in the form of negative financial results, Karl saw it as his moral responsibility to protect his legacy and make sure that the firm was not lost, like so many of his 'colleagues'.[69] I discuss the moral motivations of the business owners further in Chapter Seven.

We have seen the importance of continuing the firm according to what the business owners considered as the *right* values. This description of the moral order of a family firm encourages us to speculate what would have happened with Ikan if Karl had not intervened. Would Ikan have gone bankrupt like so many other small businesses pressured by larger corporations? Would Polly and Poul have managed to turn the firm around and make profits again? While we can never know the answer to these questions, they underscore the importance played by social values in small independent, niche firms such as those represented in this study.

---

[69] A common trait among most of my business owners was their tendency to refer to other small independent shops in the same branch as 'colleagues' instead of competitors. Large chains, however, were referred to as competitors.

## Chapter 5
## Values over Skills: The Business of Doing Good

> I am just like my mother. That's why I'm the owner of this firm today. It's the only way Toys[70] can be managed, the way we manage it.

Sally took another sip of her coffee before looking up at me to explain how her business works. Sally, the toy shop owner, is very clear about what she considers the (morally) right way of doing business. 'My business is successful because this is a moral enterprise, and I know what is right'[71], Sally told me in a conversation. As a teenager, Sally had helped her mother, Pia, in the shop. Even then, Sally knew that she would continue to work there as an adult. When Sally completed primary school, her mother Pia told her to go and live her life, to do her own thing. Pia did not want Sally to just stay working in the shop. She thought that Sally needed to have her own life experiences before she would know her path in life. Sally took her mother's advice. Aged 19, and with various personal problems, she decided to leave Aarhus. She moved to Norway for a few years, where she worked as a housekeeper on a farm in return for room and board. In the meantime, Sally had given birth to a daughter, and after some years she returned to Denmark. Later, she returned to Norway, where she completed a teacher's training course in Oslo. After completing her schooling, Sally obtained a job as a schoolteacher in the Aarhus area, and she taught for a full fifteen years. However, Sally had always had a creative side, so she decided to enrol at the Aarhus Art Academy to become a ceramist.

Soon after completing art school, Pia asked Sally if she would like to return to the business. A few years earlier, Sally's sister, a nurse working in Copenhagen, had tried to take over the shop. However, she soon returned to her nursing job. Pia felt worn out. The business was not as successful as it

---

[70] Pseudonym.
[71] Original Danish quote: 'Virksomheden går godt fordi den er moralsk, og jeg ved hvad der er rigtigt' (October 2016).

had once been, and Pia realized that a major change was needed. She had come into conflict with their main wholesale customer of many years, and their retail sales were declining.

Sally was animated when describing how she came back and revived the business: within her first year, she had more than doubled the shop's sales, and her success continued to grow steadily (this claim is confirmed by the firm's financial records over the past seven years). When Pia witnessed the tremendous success that Sally had produced, she was ready to transfer formal ownership of the firm to her daughter. However, Pia had not prepared for the transfer and was unprepared for the many bureaucratic obstacles. Laws and tax regulations specific to succession prevented Pia from simply signing over ownership of Toys to her daughter.

Transfer of firm ownership, for example of a shop, a farm or a business, requires a tax assessment of the current value of the firm. The tax assessors calculate the market value of an enterprise based on its annual revenue, inventory, and other moveable assets. An owner who wants to sell their firm must pay a tax on the income earned from the sale. An owner who wants to give the firm as a gift to a child must deal with the risk of conflict between the non-inheriting siblings. In Sally's case, her sister would have to be compensated. Sally explained that a smoother and cheaper transfer of the firm might have been possible when the firm had its low point in sales, since the amount of taxes to be paid on a transfer is calculated based on the firm's revenue, Sally thinks that the transfer would have been affordable before she took over management and turned the firm around. With the firm's market value much lower at the time, the tax assessment would have been more manageable. However, it was only after the shop's revenue had trebled that Pia considered transferring the firm to Sally. The market value of the firm was now too high for them to pay the transfer tax. Sally could also have purchased the firm outright, but this would have required her taking on a debt and was out of the question. Sally and Pia therefore ended up slowly transferring the firm in annual steps, using the model of successive transfer (*successiv overdragelse*). Pia would make annual transfers of parts of the firm, somewhat like an annual gift. In this way, they could both avoid taxes on the transfer.

Many Danish firms share this problem of transfer between the original founder and their children. This issue, known as '*generationsskifte*', is a frequent topic of political discussion among Danish political parties. Unsurprisingly, the right-wing parties want lower regulations and lower taxes so that parents can more freely transfer their firms to their children, while left-wing parties are suspicious of inherited wealth as unearned income that will increase inequality. Danish accounting firms offer a variety of imaginative solutions to these barriers to transfer of assets, and Danish middle-class households routinely utilize combinations of annual cash gifts and interest-free family loans with delayed repayment, all in order to avoid taxes.

In all modern states, but especially in social democratic welfare states, the state authorities have set up a complex web of regulations for separating business from private life, including measures to control inherited wealth. These regulations involve both gift and inheritance taxes as well as taxes on transfers of property or a business from parent to child. However, bureaucratic and tax regulations were not the only challenges facing business owners who sought to transfer ownership of their firm to their children. For some owners, the main problem was the differing career interests between generations. Many children simply did not want to follow in their parents' footsteps. The baker's son, for example, had no intention of becoming a baker; he studied journalism. The son of the fishmonger took absolutely no interest in fish; he dreamt of designing computer games.

In structured interviews that I conducted with 25 business owners, 20 of the 25 came from families where one or both parents had also been business owners. Yet only two of the 25 interviewed business owners had taken over their parents' firm.[72] The children had followed their own path. Yet the older and younger generations still had something in common: shared values.

In this chapter, I argue that in order to understand family firms, including processes of generational transfer, we need to look beyond the purely legal barriers connected with succession from parent to child. I will show that the transmission of a business from one generation to the next had more to do with transferring skills and sentiments needed to successfully manage *a* firm rather than capital or legal ownership. The real transfer was not the firm, but the transfer of something more intangible: values.

Taxes and inheritance customs create difficulties for generational transfer of resources in all societies. There has always been interdependency between different generations, who possess different kinds of resources and find themselves at different stages in the family life cycle. In Western Europe, these dynamics interact with complicated tax laws, business regulations, and gift and inheritance customs between generations (Colli, Pérez, and Rose 2003). Sylvia Yanagisako argued against the conventional

---

[72] The interviews were part of a common survey developed in the research group REALEURASIA, where all members of the research group used the same set of survey questions to business owners in Denmark, Hungary, Germany, Turkey, Russia, China, India, and Myanmar. The Danish sample consists of a random selection of Aarhus businesses: I travelled around the city and interviewed owners of primarily small, independent firms employing a maximum 30 employees. Some of the firms agreed to several follow-up interviews (between two to nine) and participant-observation.

wisdom that family firms are destined to be replaced by a more rational capitalism (Yanagisako 2019a: 2; 2019b: 229). Yanagisako argues that family firms do not measure their success purely in terms of financial outcome and accumulation of wealth. She has criticized scholars for overlooking the social and affective benefits implied in family firms, and she has argued that we need to acknowledge success as more than wealth-maximization and financial outcomes (Yanagisako 2019b: 230). Yanagisako suggested that we understand the success of family firms in terms of their social and kinship outcomes (ibid.: 230–31). For Yanagisako 'generational transfer' is not simply a juridical process from one owner to another but also a transfer of social values.

Yanagisako's insights apply well to the case of the business owners in Aarhus. The Aarhus business owners were not particularly concerned with the legal technicalities of transferring ownership of their firm to the next generation. It was certainly difficult or time consuming in bureaucratic terms, but the transfer process was not a cause of any kind of existential anxiety for the elder generation. The difficult aspect, rather, was ensuring the proper transfer of the kind of norms and values which they felt would form the foundation of their children's economic security. What factors led the parents to be more concerned with norms and values rather than the legal and economic provisions? And what were the implications of this norm-based concern for generation relations in the running of the firms? In the following, I draw out the different models for generational transition that I encountered among the Aarhus business owners. I will show that the business owners dealt creatively with various bureaucratic obstacles and regulations, juggling various forms of formal and informal ownership. Not everything went smoothly, of course. And I will therefore also describe some of the tensions and disputes that can arise in such situations where the right kind of norms and values must be ensured as a precondition for transfer to the next generation. I argue, therefore, that the focus on transferring material assets needs to be balanced by an equal attention to the kinds of family norms and values that are transferred. In other words, it is not just a business that changes hands; norms and values are also being passed on and reproduced from one generation to the next.

## The Value of Values

Peter Jaskiewicz, James Combs, and Sabine Rau (2015) has claimed that the reason why so many family firms fail to survive past the first generation is due to the second generation lacking entrepreneurial skills. Business scholars studying family firms tend to emphasize that family firms are less concerned about profit and more focused on socioemotional priorities, such as maintaining good relations among family members.[73] Following this claim, scholars agree that only those who inherit the 'entrepreneurial spirit' will succeed beyond the first generation (Jaskiewicz et al. 2015).[74] These theories stressing the necessity of an 'entrepreneurial spirit' resonate with what I found among the Aarhus firms that I studied. However, the spirit was not necessarily directed towards their parents' business. Rather, it was an enthusiasm about creating something on their own. In Danish, we might say that they should be *iværksættere* (lit. 'set-in-work'), which is used to describe a self-employed, often innovative person who is characterized by their ability to put ideas into action (in this sense, not all shopkeepers are *iværksættere*, but someone with an idea for a new kind of shop or service would be). The parental generation among my informants have norms and values which they feel are absolutely vital for the maintenance of their firm or for starting their own firm. Moreover, the parents want these norms and values to be perpetuated and ensured if they transfer ownership or management of their firm to their offspring, or if their children decide to start their own firm one day.

When business scholars discuss 'entrepreneurial spirit' they refer mainly to a priority on profit-maximizing and market orientation (e.g. Landström 2005). If we widen the scope and investigate entrepreneurship from novel angles, we discover that the sentiments I observed among the Aarhus firms may provide further nuance to the concept of an entrepreneurial spirit (Swedberg 2000: 7). In contrast to the conventional business studies understanding, I argue here that the entrepreneurial spirit should be understood as the core norms and values of the founders. These norms and values are not constant. They vary with the social and cultural context. The entrepreneurial spirit, therefore, can be more than the ability to create innovative ways of earning capital. It can include other sets of values such as freedom and creative work. I will illustrate this contrast below.

For the current generation of Aarhus shopkeepers, the succeeding generation needs to be as much engaged in the idea of the firm as they themselves were when they started. Managing a firm is hard work, and without full engagement, high *arbejdsmoral* ('work ethic'), encouraged by passion for what the firm represents, the successor will (in their view) fail (Johannisson and Wigren 2006).

This kind of argument also appears in Yanagisako's study of Italian small business owners, 'The grandfather founded (the firm), the sons develop it, and the grandsons destroy it' (Yanagisako 2002: 1). Yanagisako

---

[73] See for example Tahiri and Davis (1996), Burkart et al. (2003), Colli et al. (2003), Gómez-Mejía et al. (2007), and Berrone et al. (2010).

[74] On discussions about entrepreneurial potential, see Bill et al. (2010).

argued that when the son sees the hard work and engagement his father has invested in the firm, he will be more likely to adopt his father's skills and expertise and develop it further. Being witness to the hardworking, dedicated father, the son adopts both his father's values (hard work and engagement) as well as learning the skills and acquiring expertise. When the grandson generation was up for succession, however, the grandson had grown up without witnessing the discipline and frugality of the previous generations, who had a closer relationship with direct production. After two generations of building up the firm, the third generation stepped into a successful firm. When the grandson obtained access to the firm's assets, he ended up going on expensive vacations instead of investing hard work into further developing the enterprise (Yanagisako 2002: 1–3). Yanagisako has emphasized that we can benefit from viewing the family firm as a kinship-based enterprise that has a social life beyond that of the legal firm. She shows how the Italian family firms are embedded into the family members various life spheres. The firm is intertwined with kinship relations and influences educational choices, and its influence persists for the family long after the formal legal firm may have been sold off or closed down. Yanagisako defines a 'kinship enterprise' as 'a project whose goals and strategies are constantly being reassessed and reformulated by people who construe themselves to be connected by enduring bonds of relatedness and whose relations are shaped by a dense assemblage of beliefs and sentiments, and commitments attached to these bonds' (Yanagisako 2019: 231).

What is the difference between the Italian and Chinese firms described by Yanagisako and the Danish business owners? I would argue that the Aarhus business owners placed higher priority on the values they meant to transfer onto their children. The Aarhus business owners seemed to place more faith in the right values as opposed to having a specific skill set. Hence, Yanagisako's Italian business owners hoped that their children would learn certain business techniques in business school, and they were disappointed that the principles of capitalist rationality they learned in business school failed to work in practice. In contrast, the Aarhus entrepreneurs did not send their children to business schools at all. In place of acquiring education or a specific skill set, the Aarhus business owners acted as if their own norms and values were more important than the capitalist principles and techniques taught in business schools. The Aarhus business owners downgraded educational skills in favour of having a prudent and modest behaviour (e.g. Dahl 1986: 100).

Here again, the comparison with Yanagisako's Italian family firms is instructive. The Italian family firms, like those in Aarhus, celebrate their diligent work ethic. By the third generation, they have grown into a comfortable, prosperous bourgeoisie. The Aarhus family firm owners did not aim for wealth. They were more concerned with preserving the freedom and control involved in managing all areas of the firm themselves. The Aarhus business owners valued above all their freedom to control their own life and work, celebrating a modest consumption. The emphasis on the work ethic was thus similar in Como and in Aarhus, but the Aarhus business owners differed in such a way that they were consciously working to achieve a balance between hard work and modest consumption. Their main motivation was not to expand, grow or develop, but to lead a life where their work remained meaningful to them at the personal level, doing what they enjoyed and managing business according to their own principles were more important than profit-maximation. In contrast to what Yanagisako found among business owners in Como, the Aarhus entrepreneurs continued to live by their norms of a moderate material consumption, even when their firms had been successful long enough for them to move to a higher level of consumption and gain more leisure time. The business owners remained with their firms, putting in the extra hours as they had always done, not because they had to, but because they wanted to.

What stands out about the Aarhus firms is that they were small firms that intended to remain small. Their entrepreneurial motivations did not derive from a desire to accumulate vast amounts of wealth for themselves, nor to expand, nor for their children to live in luxury. Their project was not that of social advancement in the sense of 'working hard so my kids don't have to'. Their dream was not to build a legacy they could pass on to their children. Rather, it was to equip their children with a set of values that would enable them to make the right choices in order to live a good life. The good life was a life you did not want a vacation from (borrowing Ole's words). In later chapters, I will how the business owners prioritized values such as freedom to do what they enjoy, the self-fulfilment of creating something where they could physically see the results and the feeling of contributing to the local community by offering local products in an intimate environment. Aiming 'never to grow larger than what I could manage myself' was an oft-heard declaration of principle among all six of the business owners with whom I had intimate contact. Moreover, most of the business owners admitted that their firms would not become any sort of 'dynasty'. It would not involve future generations, and this was something their children knew. This does not mean that they did not care about their children's future. Their concern for their children's future was precisely what motivated them to ensure the transfer of what they considered important norms and values, rather than the transfer of the actual business as such. Ole, owner of a bakery business, was explicit in this emphasis on values when he declared, 'No, I'm not planning for my children to take over the business. They have to take their own paths'.[75] In another conversation, he reiterated that 'I hope my children benefit from the values we have given them'.[76] Similar remarks came from Julian, the jeweller, 'I don't expect them to take over the firm, but I hope the children will be inspired to make the right decisions'.[77]

Even though the parental generation tried their best to transfer what they believed to be the proper values to their children, there was no guarantee that the children would follow the same path as business owners or that they would adopt the same values as their parents. Perhaps in order to give their children the best possible conditions, parents therefore invested more in teaching their children the values they considered vital to succeed in life rather than focusing on the skills they needed in their particular firm. The passing on of values from one generation to the next is hardly limited to small business owners. Marianne Gullestad's (1986, 1996, 1997) generational studies from Scandinavia illustrate that the senior generation focused their energies on passing on what they believed to be the proper moral values. This transfer of values effort was not always successful, of course. In Chapter Four we saw that Polly and Poul articulated a different concept of what they considered 'hard work' than Polly's father Karl. Although Poul claimed that he was concerned with modesty, Karl did not think Poul was modest enough.

One of the ways that the Aarhus business owners attempted to transfer their values of hard work and modesty to younger generations was their refusal to make cash transfers to their children. Common to all the business owners in this study was that regardless of their parents' level of prosperity, the shop owners had received little or no financial assistance from their parents to help start their firms. This is not unusual in Denmark, where young adults may even pay rent to their parents if they remain home, and Danish parents will often expect the state welfare system or educational stipends to sustain their teenage or young adult children so that parents do not need to give their children money for living expenses. This kind of relationship changes, of course, when parents become grandparents, with the usual system of caregiving, extravagant gifts, cash advances and loans to children and grandchildren. When reflecting on their upbringing, my informants commented on how their parents had emphasized values of hard work and making your own way in the world. A common trait in these

---

[75] 'Nej, jeg planlægger sgu ik' at mine børn skal overtage virksomheden. De skal gå egne veje'.

[76] 'Jeg håber vores børn kan drage nytte af værdierne vi har givet dem'.

[77] 'Jeg forventer ikke at de skal overtage virksomheden, men jeg håber de bliver inspireret til at tage de rigtige beslutninger'.

upbringing narratives were stories about helping their parents work on the farm, in the house, making an early economic contribution to the household (from the age of confirmation at 14) or having to leave the childhood household early (age 16–18). Today, most Scandinavian young people leave their parents' home to live on their own as soon as they finish secondary school, between ages 17–20. Usually, the first time living away from home involves renting a room in a shared flat with either friends or strangers or perhaps moving together with their partner to become cohabiting (*samboende*). Leaving home right after school is common throughout Scandinavia, so much so that it would be considered strange if a person in their twenties was still living in their parents' home. The welfare state facilitates this youthful independence with welfare benefits for unemployed youth, generous stipends for teenagers or students who live outside the home, generous student loans and rent subsidies for those with low income.

In many societies studied by anthropologists, the transfer of resources either before or after the parents' death is an integral part of one's own life cycle. Among the business owners whom I studied; none had planned their future with a view toward any kind of anticipated inheritance. They tended to view any kind of inheritance as a windfall, a bonus in which they might unexpectedly inherit certain valuable material goods or cash when close kin died. Relying on inheritance to achieve one's life project was not part of the equation. Meddling with a parent's finances was acceptable only if the parent had become senile or for other reasons could not manage their own financial affairs. This attitude is also evident in the questions I asked about inheritance. The person responsible for a sick parent would be trusted by other siblings to manage the finances according to the parent's need. My general impression about the Danes I befriended, both shop owners and others, was that the money or other material assets of their parents was not anyone else's business, including one's own adult children. People thought it morally wrong to interfere with a living parent's consumer spending or if the parent wanted to take an extravagant vacation abroad; such behaviour indicated greediness and selfishness on the part of the child. Danish law outlines strict rules of inheritance, known as 'compulsory inheritance' (*tvangsarv*) that makes it impossible to disinherit widowed spouses or children, as might be the case in other countries.

Some business owners inherited property and other assets from their parents after they had already established their business, household, and family independently, while others could expect to inherit from their elderly parents when they died. Certainly, some informants had inherited money or property, and this inheritance certainly helped their personal economy or enabled them to invest more in their business. Ole, for instance, inherited part of his mother's house when she had passed away the year before. Ole sold the house, and the proceeds were divided amongst Ole and his siblings. These extra funds enabled Ole and Marie to renovate their own home without having to take out a bank loan, which they initially had planned to do. Ole explained to me that, 'We did not need the money we got from the inheritance settlement'. Nor did the inheritance lead them to invest more in their firm or make a larger renovation than originally planned. When Marie and Ole showed me around their newly renovated house, they repeatedly stressed how they have chosen a modest style, not doing more than 'necessary' and upgrading the house to be functional rather than fancy. Another example is that of Julian, the goldsmith. Growing up as one of seven siblings, Julian never encountered any extravagance in his upbringing. He got his first job when he was 12, delivering newspapers, and he continued in various odd jobs before and after school. When he had finished primary school, he worked his way up to a managerial position in a supermarket, until he finally decided to enter university. Without help from his parents, and thanks to the welfare state providing free higher education and a generous student loan, Julian completed his education as an engineer and worked his way up to a 'very well paid' (his words) management position. When he decided to change careers and become a goldsmith, he was able to do so partly because he had been able to save up capital to start a shop. Similar to Marie and Ole, Julian was, to use Ole's words, 'better at making money than spending it'. This gave him, and the other business owners with a similar lifestyle, the opportunity to do something they enjoyed in various stages of life. The enjoyment lay not in any sort of free time pursuit or hobby, but in the work of owning and managing their own shop.

These examples reveal how my informants expressed sentiments about being independent with a strong preference of being able to manage on their own, without the help of their parents. Despite very different family backgrounds, they all expressed this desire for independence. They all emphasized thrift over conspicuous consumption. And they all underscored a work ethic that allowed them to establish and manage their firms based on a personal commitment and on-the-ground, shop-floor presence. For Julian, this commitment was to his new craft of goldsmithing, for Marie and Ole it was mushroom farming and then their bakery, and for Pernille, it was handicraft. Sentiments like these are certainly not particularly Danish. Rather, they are important features of successful small business owners the world over. However, the Danish welfare state, with its bureaucratic regulations, advanced economy and social safety net, provides a very specific context for these values that is not found elsewhere. This social context may explain the rather low level of entrepreneurship (understood here as proportion of small business owner-operators) in Denmark compared to other advanced countries. In general, small business owners are often depicted as either extreme risk takers (the proverbial 'start-up') or so desperate that they cannot find adequate wage-labour. The Danish small business owners are neither extreme risk takers nor desperate low wage earners. They do not fall into these extreme categories, which is why they may be considered more of a subculture than in other countries.

Another example that illustrates the valuation placed on thrift and independence comes from Kia, a dog groomer in her fifties. Kia had paid an 'interest only' loan on her home mortgage for 20 years. The original loan was not paid off, however. In addition, as the market value of the house had increased over the years, Kia had refinanced her loan in order to renovate the house, travel, and invest in her dog grooming business. This meant that when Kia died, after having lived a comfortable life with very small housing expenses, her children would inherit a house burdened with such a large mortgage that they would not be able to keep it. Her children would have to sell the house at a very small profit. Kia explained that not having built up any savings that she could pass on to her children was a conscious decision she had made many years ago. She said that in her view, she had equipped her children with something more important than money: independence and the ability to take care of themselves. She told me that she did not feel that it was her responsibility to leave any kind of inheritance for her children. Although few business owners were as outspoken as Kia about not leaving an inheritance for their children to ensure independence, they shared her idea that children should learn to work hard in order to take care of themselves and their community, and not sit back and expect to get anything 'for free' (*gratis*).

These attitudes of raising independent, self-sufficient children dovetail nicely with late capitalist, neoliberal values of individualism, free choice, and an emphasis on enhancing profit by working hard and saving labour expenses (Ganti 2014: 91–93). However, the business owners were not concerned with profit- or wealth maximization. They had entered self-employment and started a business because they wanted the freedom and control entailed in such a life path. They wanted the freedom to work with something they enjoyed using ways and means they could control. Although Marie and Ole were concerned with working hard, articulated as constantly keeping themselves busy, their motivation was self-fulfilment, not profit-maximization. A similar emphasis on hard work and independence as a cultural value and a political ideal can also be identified in Danish welfare policies and political campaigns (Bendixen, Bringslid, and Vike 2018: 19; Larsen 2018: 248–58). Ideas about personal independence and self-sufficiency have been accepted in the population as constitutive of the idea of a Danish and Scandinavian identity, being broadly discussed in the ethnographic literature since Gullestad wrote about egalitarian individualism in the 1990s (Gullestad 1992, 2002; Larsen 2011, 2018; Bruun, Krøijer and Rytter 2015).[78] Independence and self-sufficiency, of course, are values that can be found everywhere. There is nothing particularly Danish or Scandinavian about them. Here they could be described as the core values of the successful business owner. The Aarhus business owners concern for independence and self-sufficiency had more to do with freedom and control over their own lives, than an echoing of some kind of 'Scandinavian values'. They wanted their children to be independent and hard working in order for them to have the same chance to live the kind of good life in the way they envisioned. Ole, for example, he wanted his children to learn independence and hard work in order to achieve what they wanted in their lives, regardless of what their parents wanted for them. He was convinced that in order for his children to live good lives, they needed to find their own pathway in life. Pia had followed the same logic with her daughter Sally, when she had told Sally to go and do her own thing. None of the business owners I knew in Aarhus emphasized that they wanted their children to become wealthy; they were all concerned with their children living good lives.

## Creative Solutions to Bureaucratic Obstacles

When a physical enterprise is ready for transfer from one generation to another, having 'the right values' is not sufficient. Other issues arise connected to the practicality of transfer. Whenever I visited a firm for the first time in the course of my research, my opening query was always, 'Hi, I'm looking for the owner'. This sentence proved to be an effective means of discovering the complexities of ownership. It was often the case that the person to whom I was initially introduced as the owner would later turn out to be only the operator or manager. This gave me a clue to how families deal with the process of passing on the firm from the senior generation to the junior. The transfer of responsibility, management, and ownership could take place without the actual transfer of assets, at least while the parental generation was still alive. This confusion about who was really the 'owner' of the firm, and what it actually entailed to 'own' a firm, forced me to refine my understanding of ownership as such.

---

[78] Egalitarian individualism deals with the tension between individualism and equality as sameness (Danish: *lighed*). Individualism and identity are important, but equally important is equality, here understood as sameness or fitting in. The individual negotiates their individuality in confrontation with people who are different. Sameness is achieved by avoiding sociality with individuals with whom they do not 'fit in' (Gullestad 1992).

At Ikan, for instance, most of the employees would refer to both Polly and Poul as the owners; legally, however, the real owners were Poul or Karl, depending on which firm they were referring to. Polly referred to herself and Poul as the owners, whereas Poul sometimes referred to himself as the sole owner, and on other occasions he said that both he and his wife were the owners, depending on the social context. He never mentioned Karl as owner, although legally, Karl owned the Ikan property, its inventory, and the brand. In the Toys firm, Sally would refer to herself as the sole owner of her business, whereas her mother was inclined to refer to both herself and her daughter as co-owners, depending on the context.

In Denmark, the legal business owner is the individual listed on the firm's ownership document registered with the firm's name and ID number. The owner would be the person who owns the shares of a corporation A/S or ApS (LLC), or the person who owns the name of the firm on the legal documents. In practice, the business operators with whom I interacted were the owners. However, there were various combinations: they might rent the business premises, name and brand, or they owned the name, but leased the inventory, or vice versa. In some cases, this arrangement took the form of a new business with a similar name, but with a new official business registration number or new firm in the form of an AS or ApS, as was the case with Polly and Poul. Here, the parental generation, in this case Karl, was still the legal owner of the business, and it was Karl who rented out the name, premises, equipment, and brand to his daughter and son in-law.

Because of strict tax laws requiring approximately a transfer tax of 42 per cent of the firm's market value (15–36.25 per cent if given as a gift).[79] generational transmission requires careful preparation and sophisticated legal and accounting knowledge.[80] For the small enterprises in my sample, the owners had typically not prepared for a generational transmission. This was because they did not believe that their children would actually take over their firm (as did Marie and Ole) or because they had just not thought about it (like Pia and her daughter Sally). The few business owners whom I interviewed who had experienced a generational transmission shared the belief that the most important explanation as to why many businesses failed after being passed on to the next generation had to do with the divergent aspirations of the children.[81] All the generational owners whom I interviewed agreed that it was impossible to inherit a firm in its totality

---

[79] I have no examples where the parental generation gives the entire firm to their children as a gift. The recipient would be subject to exorbitant gift taxes under Danish law.

[80] See Pilsner (2014) for a description of the laws (Danish).

[81] This is based on a questionnaire where five of 25 entrepreneurs managed multiple generations family firms.

without having to pay a sizable tax bill. If the younger generation sought to take over from the current owner on his or her retirement, they would have to purchase the business at its market value (often requiring them to take out a loan), and the parents would have to pay tax on the full amount of the sale. Alternatively, the parental generation could give the firm to the successor child as a gift, but the child would still have to pay a gift tax on the value of the gift above the tax-free-gift threshold of DKK 62,000 (per parent, per child, per year).

For small firms with little excess capital, such a transfer could entail taking out a loan in order to pay the taxes on the gift (market value of the firm) since the value of the firm is contained in inventory, goods, and future profits, not in the cash on hand. The giver or receiver would need to decide who should pay the taxes. This system of taxation implies that the parents stand to earn more from selling their firm to a large corporation (that can afford more than the market value) or by simply liquidating the business entirely. This is a system, which encourages further growth of oligopoly enterprises.[82] Unless the owners have carefully planned for succession, inheritance is an unprofitable business transaction for the small business owner.

It is tempting to explain the absence of generational transmission in terms of the tax and bureaucratic obstacles. However, my research with the Aarhus small business owners has shown that other factors are involved. Of more importance is how the owners evaluate the freedom of choice and proper social values of their children. It is the strength or weakness of these values that can explain why so many of the firm owners chose not to transfer their business to the next generation. As a case in point, we can describe Pernille's yarn shop.

Pernille was lucky enough to lease the premises from Astrid, a retired business owner who wanted to pass on her life's work. Astrid's shop had been in the area since long before it became a popular shopping street. Astrid was committed to locally produced products, close relationships with customers, and a genuine engagement for the knitting craft. Astrid's daughter, Julie, had taken over management of her design and production unit, and she leased the physical business premises, with all its inventory, to Pernille. However, Julie was not interested in managing the shop itself; she wanted

---

[82] See the list of acquisitions by Bestseller, a large clothing corporation, of nearly all of downtown Aarhus, resulting in the closure of several small, independent businesses (www.tinglysningen.dk). The information is taken from a private email between a government official and an independent shop owner who showed great engagement in her attempt to prevent large corporations from acquiring the entire business area of her quarter. In some cases, Bestseller bought the property, at other times they lease.

only to take over the design brand that her mother had developed. This arrangement left open the possibility for Pernille to open her own shop without taking out a huge loan, and it saved Astrid the taxes incumbent on a sale.

Astrid wanted her shop to remain a small, local shop that would be run according to her core values of high quality, intimate relationship with customers and in solidarity with the other yarn shops. This was why she had declined the purchase offer from the Bestseller Corporation, one of the major clothing chains that were rapidly coming to dominate the Aarhus shopping scene with cheap, mass produced apparel. Another independent merchant across the street drew my attention to a growing problem for independent firms in the area. The Bestseller Corporation had offered more than market value for the premises and was in the market for real estate owned by both individual shopkeepers and land owned by the municipality. A map of the area where Pernille and other businesses were located (map provided by the municipality) showed that many shops had sold their storefronts to Bestseller. Bestseller was eager to invest in what they viewed as an up-and-coming attractive business area. However, it was an area of the city where many of the firms were very old, many had a sentimental connection to the area, or they carried the same ideals as my business owners to stay small and carry about with business because they wanted the freedom and control that followed self-employment. Some independent merchants had come together to form an association to resist the take-over by corporate interests. This association promoted local events, collaboration on seasonal events, and otherwise sought to fight buy-outs and protect their shared interests (see Becattini 1990).

The agenda of the remaining small firms was based on protecting the small, independent, owner-operated shops. While the area had recently become attractive, property values had not yet risen to the level of competing districts, and many of the small businesses benefitted from relatively low rents. The area was a convenient location for business, and if they let go of their lease, they were unlikely to find a similarly priced location elsewhere in the city. Astrid was part of this local 'resistance group'. She and her shop had existed in the area long before it had become a popular shopping street, and her decision to sub-let the premises to Pernille can be explained by her sentiments that Pernille would carry out her 'good work' as a dedicated shopkeeper who cared about quality goods and satisfied customers. Astrid had asked Pernille if she was interested in leasing the shop after getting to know her from the local knitting community. However, the arrangement between Astrid and Pernille was based not only on shared values. Part of the agreement was that Pernille would sell Astrid's product line. In this way, Astrid, or rather, her daughter Julie, would have a reliable outlet for their products, and Astrid could rest assured that her shop was in good hands, with someone who, like her, would not allow the large corporation to buy her out (Curasi et al. 2004).

However, Astrid also had another interest: to continue her line of design. Without the physical shop, she might encounter difficulties finding channels for distribution. In order for the design section of her firm to survive, she also needed a retail outlet for her products. We may view Astrid's offer of transferring the lease to Pernille as an investment in the future of her 'brand'. This investment in her brand did not preclude the fact that Astrid also had a sentimental attachment to her shop, having spent her entire professional life running it. For Astrid, as with so many shopkeepers, her material interests overlapped with her emotional attachments. The shop was not just her enterprise; it was also her way of life.

As we can see from the example of Pernille and Astrid, the definition of ownership is legal, economic and emotional. Pernille owned the brand name of the firm; she had officially registered her own business and was the sole proprietor. The inventory was hers after she had paid Astrid the wholesale price. A third person owned the physical premises, although Astrid had a rental contract that gave her basically unlimited lease with a fixed price. The rent was cheap compared to other comparable shops.

According to the Danish Business Lease Act, the lease on a business premises can be sold (*afståelse*) or passed on to a new business within the same sector or branch without price regulation (*Erhvervslejeloven* §55, §80-83).[83] The same law protects long-term contracts with limitations on rent increases. Understandably, such price-controlled leasing contracts are attractive to any business owner desiring to rent premises based on the market value of the 1970s, '80s or '90s. The area where Pernille's business was located had such advantages. Since the early 2000s the area had been gradually transformed from a district renowned for prostitution and drug dealing to an attractive shopping street for local, small scale retail businesses and cafés. The older rental agreements, protected from rentals based on the current market price, were therefore highly attractive, and could be obtained through informal networks, sold, or in some cases with an under-the-table cash payment.

Astrid sublet her rented premises, together with the shop's inventory, to Pernille. The initial contract between Pernille and Astrid was for three years. After that, they could re-negotiate the contract and Pernille could decide if she wanted to buy the lease or continue subletting from Astrid. Astrid, on her side, could choose to pass on the permanent rental contract to

---

[83]    For    full    version    of    the    law,    see    https://danskelove.dk/erhvervslejeloven («Erhvervslejeloven» 2021).

someone who could afford it (like Bestseller), but for now, she had decided to sublet to Pernille. However, Astrid indicated that if all went well, she would sell the contract to Pernille at a reasonable price.

Pernille and Astrid's example is typical in many ways. Leasing and subletting business premises is common in an area where rentals are expensive. Knowing the worth of re-leasing such a good contract creates a temptation to sublet and earn easy profits. Nevertheless, the Aarhus small business owners seemed more motivated by moral values than profit (see Polanyi 2001 [1944], where freedom is blocked by the moral obstacle). Julian, for example, retained the rental contract from his previous shop for three years after he moved to larger premises. He did not sublet the premises, but he had developed an emotional tie to the old shop, which made it hard for him to pass on the contract. It was rare to get hold of the old, cheap contracts and he wanted to pass it on to the right person. For now, Julian lent it out to young artists and held occasional exhibitions there. Mostly, it was just empty.

Whereas Pernille and Astrid provide an example of how firms are transferred between non-family members, family firms deal with the same issues. I found that they often rely on the same creative solutions. It was common that the parental generation remained the formal owners of a firm after the children's generation took over day-to-day management, with all its responsibilities and commitments. This was the case for both Ikan and Toys, and such a delayed transition had taken place in three other firms that I surveyed. These mixed ownership firms also divided the profits so that there was no practical difference between the new managing owner and original but still formal owner.

Although bureaucratic regulations and taxes created challenges in terms of transferring assets from parents to children, careful planning could help the parents carry out the transfer without much difficulty. For example, Danish law permits each parent to give each child and grandchild a tax-free gift of 62,900 DKK (€8400) per year (and a smaller amount to son- or daughter-in-law; the amount in 2020 had risen to 67,100 DKK). A gradual transfer of cash assets was thus possible.[84] Depending on the market value of the business, owners could gradually transfer the firm to the successor, an arrangement that Sally and her mother had agreed on.

In the case of Ikan, Polly and Poul avoided inheritance taxes when they took over management of Ikan by establishing a limited liability company (ApS) using the same family name. For the customers, employees, and public, as well as in all other practical matters, it was the same business,

---

[84] See Grønborg (2017) for an explanation of family gifting laws (in Danish).

but with new owners. When the local newspapers or other media ran stories on Ikan, Polly and her husband would be described as the owners. Karl would also refer to them as the owners, and he described himself as the previous generation. In legal terms, however, Polly and Poul were the owners of another firm that only rented the inventory, employees, and business premises from Polly's father. Lawyers and accountants recommend this model for generational transition. Nevertheless, Polly and Poul's case differs from this model in one significant way, namely that their ApS (i.e. an LLC) did not obtain any of the shares or assets of Karl's multiple firms, leaving Karl the sole legal owner of all assets.

Government regulation of firms through transfer and inheritance taxes encourages creative, but potentially destructive solutions for small family firms. Although these alternative ways of transferring a firm from parents to children are legal, Ikan is an obvious example of the risk of being excluded from the firm after a period of time (losing all the investments of time, energy, and finance).

Flexible, slow transfer arrangements require a close relationship between parents and overtaking children, as well as with the siblings, who must also be compensated in some form. Although there are no formal regulations on gifts, gifts can cause trouble after the giver dies. If the amounts are considerable remaining siblings might claim compensation based on reduced expected inheritance, such as shown in the popular Danish TV-series 'Arvingerne' ('The Legacy'). When the siblings find out that one of them have received large amounts of money from their mother when she was alive, they cut off a part of his inheritance to make up for the amounts he had received as gifts before their mother passed. Slow transfer of firms as gifts, also requires the parents' trust and confidence in the younger generation, that the children will be able to manage their firm effectively. With so many risk factors involved, it was not surprising that many of the firms I encountered in Aarhus underwent major reorganizations in the wake of transmission from parents to children. The numerous methods of avoiding taxes and the transfer of ownership and management from one generation to the next placed the younger generation in a precarious position. They had to deal with the tasks of everyday management and the responsibilities of formal legal ownership. In Ikan, we saw that this involved what amounted to an exploitation of the younger generation: formal ownership and assets remained with Karl, while investment of labour and capital (capital through renovation and refurbishing of the shop) fell to Polly and Poul, who remained without legal ownership. In Sally's case, her older sister had tried to manage the family firm for a time (with her mother retaining ownership), but eventually it was Sally who became the legal owner after years of gradual transmission

According to Sally, her sister Julie had wanted to take over the firm because like Sally, she was proud of the family tradition that the firm symbolized. However, sales had declined further under Julie's management, and Sally's mother, Pia, was sceptical of Julie's business style. Julie, she felt, lacked the unique *moral* (spirit) *sjælen* (soul/spirit) and *værdierne* (values) that Pia felt were needed to carry on the business successfully. Julie was not *til stede* (mentally engaged) in the shop. She had her mind on her career as a specialist nurse. As a shop Toys is a special place, Sally and her mother agreed. Not just anyone could manage it. Management of Toys required a person who held the same values that Pia had built up over the years. Even though Julie had thought that she possessed the right values, Sally and Pia agreed that she did not. The case sheds light not only on the vulnerable position of the younger generation prior to acquiring legal ownership but also the importance played by 'the right set of values' in generational transition.

## 'With the Right Values, You Can Do Anything'

'With the right values, you can do anything', Ole said during our discussion about the future of his firm. A continuous theme running through the life of all the firms I studied in Aarhus was a concern for doing right and good. Despite the multiple bureaucratic, financial, and practical challenges confronting the entrepreneurs, they kept returning their concerns about having the right set of values. Sally, for example, was overly concerned with *moral* and made sure to remind me daily of her ethical standards and the importance of running her business in an ethical manner, of having what she called an 'ethical business' (*moralsk virksomhed*). Sally talked a lot about her ethical goals and the importance of being a *moralsk virksomhed*. Sally and her family saw themselves as a spiritual family, using the shop as an arena to practice their goodness. Sally's firm was the only business where the owners planned for the next generation to take over. Sally was a single mother, and Victoria her only child. From an early age, Victoria had accompanied her mother wherever she went. She had watched and taken part in her mother's achievements as a single parent, and she expressed that she knew from experience the importance of community, sharing, hard work, and independence. Victoria had worked in the firm when her grandmother, Pia owned it, before Sally got involved. Sally and Victoria had already agreed that Victoria would take over management one day.

Victoria was proud of Sally's achievements and told me that she strived to be like her mother: a good human being who did morally right by others. When Sally and Victoria expressed these views, they did so both in relation to pure human qualities and in terms of how the firm was being run. Sally insisted that Toys was her platform to practice doing good. Victoria hoped to one day inherit this platform and continue her mother's good works. It was as if she was learning to take on a mission, a mission of good business. Victoria described herself as a 'student' learning how to manage Toys successfully. To her, learning how to manage the firm was more about adopting the 'unique atmosphere of Toys'.[85] Both Victoria and Sally agreed that it was important that Victoria work in the shop and learn the business in order to 'know it as well as the inside of her own pocket' by the time it was her turn to take over management, in 15 years' time. Victoria would make sure that she was qualified to take over the business when the time came; mother and daughter were both certain about that. Sally and Victoria stated that they shared the same values in life as in business. They both showed that they worked to make the shop a place where anyone, regardless of purpose, was welcome, and where the business was managed according to strict ethical guidelines.

Victoria copied her mother's behaviour and opinions, and shared her concern for business ethics and compassion (*medmenneskelighed*). Like the other business owners, but more extreme, Sally had emphasized independence. They came from a family history of what Sally called independent *iværksætter kvinder* (entrepreneur women) who in various innovative ways had managed on their own. Sally described her own childhood: her mother had worked, and the children had 'just been there'. She had to take care of herself and find her own path in life. Victoria, a single mother of two, told me how Sally had never helped when she had been a student and single mother. Sally did not only not help her daughter financially, but she also never picked up the children from kindergarten or helped her daughter in other ways. 'And that's just the way it is, I never expect her to', Victoria told me. Instead, Victoria explained, 'She helped me by giving me a job'.

Marie and Ole were similarly direct about desiring to 'do good' for the public and for the local community. Although more modest in their formulations than Sally, Marie and Ole often mentioned how they took the time to talk to the customers. They also explained that they sold only ethical

---

[85] The Danish terminology, which was constantly repeated, by Sally, Victoria and the grandmother was *moralske værdier, moralsk rigtigt, unikke atmosfære, respekt* all referring to an open, free from prejudice, warm and welcoming, non-capitalist business strategy that strongly respected the individual's free will (*frie vilje*) providing guidance (*vejledning*) and expert knowledge (*ekspertviden*). As noted previously, the Danish term *moral* has various connotations: it can mean ethics, as in a work ethic; or spirit, as in the English 'morale'; or it can mean a more abstract idea of 'morality'.

products, being an organic bakery and collaborating with local farmers. These values were expressed in their actions. They spent time with each customer, listened to their employees and their concerns, and communicated in a respectful manner. These actions were reflected in the views of their customers and employees, who explained how Marie and Ole always took the time to listen to what they had to tell them, even if they were busy with a work task. Their concern for taking the time to attend to others' needs and wants, going to lengths to meet these needs, was an expression of their ambitions of being good by literally doing good in their business.

Another common trait among the Aarhus business owners was their concern for and value they placed on hard work, especially physical, visible or result-oriented work, as opposed to 'back office' work, paperwork or pure administration. Ole described himself as a multitalented man who could do anything well if he put his mind to it. What was important, according to him, was not what kind of firm he owned, but what he did with what he had at hand. Now he was the owner of a bakery, previously he was a pioneer farmer of a luxury crop (gourmet mushrooms), and he believed that his success was the result of his hardworking spirit and the values transmitted to him by his parents. Ole persistently claimed that it was not important to him that his children inherit his firm. It was more important, he claimed, that they created something of their own that gave their life meaning. Ole told me that by working towards transferring his own values over to his children, his children would be able to succeed in whatever they wanted for themselves, just as he could succeed in whatever he started.

The structured interviews I completed as part of a survey of 32 shopkeepers added further evidence for Ole's priority of transmitting values rather than the material assets of his firm. The respondents to my survey had not inherited their parents' firms. However, they brought with them their parents' entrepreneurial spirit (Jaskiewicz et al. 2015). They possessed the ability to enjoy hard work and a set of values, which (according to themselves), were essential in order to manage a firm with financial and ethical success. For Marie and Ole, these values implied taking the time to show respect for other people's needs and wishes, and a willingness to help others meet their needs and wishes (such as enlarging their product assortment to include cakes or filling a large order on short notice). For Sally, her set of values implied hard work. Hard work in Sally's case refers to her total dedication to the firm, being involved in all aspects of the business, such as customer service, web design, colouring yarn, and even cleaning the floor after closing time. But their understanding of hard work also has to do with the dedication of time. Like the other businesses, Sally claimed she was always working. She also stressed an understanding and willingness to identify and fulfil the needs and wishes of others. Julian, while perhaps less explicit about his values, nevertheless expressed a willingness to work hard to help customers acquire exactly what they had in mind when they placed an order. He also took his time with each customer and made sure he became fully familiar with their specific wants and needs. This kind of customer service goes beyond greeting a customer who comes into his shop and asking how he can help. All six businesses owners offered a product or service that opened the way toward a more intimate relationship with the customers. In Julian's case, the customers who had ordered a piece of custom-made jewellery would come by several times in the process from design to final product. Julian would sit down with the customer and they would share stories about their life and ideas behind the unique jewellery they wanted. All business owners had in common that they had taken the active choice to leave a life as wage-earner and start a business doing something they experienced as meaningful. They sought social contact with people, providing specialized products or services that made the owners feel good about themselves, knowing that they offered something unique.

Polly and Poul often expressed concern that their children cared more about their screens (i.e. looking at their various electronic devices) than they did about the business. Polly's favourite activity growing up had been to go with her father to work, learning everything she could about the business. Her own children, she complained, did not see the value of 'hard work' (*hårdt arbejde*), or work at all. They were not interested in taking part in the family firm. She and Poul were genuinely concerned that their children would not seem to acquire the proper work ethic (*arbejdsmoral*).

Why had Sally successfully managed to transmit what she viewed as the correct set of values to her daughter Victoria, whereas Polly and Poul, seemingly, had not? One possible explanation lies in differences in parental contact during their childhood years. Whereas Sally took Victoria with her for work and errands, Polly and Poul did not bring their children with them to work. The children never got to see their values of hard work and collaborative behaviour in action. The children were effectively isolated from their parents' life mode. This experience contrasts again with Marie and Ole, who managed their farm from home, such that their children took an active part in their parents' work from a young age. Polly and Poul, meanwhile, built a home far away from the firm. In typical modern Danish middle-class fashion, they separated their business from their private life. Ethnologist Thomas Højrup illustrates the importance of children's inclusion and participation in adult work tasks as the key to transmission of values and preparation for adulthood (Højrup 1983). Indeed, it is difficult to transmit values unless they are tied to concrete practices, in this case the practices of running a business on a daily basis. Polly and Poul's children grew up with their parents being away at work, without having the chance to personally witness, much less take part in, the actual work they performed. Perhaps it was this separation between private life and business that prevented their values from being passed on to their children to the extent that Polly and Poul wished. Marie and Ole, Julian, Polly, Sally, and various other business owners I interviewed could all clearly recall observing and taking part in their parents' entrepreneurial activities as part of their upbringing. Watching their parents on the job had been an important part of their childhood, and it is likely that involvement in their parents' work played an important role in the transmission of values between the generations (Højrup 1983).

The Danish concept of *dannelse* (equivalent to the German *Bildung*) might be useful as an explanatory concept in the understanding of such a transmission. In his study of the Danish city of Skive, British anthropologist Richard Jenkins (2011: xiii) translates *dannelse* as 'a holistic pedagogic philosophy or ideology, at the heart of the Danish education and childcare systems, which simultaneously emphasizes individual personal development and learning to fit in with the group'.[86] The person without *dannelse* is thus unmannerly, vulgar, or uncultivated. The closest English equivalent may be schooling, upbringing or enculturation, but these terms are not sufficient to explain *dannelse. Dannelse,* and the project to ensure *dannelse*, has a long history in Denmark and Scandinavia. It involves an educational process of learning the social norms that characterize a specific way of acting, being, and knowing. Ensuring that everyone is *dannede* is the responsibility of the family, the educational institutions, the local community, and society. It is the process of becoming a properly brought up person, a Danish person (see Højrup 2002). Historically, the concept has received influence from many different epochs and civilisations.[87] Making sure that the children are *dannede* into the right values turns out to be an important, but not necessarily conscious strategy among the business owners. By allowing children to take part in parents' life and work tasks, children become better equipped for adult life (Højrup 1983). Participating in parents' work practice becomes a technique for imparting *dannelse*. For children of entrepreneurs, involvement in the parents' work life is viewed as essential for successful entrepreneurship later in life. Work is a form of education.

---

[86] See also Ministry of Education (Folketingstiende 1975) inspired by a writing on *dannelse* (Christensen 1997).

[87] The pedagogical background began as early as the classical era, with the Greeks' emphasis on music, gymnastics, later rhetoric, and grammar. The classical tradition was followed by Roman Catholic religious influence, humanism, and national romanticism.

## Conclusion

Although the decision not to continue the parents' firm was undoubtedly affected by the bureaucratic challenges and tax laws set by the redistributive state, the strong emphasis on independence and individual self-realization also played a significant role in the low number of firms that were passed on from the founding generation to the successors. When Marie's father expressed his disappointment that she did not want to continue the family farm, she responded that she was still continuing his life's work by setting up her own firm. She insisted that by involving her in his activities, social relationships, and life world as she grew up on the family farm, her father had taught her the values of hard work, community, and reciprocity. Marie had internalized a specific kind of entrepreneurial work ethic, a modest, frugal lifestyle, and an ideal of respectful care for the environment. Marie and Ole insisted that what was most important to them was not that their children should continue the firm that they had built up together, but that they, too, would reflect the values of their parents in making their own life's work. The project here was not the firm but the values deemed essential to building up a successful enterprise of any kind, and ultimately, the values essential for building a successful life.

In this chapter, I have shown that transmission of entrepreneurial skills is essentially a transmission of entrepreneurial values. Ensuring that these values are passed on is considered by my informants as more important than passing on the physical business or its assets. The business is a way of life, and at the core of any way of life is a specifically recognized value set. Among the business owners in Aarhus, this value set centred around self-sufficiency and independence, hard work, engagement with the work, and doing good towards customers and collaborators. It was thus common for the business owners that they did not expect that their children would take over their business. The owners were more concerned with building up their own business than with seeing it passed on to the next generation. Although some hinted that they would have liked their children to carry on their life's work, none expected them to do so. Bureaucratic and tax obstacles involved in the transfer of a firm from parent to child can be burdensome to a small enterprise. The various solutions to avoid heavy transfer taxes and complicated financial transactions placed the younger generation in a precarious situation in the process of changing ownership. Owners were thus more concerned with transferring values and their work ethic; they ensured this transfer by involving their children in the activities of the firm from an early age.

By ensuring that their children had requisite knowledge, the correct values, and their parents' hard work ethic, the Aarhus business owners equipped their children for the roles of adulthood as independent, self-sufficient, hardworking individuals. That the children shared the same values as their parents meant that they, too, were bound to a certain lifestyle, and life mode; like their parents, they would disapprove of a consumption-oriented, mode of life. Both my own survey and national statistics indicate that this strategy was somewhat effective: most business owners and entrepreneurs tend to be themselves children of business owners. Most of them, regardless of the kinds of educations they acquired, ended up leaving well remunerated wage-labour and returning to the life-mode of their parents, establishing their own firms, often within completely different niches than their parents.

In her study of Italian small business owners, Yanagisako (2002) claimed that as a firm grows and expands, and as members of the second generation get involved, distrust and suspicion will emerge. This eventually leads to the division of the firm and establishment of new family firms. In my main sample, only two firms had existed for more than one generation. Ikan, the oldest of the two firms, had gone through the process that Yanagisako described, where brothers established independent firms, both with the family firm name. When we consider that nearly all the Aarhus business owners were themselves children of business owners, indicating that establishing new firms was a more common option than continuing the family firm, it lends support to Yanagisako's 'inevitability of conflict' theory. We can also confirm Yanagisako's conclusion, namely that the success of a family firm cannot be measured in assets or revenue. Later, Yanagisako has argued for a view of family firms as kinship enterprises rather than economic enterprises. She argued that viewing family firms as kinship enterprises enables us to understand that the values in family firms are measured by more than economic performance or outcome. Yanagisako suggested that we should recognize the social and affective benefits that come out of a family enterprise in order to understand the real value of family firms. More specifically, we can emphasize that the success of the Aarhus business owners relies not only on how the actual transfer took place or that the firm formally changed hands legally, but on ensuring the successful transmission of entrepreneurial values.

## Chapter 6
## 'We Don't Work, We Live': The Self-Employed Life-Mode

On the path to understanding the Aarhus business owners' social and moral values, I sought to understand their perspectives on work. I discovered that the business owners shared a reluctance to use the word 'work' (*arbejde*). Work (*arbejde*) seemed to provoke negative associations related to tasks that you do because you have to, whereas the business owners defined the work they did at, and in relation to, their business as desirable (*lystbetonet*).[88] Most of the shopkeepers were unwilling to distinguish between work (*arbejde*) and leisure (*fritid*). Moreover, the fact that they spent most of their waking hours at or in their firm certainly blurred the boundaries between work and leisure, business and private life. Danish ethnologist Thomas Højrup has distinguished between three main life modes: the self-employed, wage worker, and the career professional. Højrup argued that '[f]or the career professional the "work" is your life. The wage worker is "working" for a living. As self-employed, you are living for your "work"' (Højrup 2013: 14). The business owners viewed work as a positive, embedded activity that gave them a sense of meaningful self-fulfilment. This resembles the career life-mode, with the exception that the career life-mode requires the professional worker to continually develop and demonstrate their valuable, innovative talents to their employer or to clients. The self-employed business owner has no such burdens. The self-employed enjoyed their work activities, and consequently, found it difficult to admit that what they did was work (in the sense of drudgery). As we shall see, however, their role as self-employed also necessitated that they 'live for their work', as Højrup has emphasized. In this chapter, therefore, I investigate Aarhus business owners' perspectives on life and work. We shall see how these business owners operate without a distinction between work and leisure, living what Højrup called the self-employed life-mode (Højrup 2013). It

---

[88] Noget jeg gør, fordi jeg har lyst til det.

reveals how these business owners invest almost all their waking hours in the life of their firm, even when they are supposed to be relaxing in the privacy of their own home. Even while sitting on the sofa watching TV, they are still working via their phones. The wage-earner life-mode is the only life-mode that is structured around a clear distinction between work and free time. Højrup argued that the career professional life mode is dependent on the constant reproduction of uniqueness and expertise (Højrup 2013: 9–10). Like the wageworker, the career professional can organize their free time, but it should be productive (taking courses for example), and they should typically be 'on call' in the evenings, weekends or vacations as part of their value to the firm. The career professional and the skilled or unskilled both sell their labour – be it skills, ideas or labour time – to an employer who owns and distributes the means of production. The self-employed business owner owns her own ideas, skills, and expertise, and can hold on to them or distribute them according to her own needs and desires. Although the business owners also need to invent new ideas, strategies or expertise – they need to adjust to the market and to consumers' changing tastes – they still retain control of their ideas, skills and expertise. They can choose to remake their firm or keep it in their existing niche. They can adjust their incomes to periodic downturns in the market (or market 'shocks' as occurred with the Covid-19 closure of shops). The career professional who brings her lap top to the family dinner table is employed to produce unique expertise and ideas that are sold, commercialized and implemented into the firm she works for (Højrup 2013: 11). Both the career professional and the self-employed business owners have in common that they are intensely engaged in their work. But the career professional's work is that of crafting a 'career', typically by moving up within the firm's management structure or by finding a new firm elsewhere with new challenges or selling their expertise to other firms as a consultant. The self-employed business owner's project is completely different. It is not a project of career advancement or seeking challenges. It is a project of autonomy and security, which is often obtained only with the help of an engaged spouse and supportive family members.

A concrete example of these blurred boundaries between work and life, is that of Lone. Lone owned and ran a family firm pet shop together with her husband. Like the other business owners whom I befriended in Aarhus, Lone spent a lot of time and energy on running her business. When I discussed with her the importance of work compared to the rest of her life, she became almost indignant, 'What do you mean by "work" [*arbejde*]? We do not work. Our work is our life, so how can we define how much we work and what work is? We don't work, we live!' Statements like these were common throughout my fieldwork. To the business owners, what we normally call 'work' was such a large part of their lives that my informants could not even distinguish their 'work' from the rest of their lives, much less the concept of 'leisure time' (*fritid*). This passion for work, their immersion in the life of their enterprise, was in fact one of the main motivations to run a business. On the surface, this resembles the engagement of the career professional; the difference, however, is that the career professional is inherently disloyal to their firm; they expect and plan to move elsewhere, either to another firm, or even another country. The passion of the self-employed is to their business, not to themselves. The self-employed business owners obtained satisfaction from their work; they relished the difficulty of separating work from life in general. This, of course, is the exact opposite of a wage-earner life-mode, in which working hours and leisure are to be kept absolutely separate, with the help of unions and labour contracts, so much so that one's real life only begins when one leaves the factory or office (Højrup 2013: 7–8). In contrast, the business owners in Aarhus spent most of their waking hours at their firm. They all agreed that they enjoyed what they did, and that spending these extra hours and days in their firms was not any sort of self-exploitation (as Marx might say) but instead brought happiness to their lives.

## Work and Labour

In order to understand the Aarhus business owners' ideas of work – or insistence that life and work not be separated, I will discuss various understandings of work and labour. The anthropological literature on work is typically divided between those who focus on industrial capitalist societies and wage-*labour* (see for example Applebaum 1984a; Marx 1995; Mollona 2005a; Smart and Smart 2005a), and those who focus on *work* in non-capitalist communities, characterized by exchange relations and gift economies (Mauss 1966; Goldschmidt 1984; Lee 1984; Malinowski 1984; Gregory and Altman 1989)[89] as summarized in James Suzman's book *Work: A history of How we Spend Our Time* (2020).

Our conventional understanding of 'work' is that it is necessary labour, drudgery, something you have to do but which you would rather escape from. The opposite of work is therefore 'hobby', i.e. work that is enjoyable and self-fulfilling. The self-employed business owners whom I studied seem to fall between the two categories. Their daily work is not considered onerous. And it is certainly not a hobby. Nevertheless, they find

---

[89] These two perspectives are represented in Herbert Applebaum's two edited volumes from 1984, *Work in Market and Industrial Societies* and *Work in Non-market and Transitional Societies* (Applebaum 1984a, 1984b).

their work as something that they perform with pleasure and with a feeling of self-fulfilment. In order to explore the business owners' understanding of work as something they do because they enjoy it on multiple levels (i.e. self-fulfilment, social recognition, secure income, fulfilling desire for freedom and control), we need to first distinguish between work and labour.

Hannah Arendt (1998) formulates a clear distinction between *work* and *labour*. She describes *labour* in a manner similar to Marxist theoreticians, referring to tasks which are done out of necessity, requiring effort and perhaps even some discomfort or pain on the part of the individual. Hence, labour carries negative connotations of pain and sacrifice (Firth 1979). In contrast to labour, Arendt refers to *work* as tasks performed with pleasure and which the individual finds enjoyable or fulfilling. Where labour is rewarded with external values, work brings internal or social rewards such as prestige or self-fulfilment. Following this distinction, we could say that the Aarhus business owners were occupied with work. The alienation of man from labour emerged with the industrial revolution. Karl Marx (2007 [1867]: 708) claimed that in the 19th century industrial societies, work 'mutilated the labourer into a fragment of a man, degraded him to the level of an appendage of a machine, destroyed every remnant of charm in his work and turn it into hated toil'. Marx's theory of alienation of workers has been broadly applied and reinvented by social scientists (e.g. Thompson 1963; Carrier 1992; Parry 1999; Mollona 2005a).

While there is a philosophical distinction between 'work' and 'labour', the Danish language does not operate with this distinction. The Danish word *arbejde* can mean either 'work' or 'labour'. If Danes want to talk about wage-labour, however, they will call it 'lønarbejde'. Painstaking work or drudgery could be called 'slid' (*'slid'* literally means 'wearing down'). Hence, the Danish word *arbejde* is used in many different contexts and contains many different meanings and sentiments. For example, gardening (*havearbejde*) carries quite different meanings than *lønarbejde* (wage-labour). Whereas *havearbejde* connotes work performed voluntarily at home – privately, without salary, executed during leisure time, *lønarbejde* connotes laws, regulations, employment, unions and work tasks done out of necessity. Furthermore, *arbejde* is both a verb and a noun. The Danish word *arbejde* thus means both 'to work', 'work', 'labour', and is also the root of the word for 'worker' or 'labourer' (*arbejder*). The noun *arbejder* (worker/labourer) carries connotations mainly to industrial factory workers and is rarely used in daily conversation. Instead, Danes frequently use the word *medarbejder* (lit: co-worker) to refer to employees, staff or colleagues. If there is one kind of work that the Aarhus shopkeepers may associated with work as drudgery it is '*kontorarbejde*', the office work (often performed at home or in a back office) and associated with keeping accounts, filling out forms, or communicating with the authorities. *Kontorarbejde* is 'not real work', and in popular terms associated what in English might be called 'paper pushers' and Danes call '*bureaukrati*'.

## Living: Embedded Work Relations

Based on his Norwegian ethnographic studies, Carl Cato Wadel suggests that we define work through seven characteristics. Work involves using physical energy, it is routinized/repetitive, takes place in a certain place at certain times, the activities are necessary, they are done for someone else, and it is directed towards a product or a result. Finally, work involves a commitment (Wadel 1979: 370). We shall see that the concepts of a separation of work and leisure simply do not operate for the Aarhus business owners, because their work is their life. If I mentioned the word *arbejde* to the pet shop owner Lone, she would demand that I explain what I meant by '*arbejde*'. She insisted that she could not relate to the concept of *arbejde*, she was simply living her life. Lone's business took up so much of her time and was such a big part of her identity that she refused to define her time there as '*arbejde*'. Her reaction indicates an understanding of '*arbejde*' as 'work for others' or 'alienated work'. In this sense the self-employed work overlaps with 'hobby'. It is work for oneself, work which they control, but unlike a hobby, her shop is also a means of generating income. Lønarbejde is also a means of generating income, but it involves subservience to others (the employer). Lone's claim that her occupation as a pet shop business owner was her main objective in life and that she was 'just living' is an indication of the sentiments Højrup ascribed to the self-employed life-mode, where the business owner lives for her work (Højrup 2013: 14). Lone's husband was the third-generation pet shop owner, and the firm had been a central part of their lives together before she became a co-owner. The first years of their marriage, Lone worked in a chocolate factory, she then entered the pet shop as an employee, before she took on co-ownership. Lone had not joined her husband's family firm because she wanted to work, she told me. The business had been part of her life since they met, and when she left her job (and wage-work) in a chocolate factory to join her husband's family firm, she knew that it would not only be *part* of her life, but it would also *be* her life, she explained. Lone insisted that there was never any hesitation. She would not want it otherwise.

The same applied to Marie and Ole. In their eyes, their bakery shop was not something they had to do to 'earn a living' – their work was a part of what it meant to live. They lived to work, they lived for work, and they lived within their work. But they were not slaves to their work as a wage-labourer might be. They had no employer for whom they had to 'perform'. They had only each other – and their customers. Marie and Ole saw themselves as being 'in control' over their lives. This feeling of control was revealed in Marie's response to my question about what she felt about working such long hours in the bakery every day. She replied, 'I have grown up with farming, so I don't know anything else'. In the same conversation with Ole, he added, 'My mother was also self-employed and was always at home working, so I am used to it'. The couple often reminded me of their attitudes towards work. For example, Marie said, 'We don't view leisure time as something we are longing for, we like spending time here [in the business], this is what we do, because we want to'. A second example, 'Our firm is our life[90]; it is our moral obligation [*moralske forpligtelse*] towards the community, our customers, and ourselves'. Ole articulated the difference between their way of life as embedded in work, and the plight of the wage earner who longs to escape from their job, 'If you have a strong need to get away and have a vacation, it means you're doing something you don't really like, and that's not good'.

These attitudes towards work (work as non-labour in Arendt's terms) were common among the business owners I worked with in Aarhus. The owners spent so much of their time, invested so much of their self, and took so much pride in their sense of achievement from their work in their firms that they were both unable and unwilling to separate their private lives from their work. Making such a separation would have meant that they regarded their firm as some kind of alienated, onerous labour, as just a job, as a simple means to an end. Hence, a concept such as 'work-life balance', so familiar to those in the career lifestyle, is simply alien to the Aarhus business owners. They do not need to balance because there is no scale between the two concepts. Their work and their personal lives are embedded with each other.

To the casual observer, Marie and Ole were completely overworked. They were in their mid-50s and spent 14–15 hours at work every day, allowing themselves only a half-hour lunch break and a coffee, and only if there was time. When they got home, they did the accounting and made plans for the next day/week/month. They insisted that they liked spending time at the bakery, and that the amount of time spent there was of their own choice. Marx would call this 'self-exploitation', evidence of the 'petty commodity mode of production'. A stress expert would see this as a prelude to a stress breakdown. But Marie and Ole insisted that they were not overworked (*overarbejdet*) because they did not view the time they spent in the business as being at the expense of leisure. Ole explained, 'What else

---

[90] In Danish: '*vores virksomhed er vores liv*'.

should we do? This is what we do. This is our life. We make a point out of creating an everyday life that we enjoy. We make a point out of creating a life and a daily routine for ourselves that we don't have to take a holiday from'. Although they worked very hard, you saw few signs of stress or depression, that one typically encounters among so many career professionals.

When I asked them if they ever wanted to see their friends or family, Ole would assure me that they fulfilled their need to see friends and be social in their shop. Ole and Marie always took time to talk with every customer, most of whom were regulars. Accordingly, they knew their customers relatively well. No matter how long the queue, customers patiently waited their turn while the customer told Ole about how he spent the past weekend.

The shop was also a place where Ole and Marie's family came together. When their adult children were in town, they always came by to have a chat, and during high season, they would help out in the shop. Every December 23rd, all the regular employees had the day off and as replacements, their three children and their life-partners would come and work the entire day together in the shop. Working in the shop was not just a way of giving the regular employees a day off. It was a means of engaging the family in a sort of *hyggelig* Christmas tradition. According to Marie and Ole, it was about doing something *hyggelig* together as a family. Although the day before Christmas Eve was a busy day at the shop, a day where everyone was *working,* Marie and Ole described it as a day of nothing but joy and *hygge*. It was one of the few days of the year when most of the family was gathered. Because Marie and Ole worked six days a week, from 3:00 am until 5.30 pm in the shop and then went home to finish bookkeeping before bedtime, the couple rarely spent time with friends or family outside of work. There was no free time on the weekends, that most wage earners or those with managerial careers would expect to have as a normal part of their lives.

It was only after I had spent some time and gotten to know Marie and Ole that they admitted that they longed to have more time with family and friends. In fact, Marie and Ole had secretly started to plan a new enterprise, where they could work more on their own terms and be less dependent on physical contact with customers, but where they could still have flexible opening hours. In October 2018, Marie and Ole closed their very successful bakery in Aarhus. They signed a lease for some business premises in a small town closer to where they live and have rebuilt their barn into a home bakery. In December the same year, they opened a bakery the small town close to their home. Here they sell the bread they bake from their home bakery at limited opening hours. They are only the two of them in the shop, and they express that they wish for it to stay that way.

We may understand Marie and Ole's insistence that the time they spent in their firm (including the smaller firm that they began in 2018) was not arduous 'labour' in a negative sense, but an activity they had consciously chosen because they controlled and enjoyed it. It was work, but not the kind of work from which they needed a holiday. Marie and Ole realized, of course, that they had created a life where they had little time for anything but the firm. Although they could afford to hire help and allocate tasks that would give themselves more time off, they still had this strong need to be in direct control over all areas of the firm's production and sales. This need for control, what could be interpreted as a distrust that others could do their job equally well, seemed to limit their possibility to reduce their commitment to their firm.

Their distrust of others seemed to be connected to their distrust of wage-labour generally, a characteristic I found in all the business owners whom I studied. Their understanding of wage-labour as uncommitted (or committed only as far as you receive a wage) was evident in the business owners' reluctance to identify the work they performed in the firm with that as labour. Those they hired did labour, they themselves did work (or just lived). The business owners' sentiments about wage-labourers extended to middle managers in corporate firms as well. These managers, they believed, were not committed to the business, only towards an aim of earning a good salary for themselves. The business owners expressed an attitude where they 'Trust No One' besides themselves and family. This attitude is understandable in so far as business owners place a high value on personal autonomy. Trust, as Matthew Carey and others have argued, implies dependency. Trust is 'a redistribution of control' (Carey 2017: 7). The Aarhus business owners' desire for freedom (from an employer) and control (over work and life) make them reluctant to redistribute control, hence the distrust of others outside the immediate family. As Carey elaborated, trust necessitates risk. The risk of trusting others to take care of business was not a risk the Aarhus shopkeepers were willing to take. Florian Mühlfried (2019: 4–5) cited Nietzsche as one of few philosophers who regarded mistrust as an asset instead of a problem. Mühlfried argued that mistrust is just as important as trust to the success of Western, democratic states (2019: 8). The division of power, the role of media in monitoring state affairs, and the multiple forms of control practiced by welfare states, such as Denmark, are all built on a general mistrust (ibid.). Mühlfried (2019: 5) argued that 'in business life, mistrust of the workforce is regarded as a serious malfunction'. However, the Aarhus business owners practice their mistrust in a way that resonates well with the view of mistrust as attitude, instead of problem. The business owners show mistrust by not allowing wage workers control over what they perceive as essential, creative or demanding areas of the business (such as baking bread in the bakery). But they manage to balance their mistrust in such a way that the employees experience a feeling of trust by being allowed to work in areas of the firm that the business owners consider 'manageable' or non-creative (such as cake baking or dealing with customers). Whereas Mühlfried argued that '[d]emocracy cannot exist without trust, but also not without mistrust', the small, niche firms also need both trust and mistrust (Mühlfried 2019: 8). Carey (2017: 9) argued that trust implies both control and release of control. The business owners allow the employees control over cake baking processes, but these employees risk losing this control (and employer's trust) if they do not follow the recipe in the precise way. In this way, the owners control the employees, and trust requires compliance from the employees. The employer-employee relationship remains asymmetrical, despite the trust between them.

For the business owners who own both their means of production and labour, in the classical Marxian sense, work makes them whole. Instead of alienating work from their selves, they embed their work in their lives and selves. Instead of the 'charm and remnant' of their work being destroyed, leaving them to hate their job, they find pleasure in their work.

Karl Polanyi (2001 [1944]) argued that the commodity basis of capitalism has turned land, labour and money into 'fictious commodities' to be bought and sold. Labour can only be a fictitious commodity, however, when people are employed and work for money, i.e. as wage-labour. It might be more fruitful to view the self-employment that Lone, Marie and Ole, and similar small shops I worked with in Aarhus, as representing a type of work that existed prior to the modern market economy. Indeed, Marx called this 'petty commodity mode of production' (or simple commodity mode of production). In the eyes of my Aarhusian informants, work thus resembles 'a human activity which goes with life itself' (Polanyi 2001 [1944]: 75). The shopkeepers earn income from their business, of course. But they are not capitalist investors seeking the highest rate of profit, where they would move their capital elsewhere, the moment they could get a better return. I do not claim that my firms were not profit-oriented or that they were not part of a market economy that made profits on labour (several also had employees as well). None of the businesses in my study resembled hobbies. All were concerned with making profits in order to survive, and perhaps even growing, but not beyond more than they could control. Nevertheless, several factors besides the need to earn a living motivated the owners to spend most of their waking hours in their shops and businesses. What they had in common was an attitude about the work they did: that this work meant more to them than the work itself and the income they derived from it. The work they performed was more than a fictitious commodity (wage-labour to be sold on a market). It was more than a simple 'return on investment'. It was work they did for themselves, and not labour for others (Arendt 1998). Hence, although work was a means by which they made a living, they did not think of their activity in this way in their everyday lives. If I asked Ole how he defined himself and the work he did, he viewed himself as the personification of his firm. Similarly, Poul would refer to himself as the fishmonger (*fiskemand*), because that was what he was. He never stopped being a fishmonger, even when he left the office and went home to his family. He was his work. But he was not bound by his work. He was not a worker in chains, or some kind of a 'wage slave' in the Marxist sense.

Polanyi's theories of 'embeddedness' can assist us in understanding Lone and Ole and Marie's perceptions of work. Of importance here is the idea that they are not motivated purely by profit. In fact, it is likely that had my informants read Polanyi, they would have agreed that their way of working belonged to the classification of work as an embedded activity, indistinct from their lives in general.

Graeme Salaman (1974) has argued that people of certain occupations tend to form work-based communities where they identify as people of their occupation (anglers, for example). Although Salaman was criticized for both his methods and conceptual framework (see Cosper 1977) his framework can be useful in understanding the worldview of my Aarhusian shopkeepers and the way they regarded their livelihoods.

Pernille made a living out of her knitting hobby. She constantly occupied herself with what was now her work. She had been knitting ever since her grandmother taught her to knit as a child. Whenever she could, she knitted, she took part in several knitting circles, clubs, social networks, and most of her friends were knitting enthusiasts. To make a living, she had worked in a food canteen for 25 years. One day she decided to stop. After a few months of unemployment, she obtained a job in a yarn shop. It did not take long before she had regular customers, and she enjoyed her job. The other yarn shops in the city came to know about her, and after some time, a retiring shopkeeper offered Pernille the opportunity to take over her shop. At this time, Pernille had never even thought about opening her own business, and she declined the offer. It was at this time, Pernille told me, that she entertained the idea of starting her own business. A couple years later, she got another chance with another retiring yarn shop owner. When I met her, she had been the proud owner of her own little boutique, in one of the best locations in the city, for three years. Pernille had transformed her passion into her living. This was a common feature of all the first-generation firms in my sample. Pernille spent the time outside her shop with friends who had the same hobby. She participated in knitting events, and she knitted at home. Although we might count her leisure time activities as work, in her eyes, it was not. When I asked her if she had ever tried to sell yarn to her friends or if she promoted new products while taking part in her social knitting activities, she insisted that she never tried to push her friends into becoming her customers. However, she would of course inform them with some excitement whenever she had received new products, but this was out of pure excitement. It was not intended as any kind of sales pitch.

While Pernille claimed that she was not selling when she spent time with her knitting friends, it was clear that by making her hobby into her work, she had erased the boundaries between what we conventionally regard as work and leisure. She admitted that she never had the opportunity to knit anything for herself anymore, as she was always knitting for her shop. There was always a need for new knitted samples, she spent all her time outside the shop knitting samples to be displayed in the shops (a knitting shop operates by inspiring customers to buy materials for garments or patterns that they have seen elsewhere: in a magazine, worn by someone else, or displayed in the shop).

When I surveyed 32 different business owners, asking them what they would do if they could have more free time and keep the same income as they had today, most replied that they would spend the same amount of time in the business as they already did, or that they would try to improve their (work) skills.

It should be emphasized here that each of the shopkeepers with whom I did fieldwork carried out their work in order to generate income. No matter how many times they claimed that they were not motivated by profit, they were acutely aware that they were operating in a competitive market economy where businesses go bankrupt every day, especially small, owner-operated businesses. That they pursued stable incomes, however, does not mean that they were necessarily profit-maximisers. I argue with Parry et al. (2005) and Williams (2004), that while all small businesses necessarily operate within the capitalist market economy, and not all of them have the goal of profit maximization alone. The ethnographic examples above show that business owners can be both part of the capitalist market economy and still have *attitudes* which resembles those described by Herbert Applebaum (1984b) as belonging to people of non-market societies.

## Hard Work

Polly and Poul, like most other small business owners, were extremely concerned with promoting themselves as hard workers. Poul would daily complain about his *slidt* (worn out) body. For decades, he had been cutting fish from early morning to late afternoon. Poul continually articulated his self-perception as a hard worker with a high work ethic (*arbejdsmoral*). It was important for him that I, and the people around him, understood that although he did not do the actual fish fileting anymore, that he had done so in the past. People should know that he had been compelled to reduce his manual labour due to ill health. I experienced conversations where both Polly and Poul complained about other people's poor work ethic (*dårlig arbejdsmoral*). Although the number of hours Polly spent at the firm were fewer after they had children, she made sure to remind me of 'all the work' she had to do at home. She was responsible for laundry, hoovering, cleaning the stable (they owned horses), picking up and chauffeuring the children, and so forth. As an example of the kind of work rhythms of my informants, the table below shows the average working day for Marie and Ole (bakery shop) and Polly and Poul (fish).

| Daily rhythm | | | |
|---|---|---|---|
| **Time** | **Marie and Ole** | **Poul** | **Polly** |
| 3 – 4 a.m. | Arrive at the bakery, prepare the dough | Engage in auctions via his phone from bed. | |
| 5 a.m. | Bake. | Gets up, makes calls from kitchen while having a cigarette. | |
| 5.30 – 6 a.m. | When all the bread is in the oven, they have a short breakfast break, sharing a few slices of rye bread with cheese and instant coffee. | Gets into car with headset on and continues making calls to fish auctions while driving to the shop. | |

| 7 a.m. | Employees start to arrive. Prepare the shop for opening. | Arrives at the shop and sits in office preparing orders/cuts fish and packing deliveries. First delivery leaves at 7 a.m. Shop opens. | Wakes up after the alarm has been ringing for 30–60 minutes. Wakes children up, puts milk, cereals, and bowls on the table. Smokes a cigarette in the kitchen while the kids have breakfast. |
|---|---|---|---|
| 7.30 a.m. | Continue to bake bread all day long. | Continues as above. | Children have been fed, dressed, and are sent to school. Combs her hair, gets dressed, and packs a slice of rye bread and a cup of coffee, which she will eat in the office. |
| 8 a.m. | Shop opens. | As above. | Arrives at the office. Makes coffee and has a cigarette before getting started with the bookkeeping. |
| 9 –12 a.m. | Busy baking and handling customers | Continues preparing, signing orders, and talking to suppliers/ customers via phone. Cuts fish. | Updates order books with today's orders and other adminis-trative work. Takes several cigarette breaks. |
| 12 a.m. – 2 p.m. | Around 2 p.m., Marie and Ole take a half-hour lunch break after all employees have had theirs. Rye bread | Has lunch at office sometime during this period. Lunch is also breakfast | Sometime during these hours Polly has her lunch. Either something from the shop, or |

| | | | |
|---|---|---|---|
| | with cheese and instant coffee with milk. | and is often shared with colleagues. Eats either what Polly brought, goes out to buy something himself, or sends one of the employees. Lunch is always shared. | she sends one of the employees to buy something. Often, she has made a stop on the way to work. Lunch is always shared with employees and her husband. |
| 2 – 3 p.m. | Busy times in the shop. Second round of baking and more time with customers. | Leaves the shop to visit customers, potential customers, suppliers, or other business-related errands. | Works in office interrupted by several cigarette and coffee breaks. Might leave office in this period to avoid rush hour traffic. At home, Polly cleans the stable, takes care of animals, hoovers, cleans, does laundry, and other household-tasks. (people who live on a farm with dogs in the house hoover every day) |
| 3 p.m. – 4 p.m. | Busy times in the shop. Second round of baking and more time with customers. | Continues as above. | If she has not left the office already, she leaves the office and drives home. May stop for groceries on the way home. Calls Poul several times. At home she does household tasks. |

| | | | Children return home from school. |
|---|---|---|---|
| 5 p.m.–6 p.m. | Finishes work. Leaves the shop, and the employees close up, but Marie and Ole usually takes the daily cash receipts home. Drives home. | Makes sure everything is in order at the business before he leaves and spends an hour in traffic on the way home. May stop for groceries or other errands. Lies down on couch to rest while working via his phone. Falls asleep and naps on sofa. | Continues with household tasks. Drives children to different sports activities and is a volunteer coach for one of the children's sports teams. |
| 6 p.m.–7 p.m. | Ole does the bookkeeping of the day, while Marie cooks dinner. They eat together. | Poul cooks dinner, and the family eats together. | May cook dinner. Makes sure all children are ready for dinner. |
| 7 p.m. –8 p.m. | Eat dinner together, chat and get ready for bed. | Cleans after dinner. | Prepares the children for bed, takes in the horses. |
| 8 p.m. –10 p.m. | Go to bed | Shower, personal hygiene, TV-watching. | Puts children to bed, showers, personal hygiene, feeds and takes care of horses, TV, and knitting-time. Goes to bed. |
| 10 p.m. – 3 a.m. | Sleep | Sleep | Sleep |

Table 3. Daily work and household routines for two small business owners.

As the table shows, Poul started his workday between 3–5 am, what most people would call 'the middle of the night'. When he got home in the evening, between four and seven pm., Poul continued working via his phone in between short naps. Polly and Poul defined their life according to their business, and all friends, neighbours, and acquaintances knew them as the fishmongers. Their mind was always on the business. They both claimed that they always needed to 'occupy ourselves with something', or they would not be happy. Being 'occupied with something' did not necessarily refer solely to business activities but also to household tasks. For Polly, this could mean that she was knitting while she was watching TV, and for Poul this meant that he was constantly making work-related calls, sending texts or emailing on his phone, even while they were watching TV.

Polly and Poul did not have the kind of clear division of labour where Poul took a larger responsibility for the firm and Polly performed most of the household tasks. Their consumption was not based on any relative contribution to the firm either. They had a shared household economy where they both saw themselves as contributing equally to the household and to the business. They did not draw the same amount of salary advance from the firm to spend on personal or household items. If more money ended up in Poul's account, it was because he would simply do more of the grocery shopping this month. But they did not withdraw a fixed amount. The amount varied according to expenses. Polly and Poul thus shared responsibilities, work tasks, and material wealth. The lack of distinct mine/yours-thinking between them as a couple contributed to the blurring of the boundary between work and private life. Polly paid most of the bills, whereas Poul did most of the grocery shopping. However, their bank accounts were shared, and they did not have a strict arrangement for regulating the flow of cash between their accounts. However, Polly and Poul still maintained separate savings account, and they had a safe where Poul kept the cash receipts.[91] They were married with a shared economy, and had equal rights to each other's funds, they also owned the house together, but they had separate cars. As Poul would say, 'Polly decides how much we get paid from the firm each month, since she's in charge of the economy [finances at the firm], but I tell her what we need'. The business owners were responsible for their own 'salary' if, in fact, one could call it a salary at all. In fact, most of them took out money from their own firm only in order to satisfy their immediate household needs, and nothing more. Moreover, some of the business owners did not pay themselves a stable cash salary, either because they were reinvesting in the business or because their business was still at an immature

---

[91] The reasons for why Poul kept cash in his home will, for ethical reasons, not be discussed here. I will leave it with one explanation, which could be related to mistrust in large banks.

stage and did not yet have a stable customer flow or income from which to extract a monthly 'salary'.

Although not all business owners expressed their dedication to their work as bluntly as Lone, the pet shop owner, they articulated an image of self that was based on hard work. Hard work was a prerequisite for a meaningful life, and with it came the pride in being a hard worker. Ole stated very clearly that if he did not constantly create and develop something, he would feel diminished as a human being, 'I need to always use my creativity and create something new. It's vital for my well-being. Both Marie and I are quite innovative'. Sally, the toy shop owner, repeatedly stated that keeping herself occupied with work was necessary for her very sanity, 'I'll go insane if I'm kept from doing something'. Poul repeatedly reminded me that he had worked 10 to 15-hour shifts every day since he was 13, and that this was the only way he could live. Marie and Ole's perception of self was perhaps even more visible when we discussed why they continued to carry out all the practical tasks in their firm. In our conversation, Marie explained that 'We are hardworking', followed by, 'We both want to take part in the practical tasks, and usually, if a business gets bigger, you end up just sitting there managing'. It was as if 'managing' was not real work.

For these small business owners, work, or rather, work in their own firm, was a space of pride and self-fulfilment. These sentiments express the importance of being active in each operational area of the firm, producing something useful. We may connect this way of thinking about work to what Max Weber, discussed as the essence of modern capitalism. In his renowned work, *The Protestant Ethic and the Spirit of Capitalism*, Weber (2001 [1905]: 18) claimed that 'man is dominated by the making of money, by acquisition as the ultimate purpose of his life', and further that '[e]conomic acquisition is no longer subordinated to man as the means for the satisfaction of his material needs'. According to Weber, modern capitalists, also those who profit from capitalist enterprise, had reached a point where they made enough money to sustain a desirable level of material comfort, and instead of working less, they just kept working hard, accumulating their wealth. According to Weber, the motivation for these people to work hard was grounded in a moral asceticism that had emerged from the Protestant idea of a 'calling': the belief that worldly asceticism was a sign of salvation. Nevertheless, people lost awareness of where the drive to work hard had originated, and they continued to work hard without having economic gain as their motivation. The motivation had become the work itself (Weber 2001).

Most of the business owners I met in Aarhus would not agree that their motivation for working hard was their belief in some kind of heavenly salvation; nor did they express the belief that they worked only to make money. Most of them did not reflect upon life after death or God, and more than half of them did not even believe in God, and certainly not life after death. So, if they were not overtly religious, what was their motivation for a daily life that consisted largely of hard work in their shop? Had the work itself become the motivation for work? All my Aarhusian friends come from a background of Scandinavian Lutheran Protestantism. Most of them had grown up as members of the Lutheran state church, singing Christian songs and psalms, and if not at home, they learned about Christianity from the first year in school. The public education system transferred what Danes now call 'Christian values' onto their citizens. Despite being overwhelmingly atheist or agnostic, the discussion of immigration and Islam in Denmark has led to the articulation of an idea of 'Christian values', such that even atheist Danes can say that they are 'cultural Christians' (*kulturkristne*) that they are comfortable with having their children baptized, their teenagers confirmed, being married in a Church, attending Christmas mass, etc. However, the Aarhusian business owners seem to work hard with few apparent reasons other than the satisfaction they get from being their own boss in a small business. They act out their own autonomy. They all lived materially comfortable lives, according to themselves, and they lived on their own terms. The fact that they spent so many hours each day working in their firm (or carrying out business tasks at home on the sofa or in the car) seems to be confirmation that the activities in the firm gave them the kind of spiritual satisfaction they articulated. Their ethos, visible through their continuing reiteration of their hard work, illuminates the vitality of this ethos in the moral realization of the self (Stenius 1997, 2010; e.g. Larsen 2011).

The business scholar Rosabeth Kanter (1978) claimed that working hard, doing something that they like, gives people a motivation to work that goes beyond that of obtaining financial security or profit (see also Ronco and Peattie 1988). Cato Wadel (1979) further argued for a folk concept of work. Wadel claimed that work has a logic beyond that of simply making money to survive, 'to have a job is commonly held as a prerequisite for membership in the moral community' (Wadel 1979: 371). To understand work as a moral obligation towards group and society is thus an important aspect of the hard work self-image. It is important to show that you have a proper work ethic (*arbejdsmoral*) and that you are hardworking (*arbejdsom/arbejder hårdt*) in order to show that you are, not only a good citizen, but that you are a decent human being (Larsen 2011). This moral aspect is evident in the Danish everyday phrase '*god arbejdslyst*' ('Wishing you a good work-spirit'), a common phrase addressed to a friend, colleague, or family member who is about to go off to work or take on a task. The morality of work, the duty to have a job and 'contribute to society' is also a common theme in debates about welfare recipients and immigrants, who receive generous welfare benefits but for various reasons are not working; the inability to find work may easily evolve into an accusation that they just do not want to work (which forms the core of the new research in the concept of 'deservingness').

Marie and Ole had made it their duty to work as hard as they could in order to satisfy their returning customers every day. Equally, Poul felt that he had a moral responsibility to meet the expectations of his customers and employees by making sure that there was fresh fish in his shop every single day. In Poul's case, the importance of living up to his moral commitment in the firm and towards his family became manifest when Poul's father-in-law, Karl, felt that Poul had not lived up to the expectations within the moral community. Karl ended up removing Poul, and his own daughter Sally, from their positions as managers of the business. Pernille was present in her shop every day – even on days when her sales assistant managed the shop. She explained her presence by invoking the social connection and pleasure of being two of them at work; but it was also because she wanted to ensure that every operation of the business, every routine, was going according to the way she wanted. This is another example of the pervasive mistrust that business owners have in the ability of anyone else besides themselves to run their business properly.

For these business owners, spending an entire day at home was unthinkable. This was not necessarily because they were needed on the shop floor, nor because their profits would necessarily suffer if they were absent for some hours or a day (we do not know this because they were always present). Rather, viewing themselves as committed business owners who had to constantly work at their business did not allow them to stay home or do something 'unproductive' when they could be doing work that they enjoyed. If there was one restraint in the lives of the business owners, it was their pervasive inability to relinquish control over any area of their firm's operations. This quality may explain their behaviour when they performed and explicated their concepts of work ethic (*arbejdsmoral*).

For example, Sally reminded me every day that much of her work in her toy shop was invisible from the outside. Her reminder was always followed by a hand gesture where she pointed her finger at her head, 'A lot of the work I do happens in here. Sometimes, it might look like I'm not working, but I'm *always* working'. Sally insisted that she spent a lot of time every day thinking and analysing, and this was a heavy load on her as a person. She spent a lot of time explaining to her employees, whom she called 'her girls' (*pig erne*) that although it looked like she was just sitting there, she was always working. Sally and the other business owners' strong need to constantly remind us that reflecting on their business operations was also work confirms what has been characterised as a Western industrial-society-perspective on work (Wadel 1979). According to Wadel, work should be visible; it should produce an immediate result that one can see (ibid.). This kind of work is 'real work'. Hence the oft-cited denigration of office, managerial or bureaucratic work as 'not real work', as 'pseudoarbejde' (Nørmark and Jensen 2018) or 'bullshit jobs' (Graeber 2016). Perhaps it is more legitimate to claim that Sally, being deeply religious, was influenced by a Protestant Ethic, in so far as she felt the need to constantly make sure that no one would think that she was lazy or not working. The Protestant Ethic, the 'calling', gives one a feeling of security and direction, but it also creates moments of uncertainty, that one is not working enough, or not doing the right kind of work.

After spending many hours with Poul over weeks and months, I learned that although it looked like he was just reading the news and texting on his phone, he was in fact planning, networking, and trading goods – all through his phone. I was confused at first when he made these phone calls because they sounded more like friendly chats, including telling jokes. But in fact, the jokes were just a prelude to a business deal, and Poul concluded several such deals throughout the day. Poul had a joking and personal tone with most of his suppliers and wholesale customers, and I learned that this way of talking and joking was an important aspect of fishmongering. With time, I understood that this was fishmonger banter, a way of speaking that both parts expected. All fishmongers and people working in the fish industry used this kind of verbal style, some of which resembles the anthropological 'joking relationship'. Alongside the jokes and humour, hard business deals were being concluded. Moreover, an important part of Poul's business strategy was to have a close relationship with his suppliers, knowing them on a personal level, and talking to them in an informal manner. They were both mutually dependent on each other for ordering and delivering goods. In fact, the relationship between Poul, his suppliers, and many of his wholesale customers was decades long, having been inherited through generations. It was thus both natural and important that the relationship involved a tone that represented more than mere formalized business negotiation. This kind of informal banter gave him an advantage in terms of better deals and a chance that they might call him first when goods were scarce, or when prices at other wholesalers were too high. In the eyes of his employees, it looked like Poul was sitting on the phone, joking, relaxing, and playing around all day long. In fact, Poul was very busy, working hard, constantly monitoring the fish market, looking at prices on his phone, observing what fish had been landed and calling supplier contacts to be the first to grab the fresh fish at the best available price. Similarly, the antipathy toward office work, which is necessary for any business, has an impact on those who believe that real work is only that which produces directly visible outputs. Employees on the Ikan shop floor gossiped about Poul, for just sitting around in the office, texting, making phone calls and reading news on his phone. For someone who stopped by his office in the lunchroom for short breaks and lunch once per day, it might certainly look like Poul was simply idling. However, the employees failed to realize that the hours Poul spent sitting in his office with his phone all day was absolutely crucial element in ensuring the firm's success.

The business owners' insistence on being ever-present in their shops, while it expressed their work ethic, had just as much to do with the mistrust in anyone but themselves to manage their business. When Carey (2017) and Muhlfried (2019) equally argued for mistrust as a skill and positive quality instead of simply a negative lack of trust, their views could easily apply to the Aarhus business owners. The shop owners certainly benefitted from their mistrust in others. When Marie and Ole, for example, refused to let go of control, they simultaneously ensured that their successful business strategies were protected. This strategy consisted of personal contact between the owners and customers, along with ensuring bread baking according to their style. This particular routine could not be replaced by having an employee at the counter, and according to Marie and Ole, their experience with hiring bakers was that they made bread differently than themselves. Marie and Ole believed that the customers would feel dissatisfied.

## Hygge at Work

Work in Western industrial society lies between the most private and public relations. The Norwegian anthropologist Cato Wadel, who has researched unemployment in northern Norway, claims that we have failed to view work as a social practice. Work is in fact a relational concept (Wadel 1979: 381–2). Even when carried out alone or in isolation, it still takes place between people. Susana Narotzky and Niko Besnier (2014) have argued that in order to make a life worth living, most people focus not only on earning money, but, unsurprisingly, on living a good life. This implies that people need to 'invest in multiple aspects of existence that appear at first glance to have little economic substance but end up having economic consequences' (Narotzky and Besnier 2014: 6). The Aarhus business owners also apply aspects of their social life to their businesses, and partly for this reason, they have made them relatively profitable. By making a living out of their hobbies or passions, by filling their days with activities that they say they truly enjoy, by being involved in every phase of the business even when they do not have to be, the Aarhus shopkeepers create their version of the good life. Of course, the outcome of this good life is also economic. They want their business to make a profit. But profit as such is only a means to an end.

Take, for example, Marie and Ole and their bakery. During a normal day, they will talk about the *hygge* of their work dozens of times. This excerpt from my field notes shows how *hygge* can be used within the course of a day at Marie and Ole's bakery:

I arrive at 10 in the morning. The bakery has already been open for two hours, and everyone is busy preparing and arranging the break and cakes. When I open the door, two of the employees look up from their work and greet me by stating that they did not know that I was coming today, and that it is *hyggelig* to see me. The two young girls mixing cake dough are smiling and laughing, sharing stories while they mix the dough. I walk back to the back of the baking section, where Marie and Ole are busy with separate work-tasks. When they see me, they smile and greet me. Ole asks me about my baby at home, or what I have been doing since he saw me last. I tell him something about my baby's most recent progress, and he replies with '*Nej, hvor hyggeligt*' (oh, how *hyggeligt*). I put on an apron, work shoes, and ask what I should do. Marie tells me to make a cake and that Ludvig will help me. I walk over to Ludvig, and he responds that 'det var da *hyggeligt*' that we shall work together. We walk to the back room where we measure out the flour. While measuring, Ludvig tells me about his life, and we share laughs. We walk back to the front of the kitchen, where I cut almonds for the batter, and one of the girls walks over and comments; '*Står I her og hygger?*' (Are you guys standing here having *hygge*?). We reply by saying, 'Yes', and smile, asking if she wants to join us. She replies, 'Det vil jeg da rigtig gerne' (Of course, I'd really like to), and she picks up a knife and cutting board and makes space next to me where she cuts raisins. We cut and chat in a cheerful tone. Another of the girls looks at me over her shoulder, commenting '*Nej, hvor fint du skærer dem der mandler*' (Oh, how good you are at dicing those almonds). We take out the blender from under the table and blend all the ingredients that we have collectively measured and cut. It is just Ludvig and me; the girls have gone to do something else. However, throughout the process, any time an employee walks by or passes us to get something, they throw out an encouraging comment, often containing the word *hygge*. When the cake is in the oven, other employees walk by, take a look, and comment that it looks like it is coming along nicely. When the cake is out of the oven, everyone agrees that it smells wonderful and looks good. When we cut and decorate the cake, the employees constantly comment on each other's creative talent. When customers enter and approach the counter, they are always greeted with a smile and a comment that fits the individual person. I often hear compliments being exchanged, and the word *hygge* is frequently used to describe an act or as a comment on a story.

The tone and atmosphere in Marie and Ole's bakery are constructed around principles of hygge. The constant reference to the hygge of a work task, conversation, or situation illustrates the power of hygge in constructing a comfortable working environment. Employees' mutual encouragement, and positive comments, together with the fact that the workplace allows collaboration in most work tasks, contributes to the creation of a *hyggelig* atmosphere. The couple expend a lot of energy transferring their attitudes of 'work as enjoyable'. For example, Ole described even his solitary work task in the back as having *hygge* with the dough (*'Jeg hygger mig med dejen'*). This reference to *hygge* illustrates that the concept is important in the execution of work tasks that would not be automatically *hyggelig*. Further, Marie and Ole actively recruited employees whom they believed would contribute to *hygge* at the workplace. By convincing themselves, their employees, and their customers that their bakery was a *hyggelig* place, filled with *hyggelige* people and food that contributed to *hygge*, the business owners created an attractive place for employees as well as customers (see Linnet 2012). Most of the shopkeepers sell items which have a certain kind of hygge; buns in the bakery, toys, fish for family dinner, yarn for making personal items and gifts, pet supplies for *hygge* with pet, so the materiality of the items sold is also a factor.

Smart and Smart (2005b) argue that small businesses, or what they refer to as 'petty capitalists', in which the business owners employ a few workers and are themselves actively involved in the labour process, form a different kind of sociality than in larger, corporate firms. Marie and Ole actively took part in the multiple tasks of the business, working side-by-side with their employees. Although they would not admit that the emphasis on *hygge* was a strategy to optimise work performance, this was undoubtedly an effect of *hygge* at work. These sentiments were also evident in Højrup's work among self-employed fishermen on the north-west coast of Jutland in the 1980s (Højrup 1983) and in Robert Paine's research (1972: 35) among the north Norwegian fishermen in the village of Nordbotn in 1958. It is hardly surprising that small businesses where the owners are involved in all areas of the business will develop a more intimate sociality between owner/manager and employee than in large, corporate firms. Nor was it coincidental that so many of the employees in my study were young adults within the same age group and life situation. Marie and Ole informed me that each employee had been carefully chosen. The choice was not based on specific skills, but because their personalities 'fit' in the team (*passe ind i holdet*), and they were easy to form. When I discussed attitudes about work with the employees, they all gave similar answers to my queries. The young staff enjoyed spending time with each other at work and became friends outside of work. Coming to work was for them another way of being with friends, and they claimed that they performed their work tasks with a motivation beyond that of simply earning an hourly wage. They had a close and personal relationship with the owners and a consciousness about the importance of the work they did. In my conversations with each of them, all the employees asserted they did not feel that working there was 'labour' (*arbejde*), because they had so much *hygge*. They also claimed they had a feeling that what they did was meaningful, not just for them, but for the broader community, 'Customers are genuinely happy to be here' ('*Kunderne er rigtig glade for at være her*'), they insisted. Their work helped them make a life worth living (Narotzky and Besnier 2014). In many ways their work at the bakery came to resemble leisurely, togetherness, as much as wage work (Applebaum 1995: 67–72; Bakke 2006) (Indeed, most families have memories of baking cakes together). Work, at least some work, can be more than a task which is exchanged for a wage. Work can be *hyggeligt* (Ronco and Peattie 1988; see e.g. Etzioni 1995).

## Discussion and Conclusion: The Value of Work

Marie and Ole worked hard to 'make a life for us that we don't want a break from' (Ole). Mark Vacher (2011), in his ethnography of summer cottagers, points precisely to this separation between work and leisure. Here, everyday life associates the body with an instrument of labour, where leisure, and even a short stay at one's summer cottage, symbolizes a state of freedom (Vacher 2011: 52). The Aarhusian business owners consciously chose their life path, where one of their main aims was to avoid this feeling of a need for a break from their everyday lives.

In describing the work routines of my informants, I could have included additional examples of days or moments when the business owners were exhausted and tired. However, such a negative perspective would have been misleading. My aim has been to draw out the general tendency in these firms, which is the embeddedness of work in these people's lives. It is this embeddedness that gives their lives a sense of fulfilment that many of us in even the most stable salaried jobs can never hope to achieve. In their celebration of work over labour, these business owners and their firms remind us of the nature of work and how work can become part of our social and personal identities. The business owners held on to an ethos that included a strong emphasis on *hygge* and hard work, and their work became an integral part of their inner lives. Without invoking Weber, work was their 'calling', if not their religion.

The examples presented in this chapter suggest that when work is a source of respect and self-fulfilment, the onerous image of work as painful and unpleasant disappears. Instead, work comes to resemble more what we might refer to as passion or calling, as an emotional engagement about their business. It was this kind of emotional engagement, this passion, that kept them working hour after hour, day after day, year after year. The personal investment of creative ideas, manual labour, time, and hygge-infused sociality made the business owners feel that their life was their work. However, the same sense of ownership, autonomy and personal investment generated a mistrust that anyone but themselves could manage their firm successfully. The freedom to control their own business thus entailed a mistrust of others. This form of mistrust worked as a skill because it forced the business owners to control the way of their firms. Marie and Ole's bread never suffered from beginners' mistakes, because Marie always made the bread herself. Sally's toy shop customers were always ensured expert advice, because it was Sally who was there to help them.

The status as self-employed gives these individuals freedom and responsibility that we cannot compare to that of employees performing wage-labour. We need to consider that in the welfare society of Northern Scandinavia, the self-employed have both more autonomy, and a larger responsibility for own well-being than do wage-labourers. Tax systems, competition, and a constantly growing corporate market economy make it hard for the small independent shops and businesses to survive. The income from the number of hours put into a small business can only rarely compete with the hourly wage benefits of employed life, if one were to calculate with wage per hour worked. But autonomy is often difficult to calculate in monetary terms. The main motivation for maintaining a business must thus be found somewhere else than in a profit-oriented market thinking of hours worked and income received. This chapter has shown that for my Aarhusian friends, work was about hygge, freedom, self-fulfilment, and giving meaning to their lives. Work in this sense was the very antithesis of labour. In some ways, the Aarhusian business owners have already reached what Pahl refers to as 'the good society'. In a good society, people depend less on how much money they can get from their work, and more on how they arrange the social relations in which that work is done (Pahl 1988a: 749). Unexpectedly, I found elements of Pahl's 'good society' among the Aarhus shop owners.

*Chapter 7*
# Motivations


Karl Polanyi claimed that '[t]he outstanding discovery of recent historical and anthropological research is that human economies, as a rule, are submerged in our social relationships'. Being one of the voices in the human economy, Polanyi argued that humans most of all act to protect our social standing, not material goods (Polanyi 2001 [1944]: 48). Polanyi's claim that the economic system operate on the basis of non-economic motives are illustrated in a conversation I had with Sally, owner of the Toy shop, 'You know, there are two types of money. There is the money that has blood and human lives on them, and there is moral money [*moralske penge*]. That is not a problem for me. [As a business owner] I constantly have to evaluate what is morally and ethically right, but luckily, for me, I *know* what is right [my translation]'.[92]

What does it mean to act morally as a business owner? What is a '*moralsk*' business and how is the ideal of a '*moralsk*' business realized? In the Danish language, the terms '*moral/moralsk*' are commonly used in everyday conversations to refer to ideas about right and wrong, and combine ideas of both morality and ethics (Gundelach 2004b). Morality and the perception of a moral business refers here to the emic perceptions of what is individually understood as good and right. It refers both to the recurrent emic talk of *moral,* and to the content of what I have identified as morality. These 'goods' and 'rights' refer to a set of values that can be identified in the perceptions, actions, and practices of my business owners, and the shared values should be understood as components of the business owners' idea of a shared morality. Although these values and their articulation are subject to

---

[92] All quotes are based on interviews and several spontaneous conversations with the business owners, employees, and former employees. The interview guide was based on questions that I asked all business owners (and a different one for employees and former employees) in all the firms I studied. I was conscious and careful not to ask leading questions, and I allowed the interviewee to talk as much as possible about their own initiative in order to discover sentiments, attitudes, and perceptions untainted by my own observations.

individual, situational, and social variations, they tend to be shared by all the business owners.

The aim of this chapter is to show that the values contained in this morality function as motivation for the Aarhus business owners in their daily operations. Their ideals are part of a business strategy that they view in opposition to the mainstream, corporate-dominated market, which they view as devoid of moral values. Moreover, they understand that their strategy of differentiating themselves from mainstream market structures not only gives their lives meaning, but it is also the key to their success.

The above quotation from Sally is typical of the moral themes that pervade the business owners' market discourse. When talking about the ideals and motivations for starting or continuing a firm, the business owners made similar types of references about their wish to do good. Hence, some referred to a 'meaningful business' (*givende virksomhed*), others used formulations such as 'make others happy' (*gør nogen glade*), 'create a community' *(skabe et fællesskab)*, 'spread joy' *(sprede glæde omkring sig)*, 'do something meaningful' for people (*lave noget meningsfyldt*), 'contribute to the community' (*bidrage til fællesskabet*), and so forth. Although the specific terminology and formulations varied, they were all grounded in the same sentiments of doing something morally good for the community and thereby for themselves. Simultaneously, few business owners tried to hide the fact that their expressed desire to do good was initially a selfish desire. These business owners derived satisfaction from their conviction that their entrepreneurial activity contributed positively to the well-being of individual persons, to the community, and to their own vision of the good life as materially secure and personally autonomous (own boss).

## Modesty and Meaningful Relations

I begin this section with an excerpt from my field notes:

Ole is talking to me about values again. He tells me that they [he and his wife Marie] do not price their goods according to market value. They set a price at a level of only what they think they need in order to manage their business with profits. They do not have ambitions of growth or accumulation of capital. He thinks these values have to do with age, Ole is in his late fifties. However, in the next sentence, he states that he has always thought about things this way. He claims that he adopted these values from his mother, who ran a business from home. She offered swimming lessons, and she never took much money for it. His father always asked her to take more, but her reply had always been, 'Why should I do that? I have everything I need and can buy whatever I need when I need it. I cannot buy a red

Ferrari, but why should I have a red Ferrari?'. Ole claims that Marie has inherited the same mindset from her farmer father in West Jutland. Ole believes that it is important to contribute to society, although he feels that he does not really have time for that now. He specifies that he is thinking about volunteer work, adding that he really hopes his business is useful for society too (Excerpts from notes from conversation with Ole, December 2016).

Marie and Ole, both in their 50s, earned PhDs in natural sciences and described themselves as 'hungry for knowledge'. When their children were very young, they found that their academic careers demanded all their time and dedication. They felt that they could not be present for their children as much as they wanted. They began thinking about whether to start their own business, in the hope that it would allow them more flexibility to be with their children. They used their academic skills to educate themselves about mushrooms, and after three years of research and experiments, they finally started a farm producing exotic mushrooms. Their initial capital came from state grants and years of saving from their academic jobs. 'We didn't really spend much money, we're not good at that […] so that's why, in fact, we had quite a lot of money saved up'.[93]

The fact that Ole stresses how the couple is 'not good at spending money' is one indication that he values non-material wealth over financial expertise. He gives the impression that money and material wealth is so unimportant to them that they do not use much effort on consumption expenditures. If we look at their home, car, and personal consumption habits, one might confirm their claim of not being big spenders; they seemed to live a frugal life, buying only those goods they felt they needed, avoiding excess.

At the time when they established their first business, their specific product of organic mushrooms was rare on the market, and their farm became an important supplier for many industries, including restaurants and supermarkets. Marie and Ole were the first to introduce organic, locally grown, exotic mushrooms of various kinds to the Danish market. In this sense, they were true entrepreneurs in the conventional understanding of the word. Nevertheless, they sought to remain small, which again seems to undermine the concept of an entrepreneur as someone who wants their innovative business to grow. Although the amount of time invested in their work amounted to about the same as when they pursued their academic careers, they worked from home and felt that they were able to control the routine of the day themselves. This control over time is their major concern

---

[93] Quote from recorded interview, translated by me. In Danish: '*Vi brugte ikke ret mange penge, det er vi ikke så gode til. [...] Så derfor havde vi faktisk samlet rigtig mange penge sammen*'.

when they talk about their first firm. Their children were directly involved in the activities of the firm, and they could do much of the work when the children were away at school during the day or after their bedtime. Instead of focusing on the tremendous success that the couple had in building their brand and creating a demand for a product that had previously been non-existent in Denmark, Marie and Ole were most proud of the flexibility and self-fulfilment their entrepreneurship gave them. Their farm enterprise grew with demand, they invested in a more efficient system, and they produced 'quite a lot' of produce, Ole confirmed.

However, as the children grew and became increasingly independent, Marie and Ole felt the need for change. Their work at the farm felt almost antisocial, and they wanted to engage in a business that had more direct contact 'with people' (i.e. customers), they told me.[94] They wanted to take a more direct part in people's everyday lives and 'give of ourselves'[95], together with the products they sold. They started experimenting with innovative ideas and found a way to open a business that combined production and sales, as they wanted to take part in both. They sold their farm and used the money from the sale together with their savings (from the years of 'not spending money') to buy a townhouse in the centre of downtown Aarhus. They leased a small storefront near their new home and transformed it into a bakery. Their plan was that only the two of them would work in the tiny bakery, which had a production area and sales counter of only approximately 30 square meters. However, their plan to run the small bakery with no employees and with short opening hours quickly changed due to customer demand. Ole told me with frustration that the customers were constantly asking them to prolong their opening hours. The couple gradually met their needs by increasing their opening hours, one hour at a time, until they had reached the current opening hours, which almost met the standard of their sector (7 a.m. – 5.30 p.m., including Saturdays). Marie explains:

> Initially, we thought it would be just the two of us in a tiny shop, where people would come down to chat and buy a couple of loaves of bread, and nothing other than bread. Suddenly, we were in Denmark's second largest city with an ocean of customers who told each other how fantastic it was… Then they started to ask for cakes, and so we started to bake cakes. Next, we had to hire people, and sometimes we feel like we just do not want to be this big.

---

[94] Marie and Ole here both use the term *mennesker* (people) to refer to the consumers.
[95] 'Give af os selv' (original quote in Danish).

In the many conversations I had with Marie and Ole, they repeatedly referred to their experience of a strong moral obligation[96] towards their constantly growing customer base. 'We wanted a new project [other than the farm], because one of our main goals was to create a business where we could contribute to the well-being of other people', explained Ole. He also stated that, 'We wanted to provide the customers with a high-quality product at a reasonable price, distributed directly from the hands of its makers. We wanted to offer not just bread, but a direct relationship with the customers. We want to know who they are, and we want them to know who we are'.

This ideal proved hard to maintain when their customer base constantly grew to an extent that they could not handle the shop on their own. According to Ole and Marie, their own wish to maintain shorter opening hours and less variety in products was secondary to the desires of their customers. This claim is confirmed by the number of working hours they spent at the firm, and their tendency to prioritize the firm before personal needs. On the same topic, Ole expressed that 'even though we initially, and well, still, actually, want to work fewer hours and have fewer products, it is more important for us to make people happy... We have the shop for the sake of other people, if you understand what I mean?' Marie and Ole signalled their dedication to their initial motivation to 'contribute positively to people's lives' and offer a more authentic relationship with their customers. They articulated their own business philosophy in terms of a contrast to 'the others', described as 'concept stores' (*konceptforretninger*, brand name stores offering a unique shopping 'experience' such as adjoining cafe), as shown by Ole's statement:

> That is the thing about such concept stores. You feel how people who are educated sellers... they have learned 'that is the way it is'. That people say 'that' and you are supposed to say 'that'. You can feel it by the way people talk, you know. And I simply feel tired of hearing that. I don't think everyone feels the same way, but I think there are people who feel the same way that we do about it. It's awful to listen to. And I think that is part of what makes us special to people. We are different.

Marie continued, 'This is what make people come down to us. It means that we are engaged in our customers, right. It's fun, but it's also hard.' The couple spent most of their waking hours at the firm, and the sense of fulfilment of meeting the customers' needs was a constant motivation. The reward and incentive for Ole and Marie was the satisfaction they obtained when they received positive feedback from their customers each day. On

---

[96] *Moralsk forpligtelse.*

special occasions, the customers expressed their appreciation with gifts of wine, flowers, cards, chocolate, and the like. For example, an older woman who came twice each week to buy her bread made sure to always bring fresh fish from the fishmongers on the dock and give it to Marie and Ole. She explained that she felt sorry for the couple who always worked long hours and never had the chance to go down and buy fresh fish for themselves. Because she appreciated their bread and service so much, she had made it her habit to bring fresh fish for Marie and Ole. This involved a reciprocal relationship between customer and merchant, where the formality of an economic transaction is replaced by a customer-initiated gift-exchange (Mauss 1966; Gregory 2015: 13). Marie and Ole did not intend for the relationship between customer and merchant to extend beyond the boundaries of the firm, and the significance of the relationship can therefore only be limited (Carrier 2017).

This muddling of formal and informal transactions is a direct result of the intimacy and meaningful sociality between shopkeeper and customers (e.g. Carrier 1992; Hart 2009: 100). Because this old woman felt that she knew Marie and Ole and that their relationship went beyond that of a formal market transaction, she allowed herself the privilege of initiating a gift relationship. Marie and Ole 'suffered' from the obligation to return that comes with any gift (Mauss 1966: 10–11). The giving customer forced them to either live with the constant consciousness of not returning her gift, or give her free bread, not making profits. Although their intention behind establishing meaningful social relationships with customers was not to let their relations extend to an informal exchange relationship, this kind of mutuality may lead well-intentioned business owners into an unintended moral obligation with a persistent gift-giver.

Bloch and Parry (1989: 9) state that '*our* ideology of the gift has been constructed in antithesis to market exchange'. However, this is not necessarily an effective way to operate when analysing exchange relationships. The above example illustrates how Marie and Ole's products carried with them certain expectations that at times blurred the boundaries between reciprocal gift relations and pure cash-based transactions (Bloch and Parry 1989; also Mauss 1966: 70, on Trobriands).

Another illustrative example how Marie and Ole dealt with informal gift relations comes from the couple's twenty-fifth wedding anniversary celebration. Months before the actual anniversary, Marie and Ole knew that they would close their shop for the day of their anniversary celebration and for the following weekend. The whole extended family from near and far were coming for an informal celebration at their home. However, Marie and Ole made a conscious choice *not* to hang a sign on the shop door to inform their customers that they would be closed these days until after they had actually closed up the shop that week. They told me that the reason for not informing their customers beforehand, was because they knew that many of them would bring them gifts. Ole felt that hanging a sign on the door beforehand would imply an invitation to give, something the couple did not want from their customers. In order to avoid a large flow of gifts, the couple therefore chose to close their shop without informing anyone beforehand. 'Of course, some will be angry and disappointed that we did not tell them. They will go down here and find the shop closed, but rather that than all the gifts', Ole told me the very evening before we placed the 'Closed' sign on the door.

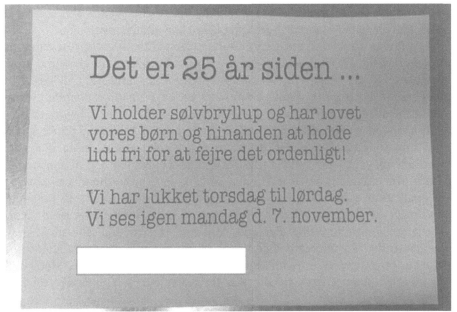

Det er 25 år siden ...

Vi holder sølvbryllup og har lovet
vores børn og hinanden at holde
lidt fri for at fejre det ordenligt!

Vi har lukket torsdag til lørdag.
Vi ses igen mandag d. 7. november.

Plate 4. Anniversary note. It says: 'It's been 25 years... It's our silver wedding anniversary and we have promised our children and each other to take some time off and celebrate properly. We will therefore be closed Thursday to Saturday. See you on Monday, 7th November' (signed Marie and Ole).

Despite the attempt to hide the event, some customers got wind of the news and as expected, brought flowers, wine, books, chocolate, and other gifts. Marie and Ole also received gifts and congratulations when they opened again the following week. The couple accepted these gifts with humble appreciation, but quietly complained to me. They knew they were appreciated by their customers, but they did not have the capacity to enter into reciprocal debt to 'all' their customers. Marie and Ole felt that such gift made them obliged to give away free goods, but the customers refused not to pay for goods, leaving Marie and Ole with a feeling of unreciprocated gifts.

Offering meaningful social relationships with customers can be a burden on business owners when the customers engage in gift-giving. The customers insisted that they wanted nothing in return; they just wanted to express their appreciation. However, these gifts cannot be understood as 'pure' or 'free' gifts, generalized reciprocity (see Malinowski 1922: 136; Sahlins 1972: 194; Douglas 2002: ix–x), or other concepts carrying similar meanings for the simple reason that they involved a sense of obligation, felt by Marie and Ole. The obligation that comes with any gift was strongly felt, although Marie and Ole did not intend on forming such relations (Mauss 1966; Gregory 2015). This kind of tension is unlikely to happen in a large supermarket chain or other establishment where the relationship between seller and customer is much more formalized and anonymous.

Having a real and meaningful relationship with all customers can thus become challenging on several levels, especially when the customer flow increases. Hence, on several occasions, I witnessed Marie and Ole hiding in the back of the store or asking employees to tell a customer that they were out of the shop, simply because they did not have the time or energy to deal with a customer who demanded more social contact than they could spare. This unwillingness to engage in informal gift relations, or more intensive sociality, may be connected to the Scandinavian preference of immediate return over more sustained relations (Archetti 1986), but there was more of an egalitarian aspect to it, in so far as there was the desire to not treat customers differently. Furthermore, the couple often expressed their frustration over how the demand for both pastry and sociality grew symbiotically. To maintain their ideal of meaningful, social relationships with customers combined with high quality and reasonable prices, Marie and Ole invested great energy in selecting their employees. The employees had to be willing to follow their 'philosophy' (as they called it) and 'fit into the team'.[97] Ole thus clarifies, 'It has happened that we've made a mistake and hired someone who did not fit in. It didn't last very long'.

If the employee did not express engagement and could not understand or adapt to the philosophy of the two owners, the atmosphere would cease to be *hyggelig*. However, Marie and Ole's engagement in selecting the right employees involved more than ensuring a good working environment. It was part of the couple's contribution to the community. 'They are like parents for us, you know', several of their employees said. Marie agreed with Ole that they saw it as their responsibility to teach the youth who came to work for

---

[97] *Passe ind i holdet.*

them about the right values. Karina, one of Marie and Ole's former employees, confirmed that Marie and Ole's bakery shop was a special place:

> It is different because they are always there, even when it runs on its own. They are not there to make money, and you notice that instantly. It is very liberating [...] Marie is the brain behind the whole atmosphere down there. She has the intimacy and the presence, the compassion. They [relationships] become meaningful and close. It is not like that in [the supermarket chain] Føtex or other large firms. [...] Customers change. They allow space [giver rum]. Even when the queue is long, and the wait is long, people do not mind. They know that the openness [rummelighed, lit. spaciousness][98] is equal for everybody, and they are happy with it. The customers change their behaviour, too. It is a gift (Quote from interview with Karina, former employee, my translation).

Karina eventually left her position at the bakery, for several reasons. One of the main reasons why she decided to resign, and not just reduce her working hours when she became a university student, was that Marie and Ole's philosophy of taking their time with every customer, offering a meaningful relationship, became too intense for her. She also found it difficult to deal with other aspects of their 'philosophy', such as the counter being designed in such an inefficient way that it compelled sellers to have more time with each customer, something she claimed they had done purposely. She also found it hard to explain to customers, who are called 'guests' (gæster) instead of the normal 'customers' (kunder) when they had sold out of goods. Karina explains:

> Marie and Ole bake only what they plan to sell every day, and when they are sold out, it is because it is supposed to be sold out. This is part of their philosophy, and something the customers should know. I believe they [the customers] understand it when you have explained it once. But I still think it's hard to explain to a guest [gæst] who has been looking forward to their little moment of happiness [hverdagsglæde, lit. 'everyday joy'].

Karina, formerly a salesperson, was now a frequent customer, and from what I could observe, her relationship with Marie and Ole remained friendly. In conversations with current employees, they expressed similar sentiments. Another employee, Ida, elaborates:

> When I started there, I had a much more materialistic view of the world. I came here because I needed money. But you know, they

---

[98] The Danish term *rummelighed* (lit. spaciousness) is often used in these contexts to connote an enhanced level of inclusivity, openness and accessibility. A *rummelig* labour market, for example, is one that provides jobs for people with disabilities.

take care of you, they treat you with respect, and you really get to know them. They make you view things differently. When I worked at [Føtex, a large supermarket], it was not the same at all. Here, I look forward to going to work every day. You can also talk to Marie and Ole about anything, they take care of you.

Marie and Ole claimed that they had always worked for a community wherever they were. When they had their mushroom farm, they had been engaged in the organisation of the village community. When they moved to Aarhus, they strived to make a community out of their bakery. Indeed, their bakery was organized not only as a workplace, but as a livelihood for them, and as a social community for their employees and in a manner of speaking their regular customers. Ole and Marie thus insisted that they spent a lot of energy establishing and maintaining this feeling of community (*fællesskab*) and *belonging* (*tilhørighed*). Customers could confirm this with exclamations such as 'It's amazing how there's space for so many people in this tiny place', or 'This is not just *my* bakery, it's my *fristed* [breakout room from a busy life]'. The social openness could also be observed through the nursing mother in the window counter (which was the only place to sit inside the shop) or the complete strangers who started conversing and accidentally shared their half-hour lunchbreak sitting at the window countertop. The bakery was not a café designed for guests to sit down and enjoy pastry. Nevertheless, customers still seemed to find ways to spend time together in the small space. The store had a window counter that was broad and low enough so that one could sit down, and customers used it as a natural place to sit and chat. Quick questionnaires that I gave to the customers revealed that several of the people standing in line together, sharing a laugh or their lunch breaks, were acquainted through their shared status as Marie and Ole's customers.

Marie and Ole had indeed succeeded in creating a space and an atmosphere that allowed for casual socializing and a feeling of community. Of the many strategies they used, the most important was the equal, friendly treatment offered to each customer. They all waited together, and they all got 'their time' with the salesperson behind the counter, once it was their turn. The limited space pushed people into an intimate sphere of physical proximity. The same limited space, combined with an atmosphere of calm, quiet acoustics and soft brick walls, encouraged a sociality and lowered the threshold for starting a conversation with a stranger (Linnet 2012b). It fulfilled the expectations about Danish *hygge* in all these ways, nourishing the authenticity and the values of equality, community, and spaciousness (Linnet 2011, 2012a, 2012b). Marie and Ole succeeded in creating an environment that both confirmed and reproduced these sentiments as a model *of* and a model *for* their values (see Bruun 2018 on models of Danishness). The fact that nearly all customers were regular, returning '*gæster*' who routinely came at approximately the same time every day, or week, was another important factor in the push towards a community atmosphere.

The strategy of emphasizing the importance of openness (*rummelighed*) was a common feature in several of the businesses I studied. Their shared values helped consolidate the existence of a common morality, mirroring Scandinavian discourses such as *hygge,* community, openness, and equality (Bruun, Jakobsen and Krøijer 2011; Jenkins 2011). These values become key factors in the differentiation between 'us', i.e. the small, independent shopkeepers, and 'them', the large impersonal, profit-oriented corporations.

## The Moral Message

'The purpose of this firm is the moral message', Sally, the toy shop owner, repetitively proclaimed. Like Marie and Ole, Sally expressed a strong self-awareness regarding her business philosophy. She had adopted the ideals from her mother, Pia, who started the business forty years earlier. Pia had started the business with a clear motive, 'I saw it already in the seventies, people were moving towards a consumer culture. People were buying into the cheap plastic. I didn't want to be like that'. While the growing consumer culture was satisfied with cheaper, standardized products, Pia insisted on quality, durability, and expertise. She sold yarn and cloth nappies together with durable, non-plastic toys. The goods themselves reflected the values she promoted.

An example of how Toys presents itself in line with these ideals is their webpage. On their webpage, Toys presented the business's history in the form of a fairy tale. It presents the story of an energetic, honest, innovative woman who had always fought tirelessly to do everything she could to create the best products for a good life. Pia and Sally had carefully chosen adjectives to bring out the moral values pioneered by Pia. It described mother and daughter as constantly fighting a battle for the benefit of ordinary people who wanted quality, against the superficial consumer society. By bringing the well-being of the customer into the centre of their philosophy, their appeal functioned as both political statement and as a marketing strategy (Linnet 2012b). They targeted the customer as a person with values, and like Marie and Ole, they reproduced those values associated with discourses of Scandinavian identity (Linnet 2011; Bruun 2018). The interior atmosphere of their shop resembled that of Marie and Ole's bakery, carefully chosen to enhance intimacy, domesticity, and informality. A shop overfilled with soft coloured toys, baby crib mobiles hanging from the roof, a soft scent of coffee blended with something indistinguishable but not intruding, comfortable temperature, the occasional music from a music box, and seasonal live candles and decorative lights, all left no doubt that here was a place with a *hyggelig* atmosphere (Linnet 2012a, 2012b). Sally's store was also attractive enough that I often observed people entering the store just to seek shelter from a rainstorm, or to just look around.

Every year, in the weeks leading up to Christmas – the busiest time of the year in the shop – journalists contacted Sally and requested her assessment of the Christmas shopping season and the growing 'Black Friday' sales trend.[99] Sally and her shop were renowned for not taking part in Black Friday. I happened to be present when a journalist from the major newspaper *Jyllandsposten* came by to interview Sally. Sally's mother Pia was also present, and she encouraged me to record the interview.

With great enthusiasm, Sally made sure that the journalist really understood the importance of her principles. Sally claimed that the large corporations were fooling people into buying unnecessary, poor quality products from constantly changing sellers who worked just to earn money and lacked any personal interest and passion in what they were selling. Sally argued that the constant pressure to simply buy more made consumers blind to quality.

She explained to the journalist that she never held sales, reproducing the reasons she had given me daily. 'We never have sales because we never have any [goods] that are obsolete. Pia added that for the 35 years she had owned the shop, she, too, never held sales. Sally continued that Toys did not exist for her to make loads of money and become rich. They already had their apartments, and they (Pia and Sally) 'do not care for shopping'. For Sally, Toys existed because she, and her mother before her, had a genuine interest in providing people with top-quality products that fit everyone's specific needs, wants, and wallet. Sally explains:

> Because we never compromise with quality and the use-value of our products, our products do not go out of style. We do not want to contribute to the 'buy and discard' [consumer] society. Our products do not vary with season, and they never stop being interesting for customers, they are always relevant, and therefore we never have to make sales to make room for new goods! By attracting customers with sales, people spend all their money on cheap, plastic [goods] that are made not to last. Many large firms think this is good business, but in fact, it's bad for business. People empty their

---

[99] Black Friday, originally the day after the American Thanksgiving holiday to mark the start of the Christmas shopping season in the U.S., has now become a global marketing event where businesses hold large sales on the last Friday in November.

pockets on sales before the holiday season, and no one pays what it costs. This creates a much larger problem of exploitation from large chains. We small firms, we cannot afford to sell our goods for wholesale price.

When the journalist asked how Sally could compete with the large chains that had major sales throughout the year, Sally gave him an ironic look. 'Very simple', she explained. 'My business offers something that the large corporations can never compete with'. Sally referred to herself and her character and continued to list all her diverse life experiences and educations. She also explained thoroughly why her background mattered. She persisted that the assistance you received when you entered her shop was unique:

> In addition, my girls [employees] know all there is to know about every single product in this shop. I do not let them talk to customers before they are fully trained. I make sure to train all of them to a level that makes them professionals when it comes to finding the right product for each individual who walks into this shop. But what is most important [raising her finger], is that the moral background of this business is not to sell goods to customers but to help individuals and give them what they need to improve their life.

During the months I spent with Sally, she repeatedly told me that her main principle, not just in business, but also in life, was that you should not try to manipulate people's free will. Sally was deeply religious (Evangelical Lutheran), and although she insisted that her religion was not what made her the person she was, she was convinced that God had given humans free will and that trying to manipulate that free will was the worst sin. This meant that she insisted on not preaching her religious beliefs to others. Her customers did not know her as a religious person, and it took some time before she talked to me about her faith. Most, if not all, of her employees, including her own daughter, were 'non-Christians' (*ikke-kristne,* i.e. not religious), and she stressed the importance of treating everyone equally, regardless of their (lack of) religious affiliation. Her religion was something personal, and being good, doing good, and preaching good, she insisted, did not imply imposing one's religion on others. This would be against her idea of people's free will. It was more important to be good and do good, and she *did* preach the *moral* message. To Sally, her firm was thus an arena for doing good, and those who knew her well referred to her as 'the priest', although I never heard her preach to others in the name of God or Jesus. Instead, she would invoke the idea of the 'good'.

Sally's religious beliefs could be seen as being in stark contrast to principles of profit maximizing that in some form or other exist in all businesses. However, Sally was convinced that she adhered to her ideal not to lure customers with sales or push people to purchase more than they needed. Sally's mother, in contrast, did not invoke religious motives in her 'mission' to do good. Both mother and daughter expressed a strong belief that their 'mission' was to do good and help anyone who asked for their help. Pia and Sally's values were not a result of any specific religious belief, although their values overlapped with Sally's religion. Pia did not stress free will in the same way that Sally did, but she believed in honesty, offering fair prices, quality products, and she trusted that customers would choose her shop over the mass-producing corporations. She trusted that customers would prefer ethically produced, fair-priced products offered by honest, personable shopkeepers. Sally was confident that her strategy of offering something most other toy shops did not – quality, expertise, warmth, together with the intimacy of being small and local – would ensure that her firm would continue its success without following what she referred to as 'immoral business strategies' (*umoralske forretningsstrategier*). Sally knew the secret of her success, 'I know why I have success. It's because I know what I'm doing, and that's good. I never pressure anyone to buy anything. The atmosphere of this shop is meant to make people feel welcome and at home, also if people come in just to get shelter from a thunderstorm'.

These kinds of sentiments, expressed repeatedly by Sally, were almost identical to those of Marie and Ole. Their perception of what was 'good', or what was good business, was shared, despite the fact that Sally's motivations lay in religion and those of Marie and Ole purely secular. Their two firms had nothing to do with each other, and the owners were not acquainted, but still, we find almost the exact same formulations around this topic. Both have recognized a certain style of service that they contrast with large, impersonal corporate supermarket chains, concept stores, and hypermarkets. Ole declared that the customer service offered in these 'other businesses' made him sick (*dårlig*). It made him not want to enter these places. Sally, similarly, observed how these 'other businesses' approached customers in a bad manner (*dårlig måde*) motivated by profit-maximizing, instead of exhibiting a genuine engagement in what service or product they offer. In a different conversation, Sally expressed that:

> The others [corporate chains] hire new people all the time. The CEO is never in the shop. She just sits in an office in Copenhagen, or somewhere. Then they hire a manager who does not care. She is not there to stay, maybe a year or two, and then she leaves for another job. To her it's just a job, and they do not know how to do it. They have no background or education in children [toys]. Maybe they have a degree in management, but they do not care. They hire people

who are there to make money. To them, it's just a job. Sometimes they [competitors] come here to steal our ideas because they know we are so successful. It's all about the money [to them]. Here, people [customers] know that they will meet someone who knows and cares. No one returns what he or she buys from us because we know how to guide people into getting what they want and need. In the busiest period of the year, we have practically no returns because we care.[100]

Ole similarly expressed that he was inspired to open a service-oriented business that was not organized according to principles used in business schools, but which instead offered genuine relationships with other human beings. During December, clearly the busiest month of the year, Toys earned a total revenue of more than DKK 700,000 (€94,000), and the total return merchandise after Christmas amounted to DKK 5000 (€671), a return percentage of far below one per cent. In addition, Sally explained that most of the returned merchandise was due to the fact that people had received two of the same gifts for Christmas. These statistics demonstrate not just the success of the firm; they show that Sally and her trained employees had the proper skills in guiding consumers to purchase what was right for them.

Of course, Sally, as well as Marie and Ole, certainly wanted to make a profit in their businesses. Sally had full control over the flow of goods into and out of her business, and she knew the quantities of nearly all goods in stock. Sally set all prices by multiplying the purchasing price by 2.5, and she constantly analysed the demand to make sure she ordered the right kind and amount of goods based on what she expected that her customers would want. She knew the Danish business tax-system thoroughly, and she strategically hired young girls whom she could pay lower salaries but who were easier to train.

Sally's personality, which I describe as charismatic, involved a great authority. A customer could have looked around in the shop for an hour without deciding what to get, and with just a single comment from Sally, they would decide what to buy in an instant. I witnessed this daily. Sometimes Sally would interfere when one of her employees was talking with a customer by simply pointing at a product and saying, 'That's what you want' and the customer would buy whatever it was that had she pointed to.

When Sally informed customers about her products, she would jump around and demonstrate the products with great enthusiasm. The tone of her voice, together with detailed knowledge about all the objects and their origin, made her a convincing saleswoman. Her engagement was the same

---

[100] Quote taken from scratch notes from conversation with Sally, November 2016.

for each of the hundreds of items in the shop, both large and small, and she placed special importance on transmitting this engagement to her employees. After witnessing her sales performances, I observed how some of her enthusiasm could 'infect' customers as well. Sally insisted, however, that she would never push anything on anyone. Most likely, because of her detailed knowledge of her merchandise and confident character, customers gladly took her advice.

Sally's strategy proved its worth. Both customers who were aware of my affiliation with the shop as well as random acquaintances whom I had made in Aarhus expressed the same spontaneous enthusiasm when I mentioned that I had been in the Toys shop. 'Oh, have you been there? You must go, it's like every child's dream' or simply 'It is just such a wonderful place'.[101] A general tendency from the customer reviews in conversations as well as online on their Facebook page, was their emphasis on high quality, good service from expert staff, and welcoming atmosphere. Comments included statements such as 'It is such a fantastic small and magical place. Quality is always in mind, and you feel welcome both with and without children… oh, and the service is also good' and 'It is the best toy shop in Aarhus, with the sweetest most helpful staff'. Many customers expressed their enduring relationship with the shop and with the owners, 'I have been coming here since 1980, when they were located in [another district], and I have never been disappointed'. The customers' views were almost exclusively positive, if not enthusiastic. The single negative response was that it was an expensive shop, but then followed by a comment assuring me that they were aware that this was due to quality and ethics. A young mother stated that 'It is a bit expensive, but I guess it has to be that way when you want quality'. A father of three comments, 'There are so many things [name of child] wants from there, but it's just too expensive. I guess it's because there's no poison and stuff in them [goods]'.[102] Sally's business was indeed financially successful. Being one of very few independent toy shops in Denmark, it also carried its own assortment of handmade, woollen children's clothes, as well as yarn. It was known to most inhabitants of Aarhus, even though Toys had never spent any money on advertising (in the history of the firm).

The children's clothes sold by Toys had a long waiting list, as they were produced by a single seamstress, and she could produce only so much. Sally could have hired more seamsters; she could have invested in a larger 'production', and even moved the production abroad to benefit from cheaper labour. The popularity of her collection was certainly large enough, with full

---

[101] '*Det er bare et dejligt sted*'.

[102] 'Poison' refers goods produced with harmful chemicals.

waiting lists for many of her products. The firm had used the same seamstress since they started, but a couple of years ago, she retired, and they had been struggling to find a new one ever since. Sally explains:

> We have tried numerous seamstresses, but none of them were good enough. I give them a few months. I give them the design patterns and the materials, and then I test them. If, after a few months and attempts, I am not content, I let them go. Now we have finally found one that's good enough. She is still not perfect, but the best I have seen so far. It takes some time to get into it, and the fabric is hard to work with. And I am a perfectionist, so there is no room for mistakes.

Sally's aim was *not* to increase production beyond what one woman could manage. Like Marie and Ole, the fact that people had to wait to get their orders was not a problem that she wanted to solve by increasing production. To her, it was important that the clothes were of high quality and that a local seamstress had sewn them. Sally applied the same rule of locality to her yarn and knitting patterns. Sally and her mother had designed several knitting patterns based on the principle that anyone should be capable of knitting the finished garments. It was a low threshold offer for anyone who wanted to learn the handcraft. Sally explains:

> The toys are where we earn money. The yarn would have been too expensive if we were to sell it with profit. It is high quality, locally produced yarn, and I want it to be available not just to those with thick wallets. It is something I do because I think it's important. It's the same with the knitting patterns. I want them to be available to anyone. Not just people who know knitting terms.

These statements, and the fact that Sally priced her yarn low compared to other yarn of similar quality elsewhere, support her claim. She had not multiplied the price of the yarn by 2.5, as she did with the other goods in her shop. Instead, she sold it at wholesale price, allowing little payment for the labour she herself put into the dyeing of the yarn.[103]

An important part of Sally's business principles was that all her wool products had to be locally produced. Sally's claim that hers was an ethical, or rather moral, business (*moralsk virksomhed*) was thus grounded not just in her declared respect for people's free will. Sally insisted that her greatest motivation for continuing the firm was her aim to do something good in the world. A high value placed on frugality and modesty was also evident in her personal life. She lived in the same apartment building as her mother but had her own unit. She drove a scooter to work, and she did not spend money on

---

[103] Sally coloured all yarn herself from her home.

additional clothes or beauty products. Her eating habits reflected a sober Danish diet consisting of rye bread and one hot meal per day. In fact, she subsisted largely on coffee and cigarettes.

Another area where Sally's moral ideals were visible lay in the great importance she placed on ensuring that all the goods she stocked in her shop had been produced ethically: without harmful substances and from contractors where employees worked under regulated conditions and received a fair wage. Most of the toys that Sally sold were either from Danish or German manufacturers, and she demanded a full accounting of the production process. On several occasions, I witnessed wholesalers stopping by with samples of new products that she politely declined with a long moralistic speech explaining why. Her explanation included a critique of the components, the production process (which she immediately investigated), employment policies, origin of the product, or transportation. She also had a zero tolerance for goods made from plastic, including all synthetic materials. Because the shop was renowned for being an ethical shop, many NGOs contacted her seeking to place items where the profits would be donated to a worthy cause. However, because of her strict policies, Sally did not accept items that did not meet her ethical marketing standards. As an example, a young woman left a sample of a handmade item to support development projects in Uganda. However, because the item was made from plastic, Sally declined the collaboration. 'I realise that these people are trying to do good, and I also give anonymously to charity, but I cannot accept plastic in my shop. I just can't'.

Ideally, Sally wanted all products to be locally produced. Her wool was spun and woven in Denmark; she dyed the fabric herself in her home with colours she knew were 'poison free'.[104] The same applied to charities, where she insisted on donating to those in need in the local community. This involved donation of yarn to knitting projects for homeless people from Aarhus or for other local organisations.[105]

## The Strength of Community

While Toys was primarily a Toy shop that also sold unprocessed wool, Pernille's yarn shop was not a competitor to Sally. They offered completely different products. In fact, all independent yarn shops in Aarhus were part of

---

[104] She only allowed colours that had passed the German standards for natural food colouring. She was convinced that Germany had stricter regulations than Denmark.

[105] The homeless in Aarhus and Denmark are almost exclusively alcoholics and drug addicts who do not meet the minimal requirements for obtaining public housing. Alternatives exist in homeless shelters that offer free food, shelter, and showers on a day-to-day basis.

a collegial community and did not identify each other as competitors. When I started spending time with Pernille, I thought she differed from the more experienced business owners. She appeared to me as more naïve than the others. For example, she would spend a lot of time helping people who came by with her knitting projects, leaving again without buying something. If she did not keep the yarn a potential customer asked for in her collection, she would not try to offer something similar from her own shop, but immediately refer them to another shop she knew kept the yarn the customer wanted. In time, however, I realized that Pernille's reasons for acting the way she did, were not because of naïveté; it was a conscious choice, a business strategy. Pernille had grown up in a divided family with little resources, and she had worked hard her whole life. Throughout her life, Pernille had learned the hard way to make a living for herself, and her personal values were strongly grounded in an idea of fairness (*retfærdighed*). To her, it was important that she treated people fairly, and she expected the same in return.

Pernille did not just sell a product. She also sold advice to customers on how to use the yarn. She viewed it as her moral obligation to help anyone who entered her shop, she informed me. Several times per day, people would come by and ask her for advice on how to proceed with a creative project or where to find the right material. Pernille did not expect that the people she helped would purchase anything from her in return for her advice. I observed how, without question, she shared her knowledge without ever asking for anything in return or trying to encourage sales. Pernille explained that the reason why she did not try to sell something that would replace what they were looking for, and why she did not even try to get people to buy something from her when they asked for her advice, was because that was not the right way to run a business. Pernille elaborated:

> We need to help each other regardless of whether we get something in return or not. That is just how it is in *this* business. I would not call the other [small independent yarn-] shops competitors. We are colleagues. We help each other, and we all give advice to people who come by and ask for help with a project. I know this from when I used to be a customer. In addition, when I worked in other shops before opening my own, I always helped, just as I help anyone who comes by my shop now. Some people remembered me from there and followed me when I took over here. I believe that if I help someone, they will remember me and when they need something [to buy], they will come back. At least that's what I am hoping.

Pernille's way of treating customers is not unique. Most independent yarn shops offer customers or knitters assistance in starting or completing their project, in the hope that they will return and purchase more merchandise.

Perhaps this is because these shops sell only the materials to produce finished goods, rather than the goods themselves.

Pernille told me how one of her favourite yarns was not part of the assortment when she took over the firm. She told me that she felt that she could not wear knitwear that was made from yarn that she did not sell in her shop, and many of her favourite clothes became unavailable to her. She felt that this was a great loss and something she regretted:

> I spend all my time here [in the shop], so when would I use them? Now they just stay in the closet. It's really a shame. I've been thinking maybe I should sell them cheap here in the shop just to get rid of them.

When Pernille contacted the manufacturer to order the yarn, she learned that another yarn shop in Aarhus had just ordered them. When I asked her why she could not also order them, she explained that, 'We do not order the same yarn. I mean, some shops have the same yarn, but then they have different colours and it's only the major brands. If I'm going to order this yarn, I want at least forty colours. Now I just have to wait. It makes me sad, but what can I do? Maybe in a few years'. This too, Pernille confirmed, was an unspoken agreement between the independent yarn shops, 'This is not something we agreed upon; it's just how it is. It's just how we do things, and we all know that. Maybe some shops do it differently, but only the large [chains], not us [small ones]'.[106]

As a principle, independent yarn shops do not distribute the same yarn, and that is something all the owners 'just know'. The same applied to pricing. Instead of multiplying the wholesale price by 2.5, whenever Pernille took in a new product, she investigated the price of the same or similar goods in other shops and priced them in this manner. The informal cooperation between these small shops illustrates that these independent business owners collaborated against the more neoliberal principles of a free, self-regulating market. Instead of thinking in the mode of market capitalism, focusing on competition and profit maximizing, they emphasized principles of loyalty, trust, and community. The loyalty in the relationship between the Aarhus yarn shop owners was unique even to my sample.

In all the sectors I worked, owners referred to each other as colleagues and were loyal to other local shopkeepers within their same 'branch'. The fishmongers on the dock, for example, would borrow fish from each other if they happen to run out. The loyalty and lack of competitiveness between the eleven independent yarn shops was the most significant example of this shopkeeper solidarity in my sample. Pernille had pulled the tie between them

---

[106] Notes from conversation, October 2016, my translation.

even closer. Pernille had organized the yarn crawl (*garnstafet*, lit. yarn relay race), a yearly event where all independent yarn shops (except three in 2016) in central Aarhus took part in a weekend full of knitting-related events. Customers received different tasks, competitions, courses, workshops, all the different shops arranged knitting cafés; attractive buying deals were offered, and prizes awarded. The aim, according to Pernille, was to encourage sociality and community in knitting and between the eleven shops. The project, running since 2012, had been highly successful and strengthened the collegial relationship between the different owners when they met regularly throughout the year to plan and arrange the event.

The friendly relationship between the yarn shop owners was also related to the fact that most of these women knew each other 'from before' (*fra inden*). Knitting is often carried out as a social activity, and eager knitters come together in weekly knitting cafés held in libraries, at the Aarhus Women's Museum (*Kvindemuseet*), and in the various yarn shops. All the shopkeepers shared the same passion for knitting as a craft, and many had gotten to know each other through knitting circles, traders' fairs, and informal social networks.

All the small yarn shop owners I interviewed shared this ideology of assisting browsing customers who had some knitting problems and referring them to 'colleagues' in other shops. Could a business really survive on this kind of reciprocal business strategy? The success of the numerous yarn shops in Aarhus proved that it could. Somehow, there were enough knitters around for all of them to earn sufficient profit, assisted by the fact that each offered different goods in a kind of niche; the combination of all these independent enterprises strengthened their enterprise, giving them an enormous inventory of yarn to meet any taste and budget. All the shops offered roughly the same kind of expertise, but it was at a level that no department store or self-service hypermarket could compete with. Their mutual loyalty made them stronger against their common competitor: the large corporations such as the yarn chain store 'Stof og Stil' and the hypermarkets of Føtex and Bilka that sold cheaper, mass produced yarn. The Aarhus independent yarn shops had successfully created an informal cooperative that made them competitive in the market, while simultaneously insisting on business strategies that contradicted cutthroat market capitalism.

Furthermore, the intimacy and loyalty they expressed towards each other and their customers, sharing their knowledge of quality yarn and accessories, reproduced an appreciation for quality over price in the customers. Customers expressed enthusiasm over the individual owners and felt that they had a relationship with the person behind the counter. The enthusiasm was evident not only in the customers' kind words to describe the shops and their owners; it was also evident in their actions.

One of Pernille's customers was a university professor who stopped by the shop to show Pernille a scarf she had just finished. Another customer came by to ask Pernille a question about her project, but it was obvious that she was there just as much to hear Pernille tell her how talented she was. Many customers came by, not to buy any items, but to chat about knitting or to proudly show off their finished projects.

In my early field notes, I wrote that it seemed like Pernille's only customers were her friends. Most of the people who visited her shop hugged her or invoked an intimate tone and conversational topic that made me think they were her friends who stopped by her shop. I later realized that this was how *all* customers were treated. The customer would often stay for between ten minutes up to an hour chatting about their families, holiday plans, their work, or health problems. Nearly all were returning customers, and they established a meaningful social relationship. Whereas the duration of a conversation and level of intimacy between seller and customer in most formal economic transactions tends to be limited and practical, the transactions in Pernille's shop were nearly all lengthy and intimate. Because the great majority of her customers were regulars, and because of the amount of time they spent there, in the intimate, *hyggelige,* and domestic atmosphere Pernille had created, their social relationship grew to become meaningful beyond the boundaries of the firm (Carrier 2017).

Regardless of the individual business owner's awareness of these circumstances, the Aarhus yarn shops benefitted from their collaboration, sharing ideals of hospitality and fairness. I sometimes observed people returning to the shop, sometimes to ask for additional help, other times to buy additional items. The way in which Pernille generously gave of her expertise proved a wise investment in customer relations.

It is worthwhile to reflect on the possibility that the shop owners who agreed to my weekly presence over months differed from other shops in trying to consciously show that they were community minded. They had agreed to let an anthropologist study them, so maybe their concern for community was exaggerated compared to other small shops. However, the community and togetherness that I observed among the yarn shop owners and beyond suggest that other small firms also seemed to share a desire that their shop also serve some kind of social function (see Bloch and Parry 1989). This was evident in the sense of community that existed across and beyond specific retail niches. For example, on the street where Pernille's shop was located, all the surrounding shop owners knew each other and frequently visited each other. They often collaborated on events to attract customers, they had coffee together outside their shops on sunny days, and they mutually reinforced each other's complaints about large, impersonal corporations. They built community on their common discontent with the large corporations they viewed as their adversaries. Julian, the jewellery shop owner, often received a bowl of wild berries from one of the neighbouring shop owners when he had been out on his regular walks in the woods. Julian often brought pieces of jewellery to the surrounding cafés and coffee shops where he bought lunch, coffee, and snacks, proudly exhibiting his enthusiasm for his work.

Most of the business owners located near each other took part in a network of informal gift exchange and helped each other if they had run out of something that one of its neighbours might have. The same applied to Ikan and their neighbouring fishmonger. If Ikan received an order for fish they could not provide, they went over to the fishmonger across the street. Borrowing items from each other occurred on a weekly basis, and the transaction was informal in the sense of delayed exchange (Sahlins 1972: 230). For example, Frode from Ikan would run over to the neighbouring fishmonger and ask for a box of mayonnaise. One of the employees there would check if they had a box to spare, and if they did, he would hand it to Frode, who immediately took it back to use at Ikan. No one wrote down the transaction, trusting Frode to return a new box of mayonnaise when he received his new supplies.

Gossip about large corporations and firms whose values were seen as different from the shared ideals of the small enterprises was a common way that the shopkeepers confirmed their sense of belonging to the community. For instance, Ole claimed the value of 'morality over money'. He had a respectful relationship with his competitors, all of whom shared a similar view on how business should be morally motivated. Ole disapproved of the large firms, 'the others', whom he saw as a constant threat to small firms like his own.

## About 'The Others'

What do the large corporations say about themselves and their own business morality? Dansk Supermarked, which operates Denmark's largest chains of supermarkets, uses an appeal to its customers that resembles that of the small business owners. On the web page of their parent owner, Salling Foundations, Dansk Supermarked states that their aim is 'to meet people's ever-changing needs and to contribute to society through donations' (www.sallingfoundations.com). Since 2012, Salling Foundations have donated more than DKK 750 million (€100 million) to charity and community projects. Although they claim that they share the aim of the independent business owners; 'to contribute to [Danish] society', their methods for doing so differ significantly from that of the small business owners. The business owners see themselves as contributing to society by offering intimate, meaningful social relationships with their customers in an inviting social environment and a high degree of trust and fidelity. Salling Foundations, representing 'the other', contributes in a much more impersonal way: through monetary donations to causes which they determine are worth supporting. The lack of intimacy and personal character in the presentation offered by the Salling corporation when compared to that of the small business owners confirms the unavoidable distance between customer and management/owners that emerges when a business 'grows beyond the size that one individual can overlook' (in Sally's words). Whereas the websites of the small firms all offered a personal history about the individual who founded and owned the firm, the large corporations told the story of anonymous corporations without an 'I' to present their story.

Føtex, a chain of hypermarkets and one of the daughter companies in the Salling Foundations, has advertisements that play on the same sentiments as those of the small business owners. Føtex is part of Dansk Supermarked A/S, with the majority of shares owned by a single family. Dansk Supermarked has grown to include hundreds of hypermarkets, supermarkets, and warehouses all over the country (and Europe).[107] Føtex hypermarkets sell food, clothing, electronics, and all sorts of dry goods. The name Føtex derives from a combination of the Danish words for food and textiles (*fødevarer-tekstiler*) and exists as a constant threat to many small, independent merchants. Moreover, Føtex is just one of many large corporations selling various types of goods, threatening to overtake all kinds of small, independent shops.

In 2016, Føtex emphasized their local products, made by their own 'experts', like a baker or a butcher. The large placards found everywhere in the city depicted a man posing as a butcher, and another as a baker, offering a personal face to their products, sold in separate sections of the store. However, their attempt to offer the intimacy of 'real' people could not compete with the small firms. Although they depicted a butcher, the butcher had no name to go with the face. Moreover, when customers entered the enormous supermarket, the butcher behind the counter was different from the one on the poster outside. Even if one shopped in the same Føtex every time, the customer was not certain that they would meet the same butcher every time, or ever again. Not only were there numerous different butchers who worked on shifts, they also worked in different Føtex stores across the city.

---

[107] The total revenue of Dansk Supermarked A/S alone, in 2016, was DKK 57,899 million (€7,773 million).

Plate 5. Føtex advertisement. The advertisement reads: 'Our own butcher: He himself cuts the good beef'.

Plate 6. Føtex advertisement. The advertisement reads: 'Freshly-baked bread from our own baker, every day'.

The butcher who would help you one day may be a polite and pleasant person, but the amount of time the customer spent with him would most likely be limited to the amount of time it took to decide which cut of meat to buy. There would be no time, nor inclination for small talk. The butcher had other things to do and other customers to assist. It was also unlikely that a customer would want to talk to him about much else than the actual meat purchase. My experience is first-hand, but it is supplemented by observations of other customers and employees working in the Aarhus small shops. One of Marie and Ole's customers told me, 'Although the cashier at Føtex might be nice, it wouldn't be natural to have the kind of conversation with her as I have with Ole'. The woman continued, 'They don't have time for [chit-chat], and it would also be weird, since I don't know them [cashiers at Føtex]'. Marie and Ole's customer, who also shopped for other items at Føtex, did not view it as realistic that she would get to know the employees at Føtex like she had gotten to know Marie and Ole. Similarly, a former employee at Føtex stated that 'We were always busy; there is always a lot to do, and so many customers. You don't even know the other employees, it's just too big'. Another customer explained, 'I like Føtex, they have a big selection, but it's not exactly *hyggelig*'.

Although Føtex advertised with their own local baker, butcher, and brands, the consumers would encounter a different face every time they shopped at their store. Further, a quick survey revealed that it was likely that the consumer spent at least 20–30 minutes in the giant supermarket, but the time they would spend face to face with an employee, looking for an item, purchasing fish or meat at the counter, or paying for their purchases at the check-out, was likely to be only a few seconds. In fact, with the growing number of self-checkout stations, the consumer could complete their entire shopping without ever encountering a Føtex salesclerk or cashier. Shopping without contact was, in fact, Føtex business model, as it is for any supermarket that wants customers to enter, shop, buy, and pack their groceries without having to burden the staff with inquiries. In the overwhelming assortment of commodities, the consumer in Føtex was alone in selecting among the dozens of breads, coffees, laundry detergents, frozen vegetables, packaged meats or canned tomatoes. The conclusion is that although Føtex's marketing campaigns attempted to tap into sentiments of intimacy, the actual design and structure of this giant hypermarket and its busy, constantly changing staff, many of whom were teenagers, represents the exact opposite of the intimate atmosphere that pervades the smaller shops.

## Conclusion

The ethnographic cases of the intimate shopping experience among the small shopkeepers compared to the more anonymous experience at Føtex shows how these independent shops can succeed despite their low level of capitalization and lack of high-powered management organization. The small shopkeepers are successful because they cultivate a personal engagement with their customers and employees. They offer an expertise and a passion that Føtex and other large retail outlets cannot match. By presenting themselves as the very antithesis of consumer alienation and capitalist profit-maximizing, the Aarhus small business owners provide a service that stands in opposition to the generalized market trend. Their focus on socializing with customers, resisting aggressive marketing and avoiding excessive competition with colleagues offers a more vital customer experience that proves attractive to customers while generating a stable income from sales. They have a stable, loyal customer base. We also see a tendency in the small shopkeepers operating within the same branch to stand together against the corporate 'other'. Time commitment, intimacy with customers, and loyalty to colleagues and community were central when these business owners started their businesses. We thus observe a priority of community over individualism, even though these shops must also operate within a competitive market.

This is not to say that these business owners do not think in commercial terms. However, they are not motivated by the capitalist incentives to constantly enhance productivity, maximize profit, accumulate capital and continuously expand. The capitalist economy is only one of many forms of economy, or *oikos*, and what is desired may vary between groups, societies, and individuals (Polanyi 2001 [1944]; Hart, Laville, and Cattani 2010). We may relate these business owners' actions to the moral dimension of the economy in the sense that they endeavour to ensure that their economic actions are morally correct (e.g. Hann 2018). Humans are social, and the need for someone to interact with about everyday matters exists even when we are not necessarily aware of these needs. This is evident in the many customers who choose to drive that extra detour on the way home to buy fresh fish from the harbour, walk the extra ten minutes to buy fresh bread from the local bakery, or ask advice from the local goldsmith's shop when their wife's birthday is coming. People do not seek out these market experiences every day (they still shop at Føtex), but they do so often enough so that these small, niche businesses can survive, even thrive. The consumers choose the more expensive, less accessible, smaller, independent shops over the anonymous, cheaper supermarket. The experience of expertise and quality takes precedence over the discount shopping at Føtex, at least for those items that they feel are important for them. Intimacy with the owners, who are also the producers and sellers, becomes a motivating factor to choose the independent shops over the corporate chains. Even if it is not the initial motivation on their first visit, the consumers end up forming a social relationship with the owners of these shops in a manner that is impossible to have in the large chain stores. In the following chapter, I will explore the resilience the independent business owners showed against large scale capitalism, remaining successful as small market actors. I will discuss how the intimate entrepreneurship we have seen in the cases presented in this chapter work as a successful business strategy for small firms.

## *Chapter 8*
## Making Small Firms Work

> Market exchange involves the removal of personal dependence
> between the members of a community when objects become
> commodities that are exchanged externally.
>
> (Bloch and Parry 1989: 4)

Capitalist market economy is built on principles of profit-maximization and
endless growth. All the business owners I studied had one feature in
common: They valued the freedom of being self-employed and defined
themselves as opposed to profit-maximization and growth, which they saw
as the main feature of the large corporations (Lundkvist 2009c). Government
policies had allowed for the growth of oligopolies and monopolies, thus
decreasing competition for the large corporations and creating a difficult
environment for small-scale, petty entrepreneurs. The aim of this chapter is
to analyse the ways in which the independent business owners resisted this
market logic and practice, while remaining successful market actors. In this
sense, they were businesspeople against the market. I argue that they sought
to create what I call 'inalienable commodities', stressing the importance of
intimacy, friendly atmosphere, and *hygge*, together with a common concern
for control over all areas of their business, as significant factors in their
opposition to the more neoliberal market trends. It is this strategy,
emphasizing the inalienable aspects of the commodities that they sell, that
has contributed to the success of these firms. Although the degree of
awareness about their opposition to the market varied, the shared values
possessed by these business owners qualifies them as true opponents of the
structural development of large corporate capitalism. They were market
actors – against the market.

### Dichotomies

Bloch and Parry (1989) argue that the dichotomy between morality and gifts,
on the one hand, versus commodity and market on the other, is a Western

cultural construct that deserves critical assessment. A vast body of social science research has shown that so-called modern market societies, despite being thought of as dominated by 'calculative agencies' (Callon 1998a: 3–7) contain just as many non-calculative agencies, involving gift relations and informal exchange (e.g. Parry and Bloch 1989; Callon 1998b). Marianne Lien (1997; 2004) took up Bloch and Parry's encouragement and investigated how marketing departments involve non-calculative agencies (see also Garsten og De Montoya 2004). Lien (1997; 2004) found that marketing departments are often blind to their own market perspective on reality. The marketing department works from a principle of 'the consumer' as a fictive character and neglects attention to the real people who were their target group. Lien's ethnography offers an illuminating contrast to the business owners of my sample. The Aarhus shopkeepers are acutely aware of their customer base, constantly assessing their customers' needs and wants, based on direct face-to-face social interaction with the individual customer. Describing the marketing department of a large Norwegian food manufacturer, Lien discussed how 'the market' was among those concepts invoked most frequently by staff (Lien 2004: 11). My Aarhus business owners, in contrast, rarely mentioned the word 'market', nor did they refer to 'the market' at all. In contrast to Lien's claim (2004: 13) that the term 'consumer' has almost totally replaced 'customer', the Aarhus shopkeepers frequently referred to their 'customers' (*kunderne*) or 'guests' (*gæsterne*). Lien focused on what my Aarhus business owners call 'the others'. She studied a large corporation and given that the same phenomenon exists in marketing departments in Denmark, she confirms the kind of otherness these large corporations represent vis a vis the small-scale, intimate capitalism of the Aarhus shopkeepers.

If we view large, profit-oriented corporations as concerned with the market and consumers, then my value-oriented business owners can be viewed as concerned with the community and customers. My argument is strengthened by Lien's claim that 'this shift in vocabulary from customer to consumer reflects a final step in a historical process of separation of the field of production from the field of consumption' (Lien 2004: 13). Lien's conclusions for Norway are replicated when we examine the position of 'the market' in Denmark (Lundkvist 2009a; 2017). Hence, a substantial majority of the firms of my sample combine production and distribution activities, in the sense that the place for production and sales is shared. In this sense, we can view them as being opposed to the market. They do not go as far as the angler himself selling the fish directly from his pram on the dock, but to the extent that the bread sold at the bakery is baked on location (by the owner), that the ring sold by the goldsmith is designed and made (by the owner) in the workshop, we see the merging of production and distribution in a socially intimate setting with customers who practically participate in the process, begging for extra time with the producers. At Ikan, for example, the fish is cut, prepared, smoked, and packed directly there at the premises (by the owner or under his direct supervision). And the sellers and buyers discuss the product, its origin, how to prepare it, etc.

It is especially corporations and franchise shops that are perceived as the biggest threats to these small businesses. Julian, the goldsmith articulates this fear:

> You know, I cannot just make jewellery. I should pay attention to what the big actors do, too. I don't really care what they do; I just want to do my own thing, and I do not spend my time looking through their collections. […]. But it has happened that I get letters where they threaten to sue me because I have made something that resembles one of their mass-produced jewellery. You know, I don't pay attention to them, and I did not know. I just made something that I had designed on request from a customer. You know, I make *unika* (unique, one-of-a-kind handicrafts), and I forget that I must pay attention to the mass producers to make sure I do not make something that they have claimed rights to for mass production.

The goldsmith also admitted that sometimes the copying goes in the other direction:

> I had a girl in here, too. She took my design and brought it to [name of a large chain]. They mass-produced it, and it's really my design. It's quite funny. I didn't even know; it was a coincidence that I found out. I don't care as much as they do. I just want to do my own thing here. But you know, these things happen. Maybe I should be more careful, but it's very rare.

In these quotes, we see how Julian was careful to distance himself from the mass-producing jewellers by claiming that he was ignorant of what they were producing and selling and that he just wanted to do his own thing. He hinted at the difference between himself as an artist concerned with the process of creation, and the chain stores as anonymous corporations concerned only with quantity over uniqueness (quality) (see Gregory 1982: 41). Although Julian did not explicitly mention the difference in his motivation to create and the corporations' motivation to generate sales, the way he told his story bears witness to precisely this dichotomy. He strengthened the argument when he added that his design had also been stolen, but that in contrast to 'the others', he did not bother to do anything about it. He was not motivated by profits but by the freedom to act for himself and create his jewellery undisturbed by intense market competition.

Furthermore, Julian acknowledged that chains of mass-produced jewellery were his competitors in the way that some customers were likely to end up purchasing cheaper, mass produced jewellery than his more expensive, handmade *unika*. In addition, he rejected having any resemblance to the large corporations when he claimed that he did not put on part with his own skills. Julian explains:

> You know, people can shop wherever they want, and I am not offended if people go there [to shop in the large chains] instead. Some customers want me to make something I cannot stand. Most often, it has to do with quality. I only make quality jewellery. If people do not want quality, I send them away. Some people get angry when I say, 'No', but that's OK, they are not my customers. People who want mass produced jewellery are not my customers. I am doing OK, and what you get here and what you get there is completely different. I make everything by hand, here, in my little workshop. The customer can come here with an idea, and we design something together. There, people just come, see something they like, buy, and go. I *make* something… and I only sell something I believe in. It's not the same.

By placing great value on their 'uniqueness', these businesses survive in a world of a constantly expanding corporate economy dominated by large, homogeneous chains selling uniform, mass produced products. In direct contrast to the franchise, which all sell the same products, these business owners emphasise the uniqueness of their goods. They all offered something special, something 'unique', something incomparable with the mass-producing corporations. Moreover, the small, independent firms offered personality, meaningful social interaction, the possibility of ongoing relationships, technical expertise, and the kind of passion that could hardly be found in large chain stores, where the owner (or rather, manager), was so alienated from what was going on the shop floor that the customer had no idea who the manager was. This kind of customer alienation is likely in the large corporations where the owners are multiple shareholders, such as Bestseller, a firm that owns a number of clothing shops, or Salling Foundations, which has gradually taken over most of Denmark's shopping malls and supermarkets.

## Security and Control

The small, independent firms survive in a world dominated by corporate firms partly because they offer something found only at the small-scale level. Sally offers a good illustration of this point when she repeatedly reminded me that although customers constantly requested that she open several branches, she resisted, saying that she could only be at one place at one time. For Sally, her business was successful because *she* was in control of everything that took place in her shop and because *she* was physically present every day. Although she trained employees to work towards the same values, only she and her mother before her had the spirit needed (i.e. the work ethic and the right values) to succeed. If she were to open a second or third store, she would not be able to be there personally and control everything, and with that, the moral principles and spirit of the firm would die; of this she was convinced. Sally often reminded me that on several occasions she had to turn down offers of expansion because she could not manage it all. Her mother had once tried to operate two shops but felt forced to shut one down because the person she hired to manage the other shop had begun to deviate from Sally's personal management style. Sally refused to run a business on any other principles than her own. The same happened to Marie and Ole when, in an attempt to have more flexibility, they hired another baker to bake their bread. The employment arrangement did not work out, and the explanation given by Marie and Ole was that the new baker had too many ideas of his own. He was not willing to make bread *their* way, and any other way was not an option to them.

Kathrine Browne (2009) draws attention to James Carrier's (1997) claim that choice is a moral good. In the market economy, the consumers have the choice between different goods, prices, and retailers. Carrier goes on to discuss how consumer and producer make rational choices. The examples presented above explore the choices some Aarhus business owners make. The fact that these business owners have the choice to act as they do, insisting on a 'moral business' (*moralsk virksomhed*), might be partially the consequence of them living in a capitalist welfare society.

However, this does not explain why these business owners resist market development so strongly. Why do they not try to expand? Most of the firms I worked with were extraordinarily successful. Their skilfulness and frugal lifestyle would certainly allow their businesses to grow and expand – if they had wanted to. So why did they resist? A simple explanation to this lay in their inability to let go of control. A common trait among all the business owners in my sample was that they expressed the need to control and be responsible for all areas of their firm's activities. Several had attempted to delegate responsibility to employees, but they could do so only for a brief period before taking back control. Even at Ikan, the largest of my firms, Poul was constantly controlling what the employees were doing via his surveillance system. In addition, Karl, taking back the firm from Polly and Poul, was an even stronger example of the business owners need for control. Common to them all was that they did the bookkeeping themselves (or in Pernille's case, with her husband).

One explanation of this tendency to retain control can be their shared backgrounds, all from lower-income families, combined with an upbringing where they learned to be independent from an early age. Despite their own appraisals about the importance of trust and equality, when it came to managing their own business, they did not show much trust in anyone but themselves. The owners presented their need to be in control of all the areas of the firm as a conscious choice. They all claimed that they *wanted* to be involved in all areas, that they wanted to remain small, and that they had no desire to obtain a more luxurious living standard. All the business owners claimed that they were content with their material living standard and that purchasing more things would be extravagant and not right. However, after observing these owners and their actions over several months, it became clear that an important reason why these businesses did not expand, despite persistent requests from customers and available capital, was due to their unwillingness to release control of any aspect of the firm. This means that regardless of whether these business owners wanted to grow, they could not grow larger than what the individual (or couple) felt capable of managing.

Most of these business owners had experience from having had salaried employment, and their valuation of the freedom and control over their own enterprise was so great that they were unwilling to sacrifice this freedom and control for the growth of the firm. However, this is not the sole explanation for why these business owners did not grow. Their life-style choices and their material consumption patterns reveal that most of them were simply uninterested in increasing their material wealth. Marie and Ole could have afforded a larger house, a larger car, more expensive interior, clothes, and so forth, but they chose not to, with the explanation, 'Why would we?'. Sally could have taken more money out of the firm to renew her wardrobe, drive a car instead of a scooter, or move to a new apartment or house, but she chose not to. The simple explanation for her choices and values is that she had other priorities in her life than greater material comfort. Polly and Poul, who had fulfilled their ambitions of having a large house and expensive cars, looked for the cheaper alternatives in the grocery store, they bought their clothes on sale, and they did not 'waste' money on expensive restaurants (or other luxuries they felt were unnecessary). Poul acted generous when he thought it mattered, and on all other matters, he acted frugally. Like the vast majority of the other business owners, his wardrobe was limited to a few, simple outfits. He wore the same fleece jacket every day all through winter, he did not spend his money on what he would call vanity, and the couple survived half the day on instant coffee. The coffee machine was used only on special occasions, when guests were expected.

A blend of 'Jante law', combined with nostalgia and an inability to relinquish control, might thus summarise the reasons why these firms insisted on resisting market expansion. However, explaining their lack of expansion simply on the basis of character traits as 'an urge to control' is not sufficient. Of the six firms in my main sample, several of them were actively involved in countering the development of the market and claimed to do so out of concern for 'the good of the community' (*det bedste for fællesskabet*). Marie and Ole were self-proclaimed 'greens', supporting left-wing politics and a greener future (in concern for the environment). Sally was concerned about poverty and the most vulnerable members of (Danish) society. Pernille had grown up in a socialist family, and although she was not politically active, her values were clearly of socialist character. Similarly, Julian, who had had a good income in his salaried career, and at times admitted that he missed his €80,000 car, was not willing to trade in his current goldsmithing business for a more materially comfortable lifestyle. He and his wife had moved out of the city, they shared a car and took turns commuting by train and bike. Julian was also engaged in a community of independent small businesspeople who worked for the protection of small independent shops against big business; specifically, corporate firms buying up properties and replacing the independent shops with international chains such as H&M, 7-Eleven, Magasin, Bertoni, Bolia and others.

A quick search on Google confirms that the area where Julian's shop/workshop was located was dominated mainly by independent shops and small service businesses. The neighbouring district, however, stood in stark contrast to the businesses in Julian's area, with only two independent businesses, the remainder being large, mostly international, retailers such as the women's clothing firm Gina Tricot, Nille, and the German Aldi supermarket chain. The business owners who were actively concerned with protecting the area from takeover by large corporate actors used the neighbouring district as a negative example of what they were fighting, 'We don't want to become like downtown, right'.[108]

It seems reasonable to assume that in societies with a high level of social and economic security, small business owners can more easily afford to be concerned with values other than money (Graubard 1986: 11). However, we can discern that their concern for protecting small business as a way of life is also a concern for protecting their own existence. I have shown how the business owners express the view that they wish to remain small and

---

[108] '*Vi vil vel ikke blive lige som nede i midtbyen, vel*' (Danish original).

that they reject corporate capitalism. However, this option is in fact limited. The possibility for them to expand and become a large corporation themselves is rapidly decreasing together with the growing domination by already existing monopolies and oligopolies. It is more likely, and more common, that existing corporations will acquire independent firms rather than small firms expanding to become corporations. Some firms have indeed done so, and others will continue to succeed even as they remain small, but a growing number of retail branches are simply collapsing under the onslaught of large corporations. The name and appearance of the shop may trick the consumer into thinking that they are choosing an independent shop, because they kept their old logo and design after being acquired or coming into a franchise arrangement. A closer look into the organisation of a firm, however, reveals that in many branches, the 'owners' do not really own their shop anymore. That was not the case for any of the six main shopkeepers in this study, and for sectors such as cafés and yarn shops, independently-owned and managed shops still dominate. In other branches, however, such as florists, pet shops, and grocery stores, there remain no independent shops of these kinds in Aarhus, that I am aware of. The former owner of a second-generation pet shop told me that her firm was forced into a corporate chain because they could not afford to buy their products directly from the supplier without membership in the corporate supply chain. The large corporations had ensured competitive price deals with the suppliers, effectively preventing small firms from being able to compete; the wholesale prices offered to the small firms were simply too high.[109] She and her husband now managed their pet shop as before, but they did not own it anymore. They were employed managers in what had formerly been their own shop. They still referred to themselves as the owners, but on paper (formally), they were not. Seeing and becoming aware of this development, the other small business owners need to be constantly concerned with offering the kind of unique shopping experience that large corporations cannot offer.

The question arises as to whether this emphasis on moral values represents some kind of luxury when material survival is assured. If my argument is true, then morality would have a higher value in Scandinavian welfare states than in societies where the livelihood of a small business owner or shopkeeper is more precarious, such as Hungary or Myanmar. Would small business owners in other countries place the same amount of importance on moral economic behaviour as they do in Scandinavia? The results show that despite variations in motivation, moral principles of

---

[109] In 2018, this shop was closed. Aarhus now has four stores operating as part of the Petworld chain and one operating under the Maxi Zoo franchise. Most of the Aarhus florists are operated under the Interflora label.

fairness and trust are important in business life including in countries without a developed social safety net such as Myanmar where Laura Hornig (2020) showed that business owners were continuously guided by the religious morality of Buddhism. The business owners in Hornig's sample used great effort to implement morality into their business activities through prayers, ritual offerings, and caring for their employees far beyond what I witnessed in Denmark (Hornig 2020). In fact, Hornig shows how business owners took on a moral responsibility for their employees as a result of the lack of a welfare state providing social security. In Myanmar, the business owners took on the (moral) responsibility providing social security for their employees, helping with hospital bills for sick family members, providing childcare, and even accommodation. Hornig's description of how Myanmar small business owners' emphasis on ensuring prayers and ritual offerings at the place of business shows another way of being a morally good business owner in Myanmar. Despite different motivations on the moral behaviour, the business owners in Myanmar and Aarhus were both concerned with being morally good in their role as business owners.

Moreover, operating a business with principles of being fair, offering trust, and a reciprocal relationship with the customers is to the Aarhus business owners an important strategy for economic survival and generating income (Browne 2009, see; McCloskey 2006). Similarly, it was important to the Myanmar business owners to consult religious experts and make religious offerings, acting as a morally good Buddhist to ensure profit (Hornig 2020). Consider Marie and Ole and their bakery: they have enough material wealth to live comfortably without necessarily expanding their enterprise. Of course, they live from the profits of their business, but they claim that they care more about doing something they like, something that is also good for the community.

The Aarhus business owners live in a society where all basic needs are covered by the state and social security well developed. However, the presence of a social safety net does not explain their concern for moral behaviour. Business owners in Myanmar, where there is no welfare state, are concerned with their moral economic behaviour as well. One might argue that the reason why they choose to be concerned about moral economic behaviour is due to their close relations with their customers, but such an explanation would be tautological. They are close to customers partly because they believe in the moral project of their firm. The similarity between the moral behaviour of the Myanmar business owners and the Aarhus business owners may be explained by the simple fact that morality is ever-present in social life. Hornig argues that the Myanmar business owners took care of their employees in order to present themselves 'in morally good terms' (Hornig 2020: 124).

Robert Paine (1972 [1963]: 52) distinguishes between two kinds of entrepreneurs in Nordbotn, Northern Norway. He classifies one as the 'free-holder type' who 'are prepared to accept responsibility in associations in order to help raise the productivity of the community'. The other type he calls the 'free-enterpriser type', which 'may not work in either of the principal livelihoods of the community'; the free enterprisers' 'characteristic interests are of a speculative kind and they pursue them in disregard of local values' (Paine 1972: 52). All the enterprises I visited in Aarhus were integrated into the local community and had an interest in respecting the norms and values of the community, working towards a good community. The boundaries of the community differed among the owners to include that of the neighbourhood, the city, the region, Jutland, or Denmark. Regardless of how broadly defined the boundaries are, Paine's (1972) categories are useful in understanding their behaviour, and they all resembled that which Paine describes as free-holders. Their motivations come from deeper social incentives that existed prior to their founding or taking over their current business. Their motivations lay behind their starting a business more than any incentive that grew after the business succeeded. Sally's mother, for example, claimed that she started her business as a reaction to the development of consumer culture. Likewise, Marie and Ole started their business based on a desire to offer something more than quick exchange (together with flexibility for themselves). And Pernille continued to promote the utilitarian knitters' community. Polanyi argues that economic actions are always firstly social,

> The outstanding discovery of recent historical and anthropological research is that human economies, as a rule, are submerged in our social relationships. We do not act so as to safeguard our individual interest in the possession of material goods; we act to safeguard our social standing, protect our social claims, or ensure the maintenance of our social resources. We value material goods only in so far as they serve this end (Polanyi 2001 [1944]: 48).

We can say the same about moral choices. Morality is social, it is about our relations with others; and it is the sociality that makes people choose to follow what Abraham Edel referred to as a 'moral path' (Edel 1962: 59). The Aarhus shopkeepers are convinced that their business activities have been and are motivated by a will to do good. This willingness to do good is encouraged by an awareness of what they view as the social benefits of 'being a good person'.

## Atmosphere, Loyalty, and Meaningful Relationships

In a newspaper article from March 2015, the atmosphere, customers, and employees at the Ikan fish shop are described in the following words, 'A common trait shared by all of them [the sales staff] is the smiles on their lips, and their mutual love for fresh produce, the delicacies, and the good atmosphere the place offers' (my translation). Descriptions like these testify to the positive atmosphere in the shop.

In the independent shop-owners' constant effort to offer something different from 'the others' (the large corporate chain stores), having the right 'atmosphere' (*stemning*) is an important aspect. Whereas the large corporate chains such as Dansk Supermarked attempt to appeal to the consumer with images of their local expertise and locally sourced products, the size of their shops alone prohibits them from achieving the same kind of intimacy or independent atmosphere as that of the shopkeepers. The Føtex supermarket chain has tried to create a more relaxed, intimate atmosphere by installing softer lights in certain sections, soothing music, and warm colours. Nonetheless, the customer ends her shopping trip at an illuminated checkout counter with florescent lighting, often accompanied by loud music, always blended with the noise of items moving along the check-out belt, beeps from the cash register, money falling into the automated counting machine, and the rush to pack up to make way for the next customer, not to mention the constant summing noise of people, and food trolleys being pushed around. The large chains' attempt to achieve the same *hyggelig* atmosphere is simply no match for the small niche shops with their personalized service offered by an owner with intimate knowledge of their product.

Marianne Lien (1997; 2004) discussed how the marketing departments within a large, Norwegian retail corporation attempt to understand 'the consumer' without realising the consumer's subjectivity. Linnet (2012b) discussed the importance of atmosphere in marketing. But no matter how much emphasis marketing departments place on the soft lights, seductive product placement, relaxing sounds, etc. they cannot achieve the same intimacy as the small firms due to the simple fact that they are not small. The employees in these large shops will vary to a much larger degree, they will be much harder to supervise than in the small firms, and the simple lack of the owners' presence at the place of transaction immediately removes the intimacy between customer and firm. An employee working in one of the small Aarhus shops stated that when there is more than one level between owner and employee, the entire social situation changes. She meant that when the owner is not present to support, guide, and supervise the employee, and the manager is someone other than the owner, it creates a form of hierarchy and inequality that is destructive to the social atmosphere at the workplace. Her experience was that in the larger firms, with several hierarchal levels, the social relations between colleagues was limited and impersonal. She believed that this was due to the levels of hierarchy. In smaller firms, the owner was also the manager, such that the lack of hierarchy among employees created a much more intimate social atmosphere and a *hyggelig* workplace where 'the employees enjoy their work and each other'. Surely not all small workplaces are *hyggelig*. They can be horrible if the relations between boss and employees is bad or there is exploitation, all of which is not the case with the Aarhus business owners. Small is not always beautiful by definition, but the Aarhus business owners' way of business, is.

The ability to establish meaningful relationships with customers in the way Pernille, and Marie and Ole had managed to do was a common feature shared by all the firms in my sample. Although Sally and Julian had the same principle, the relationships between Sally and her customers took longer to establish and were not as deep. This can partly be explained by the simple fact that although Sally had return customers, people do not buy expensive toys on a regular basis, whereas bread, fish, and yarn are products that would allow more frequent return visits by loyal customers. With Pernille's yarn shop, for example, the fact that customers returned for help and confirmation regarding their creative project allowed for more frequent socialisation than was possible at Sally's. In the case of Julian, the goldsmith, he designed and planned his orders together with the customer, which often entailed several visits over a period of some weeks; this allowed for relationships that could become more personal. At Ikan, the relationships with customers varied. This was a larger firm, and some customers had a closer relationship with the employees and owners than others. However, Karl's emphasis on taking time with each customer was acted out at Ikan. These sentiments are also confirmed in quotes from customers who praised Ikan for its 'fabulous service and they always give good advice on the way, even on a very busy New Year's Eve day. I also want to make a shout out to the nice fishmonger (*fiskemand*) with the good humour who reminded the customers in line to smile'. Another customer declared to me that it was 'always a pleasure to come to Ikan, both privately and with regards to business'.

Ole explained how intimacy and meaningful relationships in the business were a conscious goal and a common motivation for when he and Marie decided to change their business project from farming to the bakery. As their business grew, however, their investment in meaningful social relationships had now become a burden. The customers wanted them up front, at the counter, but they needed to be in the back, preparing the dough.

The nature of the work pace in a bakery versus a yarn shop was significantly different, and on most occasions, Pernille had sufficient time and energy to engage in lengthy conversations with customers. The shopkeepers all sought to create an atmosphere or mood that gave the customers a feeling of 'being inside' (Linnet 2012a: 404). This sense of being inside, of being included in a special, *hyggelig* space of the café or shop, was the expression of this atmosphere. This intimate atmospheric, what Linnet describes as an aspect of *hygge,* may also be related to Gullestad's theory of equality as sameness, where people are let 'inside' a community as recognition that they are among equals (Gullestad 1992). The shop represents the community to which one becomes a member, and by being a returning customer, you enter this communal space (Linnet 2012a; 2012b). This would not apply to all customers, but for the loyal, regular customers. Linnet argues that the 'subjective awareness of a spatial, temporal or symbolic contrast to the outside world facilitates the experience of pausing in a pleasurable, safe and invigorating environment'; this is a consequence of the intimacy in the small, Aarhusian businesses (Linnet 2012b: 29). The ideas about sociality and community, inclusivity (*rummelighed*), and *hygge* that are created in these firms, not only connote ideas about Danishness that are constitutive in these concepts; they also operate as a model for and of society (Bruun, Jakobsen and Krøijer 2011; Bruun 2018).

These business owners' success in creating intimate and meaningful relationships with customers thus form a core feature of their business activity, and an important element in their financial success. Many of Sally's customers commented on the atmosphere in her shop with statements such as, 'It's such a lovely shop, with a broad selection and a *hyggelig* atmosphere, and you are met by broadly smiling and engaged staff who know their products'.

Lillian's customers in her café gave her overwhelmingly positive reviews, emphasising the *hyggelig* atmosphere, Lillian's friendly character, and the high quality of her homemade products. Among the comments I gathered were statements such as 'The best and most *hyggelig* coffee shop in town! Everything is homemade and delicious… Not to mention the very sweet owner who completes the place with good Karma'. Another comment: 'It's a super *hyggeligt* place, super delicious homemade cakes, and a super sweet staff.' Not one of the customers made a statement about Lillian's café without mentioning *hygge.* The focus on the atmosphere seemed just as important as the products. This was a repeated compliment among customers in all my firms and confirms the importance that having the right atmosphere plays in creating the successful customer experience (Linnet 2012a; 2012b).

## Inalienable Commodities

The complex anthropological debate on gifts, commodities, goods, and objects deserves some mention here because these distinctions have a relation to the way the Aarhus shop owners express their opposition to the market. Part of this opposition involves the relationship with the objects they produce and/or sell.

In the afterword to *Economic Moralities,* Bill Maurer (2009) reminds us of the need to be aware of, and account for, the possibility of unintended consequences that might appear in an economy. He refers to Max Weber and the capitalist incentives that emerged as an unintended consequence of Protestant asceticism, claiming that 'every apparently capitalist formation seems to generate its own accompanying forms of the gift' (Maurer 2009: 266). In the ethnographic examples in the previous chapter, I addressed a similar kind of moral economy that I call moral motivations. Reviewing Marx, Mauss, Simmel, Polanyi, and other critics of monetary economy illuminates how the business owners I worked with all shared the desire to offer something beyond that of an alienated commodity sold through a simple cash transaction (Carrier 1992).

The intimate sociality between seller and customers in these small firms challenges the idea of a strict distinction between gifts and commodities (i.e. Gregory 2015). Mauss' (1966) theory of the gift refers to a reciprocal system of exchange that involves both material objects and abstractions that are exchanged between friends, family, neighbours, and acquaintances in a *prestation totale.*[110] It involves the entire social network of the giver, with the accompanying obligation to receive and then reciprocate a gift. Chris Gregory (2015: 13) described the gift economy as a debt economy. Gregory thus characterised commodity exchange as 'an exchange of *alienable* objects between people who are in a state of reciprocal independence that establishes a *quantitative* relationship between the objects exchanged, [while gift exchange] is an exchange of *inalienable* objects between people who are in a state of reciprocal dependence that establishes a *qualitative* relationship between the transactors' (Gregory 1982: 100–101). Mauss (1966) opposes the gift to the commodity, claiming that the gift always retains some element of the giver, whereas the commodity, paid for in money, represents a non-relational exchange.

This view of gifts and commodities, based on a dichotomous ideal, may work at the general level, but it is difficult to apply in the concrete ethnographic reality of my sample. Moreover, it is not enough to state that

---

[110] Due to the misconceptions that have appeared through the English translation of this concept, I refer to the original French term formulated by Mauss himself.

'goods' are objects made in a market economy, which receive the qualities of a gift when exchanged in a gift economy. The objects produced and/or sold in these businesses are not traded within a gift economy (although the toys are often bought to be given as gifts). They are bought and sold within a market economy, they are sold in a formal business, and the exchange is generally balanced by the immediate payment of money for the specific item (Sahlins 1972: 194; Gregory 1982). Nevertheless, as I have described, many of the transactions involve qualities ascribed to various forms of gift exchange, such as inalienability and an unspoken obligation to return (i.e. Pernille and her 'free' knitting assistance, and Marie and Ole's inalienable bread) (Mauss 1966; Gregory 1982: 101). In addition, although they are monetary transactions, there is an intimate sociality associated with the greeting, informal banter, and sales advice between seller and customer, not to mention the customer who just happens to stop in and browse or show off her latest knitting project.

For example, the bread that Marie and Ole sell in their bakery can hardly be classified as gifts. However, the bread is hardly a pure commodity, since it is sold in a specific social context that in some ways resembles gift exchange. The same social context resembles the interaction surrounding the purchase of Julian's jewellery. Whereas the objects are sold for money, the sociality in the way they are ordered, discussed, produced, and sold (Julian's meetings with customers to learn about their tastes) does not deserve the simple label 'commodity'. In the context of these sellers, we can therefore benefit from the ideas of sociologist Alain Cailleé (2010: 183) who argues that 'the characteristic feature of the modern gift is that it is also a gift to strangers'. The gifts that Marie and Ole receive from their customers, who are not necessarily strangers in the anonymous sense, and the 'free' service Pernille offers both her potential and regular customers, both involve a relationship of exchange that takes place within a formal economic exchange setting, but which simultaneously involves reciprocal relationships between people, 'strangers' or not. The transactions involve goods (objects) and services that are produced as commodities in a market, and which could be sold anywhere; but here they are treated and traded as socially valued commodities in the sense that the commodities are valued and adjusted to the customer's personal needs as assessed by the seller, including a special social significance. This kind of gift-like transaction blurs the boundaries between economy and society, home and work (see Carrier 1995: 197). In fact, it challenges the strict differentiation between commodities and gifts and between market and gift forms of exchange. Jonathan Parry is frequently mentioned as a pioneer in articulating this dilemma, with his discussion about the 'alienable gift' in the ritual *danadharma* (Parry 1986: 461).

Similarly, but in contrast to Parry, I suggest that the Danish shopkeepers in Aarhus strive to make commodity objects inalienable in their exchange by adding a portion of their 'spirit'. The success of making their commodities inalienable, of giving objects a kind of spirit, may vary, but their common intention, and attempt to promote such a form of exchange, is vital in demonstrating their resistance to the impersonal market and an inherent element in their shared morality of doing good by customers (Bloch and Parry 1989: 8).

Where Mauss discusses *hau*, defined as the spiritual relation between giver and receiver, we can draw a similar link between the Danish expression *at give af sig selv* ('to give of yourself'), an aim that was shared among the business owners. They were concerned not only with selling commodities in a market or with contributing to the community; they wanted their objects to contain a part of themselves. The objects were part of themselves in the manner that Julian created unique jewellery in his own personal style; or in the way Ole and Marie baked bread and pastry that in taste, texture, and sales method (and low price) differed from other breads on the market. But it was not just bread; it was Ole and Marie's bread. Of course, we could argue that the objects these business owners produce and/or sell are inalienable only to themselves, and not to the customers (Carrier 1992). Indeed, we can certainly say that Marie and Ole worked hard to transfer their 'spirit' into their bread. Julian equally transferred a part of himself into his jewellery when he spoke of his work as 'a part of myself'.[111] The Aarhus business owners seemed to believe that their spirit (what we might call a Danish *hau*) was necessary in order to ensure a good product and a satisfied customer.

It is only by observing the customer that we can know whether the shopkeepers have been successful in creating inalienable commodities, in the sense that the customers feel their 'spirit'. My data indicates that the Aarhus small business owners have largely succeeded in doing so. The unique jewellery Julian produces, and the relationship between him and customers, is confirmed when the customers send individual thank-you notes, pictures, or when they stop by just to show him how they look and feel with their new jewellery. The relationship is apparent in customer statements such as 'Julian is a totally unique goldsmith... I can only recommend a visit to the small, little shop. We had the best and most personal service and the most beautiful wedding rings we could imagine'. Marie and Ole's success is visible in the gifts and cards their customers occasionally bring, sometimes for no special reason, other than to show their appreciation. Not many bakeries can

---

[111] *'En del af mig selv'* (Danish original).

generate this kind of social connection with their customers. For Pernille as well, her returning customers show their connection to Pernille and their craft when they stop in to show off their knitting-work in progress or finished garments, or even 'tagging' Pernille on social media when they post pictures of their completed garments.

## Conclusion

This chapter has discussed how independent small business owners focus their energy in ways that stand in opposition to market principles of profit maximizing and growth and to the anonymous experience of cash and carry in large, impersonal stores. The small business owners accentuate the differences between themselves and the impersonal corporate firms and the impersonal market. We have seen that community and ideals of modesty and non-materialistic values are not the only reasons why these business owners remain small and independent in opposition to the market. Another important factor is the owners' inability or unwillingness to let go of control. In fact, lack of trust in other people to do their job properly prevents the business owners from growing beyond the size that one person can handle. Their obsessive need to control and take part in all areas of the firm limits their growth, regardless of their success. It seems that they can only remain moral businesspeople if they are small.

Another element of their success, and an element that distinguishes them from the general market, lies in the atmosphere and the social relationships that grow out of these firms. The intimacy of being small, low key, and able to offer a meaningful social relationship with customers is a vital strength in their business. We can closely relate this to their ideal and success in creating what I refer to as inalienable commodities. The products traded in these businesses involve more than just the use-value of the object itself. Mauss aside, there is also plenty of *hau* in Aarhus.

*Chapter 9*
# Conclusion

The ethnography of this work has shown how a selection of independent business owners struggle to fulfil personal desires for freedom to control their own lives in a self-employed life mode while simultaneously living up to their own expectations of a moral business economy. I have argued that the business owners featured in this work are exceptional in the way they organise their firms according to a shared morality and a philosophy that deviates from the norms of the commodity market. They oppose general ideas of capitalist enterprise through their shared goal *not* to grow beyond a handleably size. They place significant value on the ability to control all areas of the firm, from on floor work, to administration and book-keeping. Part of their aim as business owners is never to release control over any area of the business. Their primary motivation is the self-actualisation they experience in direct contact with customers, as well as production. They are concerned with presenting themselves as business owners, whose primary motivation is not profiting or prestige, but success living up to values of community, modesty, and hard work; acting according to the ideas of their moral community.

The introduction and the first two chapters introduced the background that these business owners act within. The introduction covers methodological implications where I reflect upon my role as a Norwegian in Denmark and the consequences this has on my role in the field. I emphasise a methodological path with participant-observation at the centre. Acknowledging the challenges involved in urban fieldwork in a modern, Northwestern society, I show that the aim of a holistic approach is not as impossible as fellow Scandinavian ethnographers tend to express. I gathered the data over twelve months fieldwork, divided in two parts, one where I spend most of my time in one firm and family. I spent the second half of fieldwork in five different firms in different niches across the city.

Chapter 2 elaborates how the business owners I studied acted within a nation-state that has developed into a social democracy defined by a capitalist welfare state. I discussed the security provided by the welfare state, and how doing business within such a system affects my interlocutors. Morality, or the Danish *moral,* is an important aspect of the business owners' perception of how to do business (morally good). I argue that this morality is recognizable in historical, public, and ethnographic discourses about Danish and Scandinavian society, and I discuss how these values represent ideas that have played an important role in the social construction of a popularized, politicized 'Danish identity'. In the third chapter, I went through the many ways in which we can understand morality. I landed on an analytical definition that combined theories from Edel and Edel (1959), Durkheim (2010), Howell (1997), and Robbins (2009). Here, I understood morality as common beliefs and actions that are situated culturally and temporarily, and which needs to be understood as a combination of reflexive free choice and routine. The values I discovered as shared between the independent business owners involved values of freedom to control your own work and life, hard work, community, and justice. These concepts have been tirelessly reproduced and recognised in Scandinavian popular, political, and social science discourses (e.g. Lien, Lidén, and Vike 2001a; Gullestad 2002; Bruun, Jakobsen, and Krøijer 2011; Jenkins 2011; Bendixen, Bringslid, and Vike 2018a).

In the first ethnographic chapter, I laid out the family history of an old family firm, one of my main firms. This firm differed from the other businesses both in being an old, multiple-generation firm, and because of a replacement of the owners. The previous owner intervened with the successor's business strategies and took the firm back from his daughter and son-in-law. The chapter discussed how this event illustrates the importance of obeying the moral code of business, here set by the previous generations. This case sheds light on the possible consequences that may occur from deviation from what the business owners consider as important values and business strategies, stressing the importance of moral obligations towards the family. The example provided data on conflicts around thrift and hard work, supporting the leading argument of this work.

The fifth chapter discussed various challenges associated with generational transfer of firms. Reviewing the numerous bureaucratic challenges that involved a generational transfer may suggest the complexity and financial challenges involved in a formal transfer was the reason why so few firms survive past the first generation. However, my material suggested that most independent business owners did not picture their children as the future owners of their firms. Instead, they were concerned with ensuring the transmission of what they believed were the right values. There existed a mutual perception that if their children were equipped with the right set of moral values, they would be able to create good lives for themselves either as future entrepreneurs or pursuing other desires. Values of free choice, independence, and the belief in their children's ability to choose good and right, triumphed over physical transfer of material firms. The business owners had in common that they grew up learning a keen sense for hard work, independence, and a belief in doing good, for both themselves and their community. Although the decision not to continue the parents' firm was, in many cases, undoubtedly linked to the bureaucratic challenges set by the redistributive welfare state, I argued that the strong emphasis on independence and individuality that dominates Danish public discourse also played an important role (Bendixen, Bringslid and Vike 2018b: 19; Larsen 2018: 248–58). I concluded that transfer of these values proved to be what was most important to the business owners.

The sixth chapter discussed the ways the independent business owners view work. I argued that all the owners in my sample lived embedded lives. A minority were financially embedded in the sense that the firm and family had a shared economy. However, I argued that the embeddedness was economic, whatsoever, given the amount of time, energy, and creative passion invested in the firms. The personal investment in the firms, financially, but mostly in terms of time, creativity, and personal engagement, blurred the boundaries between the person and the business owner, placing them in the self-employed life mode category. The business owners themselves expressed difficulty in dealing with questions about work (*arbejde*). This may be partly because the Danish word *arbejde*, although technically carrying numerous meanings, seemed to provoke associations with labour rather than work, in the owners. When confronted directly with questions about *arbejde,* none would admit that their occupation in their firms was *arbejde*. Simultaneously, the same business owners would stress their concern for hard work (*arbejdsmoral*), and daily reminding me of the amount of time and energy they invested in their firms. I also saw a tendency to relate the Danish concept of *hygge* to work and work tasks, creating a positive association to work. By emphasising *hygge*, work became something pleasant, both for the owners and the employees. Although the business owners were tired from working too much or spending more time than they personally wanted on the firm, they were reluctant to admit that their occupation was *arbejde*. This reasoning was grounded in their acute consciousness about their entrepreneurial activity being a conscious life path that stood in opposition to the unfree, employed life of the wage worker, and also in contrast to the career life mode, where the worker was bound by the expectation to constantly produce new ideas. The business owners owned the means of production and the modes of production, equipped them with the perfect balance of freedom and control.

In the context of motivations, chapter seven presented four cases that builds up the main argument in this work: namely that these business owners were motivated by shared moral values that benefitted their business and enabled them to subsist outside of market principles of growth. I argued that the small businesses offer of intimacy, community, collegiality, and do what they believed was morally right in business, as in life, was what made these businesses successful in a market dominated by large capital. They offered something else than mainstream corporate firms, a uniqueness in hand made products, quality, and the business owner's expertise offered to the customers directly from the source. My data suggest that by opposing alienation and capitalist ideals of profit maximizing, these business owners stood in opposition to the corporate market development. It also illustrated that the community between the small business owners, across and within the same niche, and their choice to co-operate instead of competing, proved important in their strategy to stand strong against large corporations.

The last ethnographic chapter continued the discussions in chapter seven, adding some aspects to their motivations. I argued that it was not necessarily or solely the conscious opposition to large capitalism that differentiated these business owners. We also saw that an important reason why they did not expand beyond a certain size was simply that the owners could not let go of control. When the business owner was unwilling to distribute responsibilities to employees, the firm could not grow larger than what one individual could manage. Furthermore, my data showed that atmosphere and the social relationships offered in these firms played a significant role in their success, and once again, it differentiated them from large firms that were unable to offer the same standard of intimacy. I argued that the fact that these owners were able to offer what I term inalienable commodities was an important business strategy and an important reason why customers chose to return. Invaluable commodities refer to a lack of clear distinction between gifts and commodities that I argue to occur when the business owner offers meaningful relationships and goods that contain some of the spirit of the producer. I found that this form of exchange relationship, or business strategy, provoked a moral obligation in the customer to return, and an important reason why these businesses were successful.

## The Independent Business Owner

> One must remember that bankruptcy, or absorption by a more
> powerful firm, is the daily bread of capitalist enterprises (Wallerstein
> 2004: 27).

Denmark is not alone in having an economy where large corporations
dominate the financial market. Multinational corporations spread across the
world and dominate capitalist markets globally (Wallerstein 2004; Tsing
2005; Eriksen 2016). The independent merchant is becoming a rarity not
only in North-Western Europe but also across large parts of the European
and North-American continent, overwhelmed by large corporations with
their competitive prices, large warehouses, and attractive locations. This
development has for long been recognized as globalization and the
accessibility of standardized goods can be found in nearly all corners of the
world (Eriksen 2016). Scholars disagree whether this is a positive or a
negative development, but the sensation of buying a Coca Cola in the
Marshall Islands, buying IKEA furniture in Dubai, or eating at McDonalds
in Denmark, is confirmed by their popularity among the consumers (Eriksen
2016).

Globalisation and neoliberalism are two closely interconnected terms,
and the development of global financial markets plays an important role in
the challenges independent business owners experience globally (Eriksen
2016: 18–21). In fact, Thomas Hylland Eriksen argues for
'alterglobalisation' in a criticism of an overheated world because of
globalisation in a neoliberal market economy. In many ways, we can relate
my business owners to a movement of alterglobalisation. They are not
consciously against globalisation or even a neoliberal market economy, but
their moralities, as I have presented them, oppose the current development.
They resist consumer society, and indirectly, therefore, also capitalism
(Wallerstein 1983: 144; Tsing 2005: 4). My data have shown that my
business owners are concerned with using and protecting local products and
production, modesty in consumption, and a frugal life where money as well
as other resources is wisely spent.

By insisting on never holding sales, for instance, Sally opposed liberal
values of competition and disgust for gluttonous consumption
(*forbrugersamfundet*: consumer society). Although her private reasons were
of a religious character, she inherited her ideas from a secular motive in her
mother. Similarly, when Pernille insisted on an informal cooperation with
the other independent yarn shops, she opposed neoliberal values of free
competition and profit maximizing under the idea that they were stronger
and safer together, against the anonymous other (corporate firms). My data

indicate that these components were among the main reasons for the small business owners' survival in a world where corporate capitalism dominated more and more of the market. What is more, they offered niche products that were unique either by being hand-made, made with local ingredients, or through the pedagogical expertise of the salesperson. The owners were also different, if not unique, in establishing a reciprocal relationship with the customers not just as an act of kindness or hospitality, but as a business strategy to make customers return. Moreover, when I argued that they worked 'against the market', I referred not necessarily to socialism or anti-capitalism. It referred to their wish to protect and preserve the individual merchant. The business owners believed that the intimacy, sociality, and community they offered could only exist in a small firm where the owner was directly involved in all areas of the business. They wanted to protect the freedom and responsibilities that are involved in being your own boss in a small firm.

Data presented in previous chapters have shown that although undoubtedly part of the market economy, all business owners worked hard to keep an element of themselves in the goods they sold. I have argued that this relationship between customer, owner, and goods involved a resemblance of the *hau* (the spirit of things) in Maori gifts (Mauss 1966: 9, 86–7), opposed to the alienated commodity that symbolizes a capitalist economy. Simultaneously, I have argued that we should certainly not understand their transactions as gift exchange. Instead, my data illuminate how these forms of transaction blurred the boundaries between gift and commodity. By challenging perceptions about commodities and formal economic transactions, these transactions involved what I call inalienable commodities. I have argued that this valuation of goods, stands in opposition to the alienation that is often associated with commodities in a neoliberal market (Carrier 1992).

My material revealed that the development of the market towards a growing corporate capitalism, with the resulting oligopolies and monopolies in several sectors (e.g. Arla Foods and The Salling Funds), has provoked the business owners to feel responsible for the protection of the individual merchant against the neoliberal corporations. A commonality between the owners was that they had experienced how the development of the market negatively affected the values contained in their idea of a good (moral) economy. They had lived to observe the development from when the market was flourishing with small, independent shops that collaborated through real (*ægte*), small cooperatives, based on ideals of equality and community, to a competitive, liberal marked economy, based on principles of survival of the fittest. Finally, they live to observe a state liberalism that encourages and supports privatized oligopolies and monopolies (Lundkvist 2009a; Bruun 2018).

What does the road ahead look like for these business owners? If globalisation, financialization, and neoliberal market principles continue to dominate and expand globally, it is unlikely that the small business owner will exist in the future. However, this is not a sufficient conclusion. If we look beyond the borders of North-Western Europe, or move even further, to more South-Eastern part of the Eurasian continent, we will easily detect that the independent merchant is very much alive and numerous. It is not on the cost of globalisation. We find the same large brands in India, Turkey, and Germany. The differences between these countries are many, but the way the state controls and regulates the market is undoubtedly important for the existence of the independent business owner (Wallerstein 1983: 142–7). Bureaucracy makes it more demanding to be a small business owner in Denmark than in Myanmar where the state is less bureaucratic than in western Scandinavia (see Hornig 2019). In order to understand the differences, we would need in-depth knowledge about all these economics, knowledge I alone do not possess. If we look to the other contributions in the REALEURASIA research group and view them jointly, we might find useful comparisons that can help us assist in the search for future solutions for independent merchants. However, new small-scale entrepreneurship keeps coming also in Scandinavia.

Why is it important to preserve this form of entrepreneurship? Why should we all have an interest in keeping the independent merchant? These questions bring me to reflections beyond entrepreneurship. In Eriksen's concept of 'overheating', he brings together various, global structures in a critical analysis of change and overheating (Eriksen 2016). Overheating is contextualised in the idea of the Anthropocene and how we humans have overexploited the world and its resources. Eriksen draws a link between population growth, $CO_2$-emissions, world energy consumption, urbanisation, poverty and refugees, waste, and social media.

My ethnography has prompted me to think in a similar vein. The business owners I worked with in Aarhus were resisting a development that supports further overheating of the world. Although they were not active in environmental politics or alternative economies, or even necessarily voted for political parties that supported limited growth, their values, choices, and actions all spoke for a more ethical, sustainable future where production is local, products are made to last, and we produce only what we need (e.g. the bakers who never produce more than they expect to sell). The business owners had in common that they were concerned with the local, the small, and the intimate. They avoided overspending and they were all concerned with sustainability in different ways. Sally's whole business was built up around the idea of durability. She only sold goods that were durable through a whole life and which were made without harmful toxins. She bought Danish-produced goods as much as she could, imported only goods produced in Northern Europe, and where she knew that the employees worked under fair conditions.

Lillian focused on local supplies and made all her pastry herself, emphasising the importance of avoiding additives. Her motivation when she decided to open her café was to offer affordable products of high quality. She wanted her café to be accessible to all layers of society. Marie and Ole had similar motives when they wanted to offer products of high quality to a price that made it available for a broader group of the community. The direction these business owners take, and the broader social consequences their effort entails make them sustainable in more than one way.

Climate change is an increasing global threat that leaders in most states has recognised. However, powerful leaders across the world expel the same reluctance to properly deal with these problems, and the enormous power held by a few, very large actors are responsible for a major proportion of the global $CO_2$-emissions (Griffin 2017). Simultaneously, we see that large corporations refuse to take responsibility and reduce emissions or act more ethically (Abend 2014). In fact, lack of responsibility is a direct result of global financial crisis, such as the breakdown of the American stock markets in 2008 (Abend 2014). The growth of the business of business ethics is an incentive to prevent repetition of such large scandals (ibid.). However, the global results of the business ethics business, is difficult to detect. Gabriel Abend connects this to the variety in moral backgrounds, pointing out two main categories of namely Standards of Practice and The Christian Merchant (Abend 2014). My experience is that small variations can have enormous impact on perceptions about morality. However, my data document the perceptions of the existence of a morality, which the small, Aarhusian business owners adhere to in diverse ways. Hence, the overexploitation of natural resources, as Eriksen (2016) points out, is closely connected to other global problems such as social differences and poverty, insecure financial markets, and a precarious labour market.

The problem, I suggest, is that regarding moral entrepreneurship or business ethics, size matters. My data has shown that my small, independent business owners' express an acute sense of responsibility for their actions and the consequences their business has on the broader surroundings. Be it the civil society, social community, or the environment. When a business grows beyond what one person can manage, the owners need to share responsibilities between several individuals. My observations and experience from working together in a team where a larger group share responsibility, is that keeping one person accountable for a mistake is increasingly difficult the more people are involved. When large corporations are pushed to take responsibility and be accountable for the consequences, no one takes responsibility. Strong in capital, the corporations can pay a fine and continue their activities free from responsibility.

In his research on global financial advisory corporations, Cris Shore discussed how large, international corporations knowingly break laws. Internal experts calculate the risk of being caught in fraud and other illegal economic actions, and the potential loss of capital against the amount they gain if they are not caught. For these corporations a billion-something dollar fine is nothing against what they earn through their illegal activities and they can therefore afford to act unethically (Shore 2018). Economic power is political power, and when large corporations are directly involved in, supported by, or even partly owned by states, they have the strength to control and manipulate international markets. We can ask why none of the actors within the large corporations feels responsible (or do they?). Economic interests do not explain in full why these corporations fail to take responsibility. If that was the case, we must accept that economic man is a fact too. It has been established in social scientific discourse that a human economy triumphs over economic man (Hart, Laville and Cattani 2010). Nevertheless, the individual actors within large corporations are human too. So why does seemingly no one feel responsible?

I suggest that the distance between production and management, together with the substantial number of shareholders, are important reasons why these corporations fail to act. Take for example ExxonMobil Corp. The management is divided between four individuals but with 70,000 employees globally. All listed shareholders are other corporations and finding the actual people who own the corporation is several layers down (or up). The board and the managers are miles away from witnessing, with their own eyes, the actual processes their firm involves. When firms are this big, it is nearly impossible to get the individuals behind the decisions to feel on their bodies the actual consequences for which they are responsible. I suggest it is just as problematic when companies are state owned, because who is the state? Is it the people? We cannot expect every single citizen in a country to control and be responsible for state corporations. Such an extent of democracy does not exist.

Indications from my own work with independent business owners demonstrate that the distance between production and distribution need not be very far before the feeling of responsibility declines (see also Eriksen 2016, 2017). On such matters, my data suggest that the values of the small, independent businesses and their wish to do what is right, may be important if we want a more ethical business life. If strong states regulated the market in ways that encouraged the values promoted by the owners in this sample, could we see a more moral, human economy than the last decades have witnessed?

Before we can land at such a conclusion, we need more research. What can we learn about similar firms in other places? My experience from my previous fieldwork in Indonesia is that independent street vendors felt no responsibility for the litter they left on the street when they closed in the evening. Perhaps because they trusted that street sweepers would take care of it? A look at the Jakarta River witness that that is where a lot of the garbage ends up, not properly handled by sweepers.

There is no doubt that Danish business owners know their privileged status as citizens of a well-functioning, social democratic welfare state. They can afford to be concerned with morality because they are in a stable financial situation, secured by the benefits of the welfare state. However, one should think that Exxon, KPMG, McDonalds, Asia Pulp and Paper, and other international corporations could have afforded to act more ethically too. Perhaps not without a cost, but they should be financially well enough to be able to set an example.

Data from other researchers in the REALEURASIA group can tell us about the circumstances of small business owners in other areas, but what about neighbouring nations such as Finland, Sweden, and Norway? What about the rest of the world, can we find the same mentality there? What can we find out about businesses in other niches, do plumbers have the same concern for the independent business owner?

The Norwegian Pension Fund International owns shares in large, influential corporations all over the world, and in many of these firms, their shares are of a significant size. Although Norway is a small state, the strength of this fund in the international market, could make them influential actors in a global campaign against accelerated change. However, we witness year after year reluctance to present demands. The repeating argument is economic interests, but this explanation is not sufficient. If the international market wants to persist, we need to collaborate on a new system. Among those who argue for an alternative economic system to capitalism is the leader of one of the world's largest funds, the Norwegian Pension Fund (Reinertsen and Solbø 2018). However, other leading economists (such as Adam Posen) do not agree to change directions. That leading economists are unwilling to look for alternative options becomes a problem in an overheated, globalized economy.

The Aarhusian business owners are business owners who all subsist within their own niche. They all come from one of Europe's richest countries, which happen to be a re-distributional welfare state. There is no doubt that these business owners have advantages, both in their business and in their lives in general. That is, if we compare them to similar individuals in other states. However, I wish to conclude with a suggestion and a question.

I suggest that if we want to move away from an economy that evolves around principles of endless competition, exploitation, and overheating, we need to protect and provide fertile ground for small businesses. However, this kind of entrepreneurship cannot evolve unless states act to limit the power of large corporations and allow small entrepreneurship a larger role in the market. We need to remember that the development of the market as it is today is a recent development. Consumers in Denmark, India, or Germany were not dependent on Lidl, Netto, or other corporate, low-price chains only a few decades ago. I am not suggesting that we should go back in time to before the industrial revolution when all businesses were independent or parts of cooperatives. Instead, I argue that we could learn from understanding how small enterprises work and operate, not just in Denmark, but also in other parts of the world. Business should be based on local production, products made to last, and production that is regulated after demand – perhaps on order. Do similar, small business owners in other places have the same closeness to their work, do they express responsibility for their actions in the way the Aarhus business owners does?

The independent business owners have shown that they care about the consequences of what they produce, and the actions of their firms have on the broader society. They are concerned with creating and contributing to an economy that allows for intimate relationships between seller and buyer, between products and their owners. They oppose market principles of competition, marketing, and accumulation of commodities, as well as capital. They are concerned with limiting the distance between production and consumption, hoping to create what they believe to be a better world. How can this kind of entrepreneurship be available at a larger scale and in other locations?

# Bibliography

Aakjær, J. 1920. *Samlede Digte II* [Selected Poems II]. Kjøbenhavn og Kristiania: Nordisk Forlag.

Aarhus Kommune. 2011. *Iværksætterstrategi for Aarhus Kommune* [Self-Employment Strategy, Aarhus Commune]. Aarhus: Aarhus Kommune.

——. 2015. *Beskæftigelsesplan 2015 Aarhus Kommune* [Labour/Employment Plan]. Available online, www.aarhus.dk, accessed 18 January 2016.

Abend, G. 2014. *The Moral Background: An Inquiry into the History of Business Ethics*. Oxfordshire: Princeton University Press.

Abrahamson, P. 1992. Poverty and Welfare in Denmark. *Scandinavian Journal of Social Welfare* 1 (1): 20–27.

Albæk, S., P. Møllgaard, and P. B. Overgaard. 2003. Government-Assisted Oligopoly Coordination? A Concrete Case. *The Journal of Industrial Economics* 45 (4): 429–43.

Andersen, P. B., and P. Lüchau. 2011. Individualisering Og Aftraditionalisering Af Danskernes Religiøse Værdier [Individualisation and Detraditionalizing of Danish Religious Values]. In P. Gundelach (ed.), *Små Og Store Forandringer: Danskernes Værdier Siden 1981* [Small and Big Changes: Danish Values Since 1981], pp. 76–96. Copenhagen: Hans Reitzel.

Andersen, S. K., J. E. Dølvik, and C. L. Ibsen. 2014. *De Nordiske Aftalemodeller i Åbne Markeder – Udfordringer Og Perspektiver* [The Nordic Models for Open Markets]. Fafo.

Andersen, V. M., and Z. Bosanac. 2016. *Danmark Er Fortsat Dyrest i EU* [Denmark is Still the Most Expensive Country in the EU]. Available online, https://www.dst.dk/da/Statistik/nyheder-analyser-publ/nyt/NytHtml?cid=20673, accessed 4 August 2017.

Anderson, J. 2016. *The Happiest People in the World Define What Makes Them That Way.* Available online, https://qz.com/860659/why-is-denmark-the-happiest-country-in-the-world-a-survey-asked-danes-to-define-their-top-10-values/, accessed 25 August 2022.

Applbaum, K. 2005. The Anthropology of Markets. In J. Carrier (ed.), *A Handbook of Economic Anthropology*, pp. 275–89. Cheltenham: Edward Elgar Publishing Limited.

Applebaum, H. (ed.). 1984a. *Work in Market and Industrial Societies*. Albany: State University of New York Press.

——. (ed.). 1984b. *Work in Non-Market and Transitional Societies*. Albany: State University of New York Press.

————. 1995. The Concept of Work in Western Thought. In F. C. Gamst (ed.), *Meanings of Work. Considerations for the Twenty-First Century*, pp. 46–78. Albany: State University of New York Press.

Archetti, E. P. 1986. Om Maktens Ideologi – En Krysskulturell Analyse [On Ideology of Power – A Crosscultural Analysis]. In A. M. Klausen (ed.), *Den Norske Væremåten: Antropologisk Søkelys På Norsk Kultur* [The Norwegian Way of Being: Anthropological Spotlight on Norwegian Culture], pp. 45–60. Trondheim: J. W. Cappelens Forlag.

Arendt, H. 1998. *The Human Condition*. (2nd edition). Chicago: University of Chicago Press.

Árnason, J. P. 2009. A Mutuating Pheriphery: Medieval Encounters in the Far North. *Gripla XX* 20: 17–47.

Árnason, J. P., and B. Wittrock. 2012. Introduction. In J. P. Árnason, and B. Wittrock (eds.), *Nordic Paths to Modernity*, pp. 1–24. New York: Berghahn Books.

Bakke, D. W. 2006. *Joy at Work: A Revolutionary Approach to Fun on the Job*. Seattle: Pear Press.

Becattini, G. 1990. The Marshallian Industrial District as a Socio-Economic Notion. In F. Pyke, G. Becattini, and W. Sengenberger (eds.), *Industrial Districts and Inter-Firm Co-Operation in Italy*, pp. 37–51. Geneva: International Institute for Labor Studies.

Bejder, P., and B. Kristensen. 2016. *Velfærdsstaten og de universelle rettigheder, efter 1849* [The Welfare State and Universal Rights after 1849]. Available online, http://danmarkshistorien.dk/leksikon-og-kilder/vis/materiale/velfaerdsstaten-og-de-universelle-rettigheder/, accessed 26 January 2018.

Bendixen, S., M. B. Bringslid, and H. Vike (eds.). 2018a. *Egalitarianism in Scandinavia: Historical and Contemporary Perspectives*. London: Palgrave Macmillan.

————. 2018b. Introduction: Egalitarianism in a Scandinavian Context. In S. Bendixen, M. B. Bringslid, and H. Vike (eds.), *Egalitarianism in Scandinavia: Historical and Contemporary Perspectives*, pp. 1–44. London: Palgrave Macmillan.

Bennike, C. 2016. *Hygge Har Ikke Gjort Os Til Verdens Lykkeligste Folk. Tværtimod* [Hygge has not Made Us the Happiest People in the World, rather Contrary]. Available online, https://www.information.dk/kultur/2016/10/hygge-gjort-verdens-lykkeligste-folk-tvaertimod, accessed 7 October 2016.

Berrone, P., C. Cruz, L. R. Gomez-Mejia, and M. Larraza-Kintana. 2010. Socioemotional Wealth and Corporate Responses to Institutional

Pressures: Do Family-Controlled Firms Pollute Less? *Administrative Science Quarterly* 55 (1): 82–113.

Berta, A. E. V. 2014a. Kvinner Og Makt: Et Eksempel Fra Regnskogen På Sumatra [Women and Power: A Case From the Sumatran Rainforest]. *Betwixt & Between* 24: 143–59.

———. 2014b. *People of the Jungle: Adat, Women and Change among Orang Rimba*. M.A. Thesis, University of Oslo.

Beskæftigelsesministeriet [Ministry of Labour]. 2018. *Dagpenge* [Unemployment Money]. Available online, www.bm.dk, accessed 21 January 2018.

Besnier, N. 2009. *Gossip. And the Everyday Production of Politics*. Honolulu: University of Hawai'i Press.

Bill, F., B. Bjerke, and A. W. Johansson. 2010. Demobilizing or Mobilizing the Entrepreneurship Discourse: Something Else or None of It? In F. Bill, B. Bjerke, and A. W. Johansson (eds.), *(De)Mobilizing the Entrepreneurship Discourse: Exploring Entrepreneurial Thinking and Action*, pp. 1–11. Cheltenham and Northhampton: Edward Elgar.

Bloch, M., and J. Parry. 1989. Introduction: Money and the Morality of Exchange. In J. Parry, and M. Bloch (eds.), *Money and the Morality of Exchange*, pp. 1–32. Cambridge and New York: Cambridge University Press.

Borish, S. M. 1991. *The Land of the Living: The Danish Folk High Schools and Denmark's Non-Violent Path to Modernization*. Nevada City: Blue Dolphin.

Børne- og undervisningsministeriet [Ministry of Children and Education]. 2018. *BEK nr 853 af 22/06/2018 Bekendtgørelse om pædagogiske mål og indhold i seks læreplanstemaer* [Announcement of Pedagogical Goals and Content in Six Topics in Pedagogical Teaching Plans]. Available online, https://www.retsinformation.dk/eli/lta/2018/968, accessed 30 September 2022.

Borre, O. 2004. Politiske Værdier [Political Values]. In P. Gundelach (ed.), *Danskernes Særpreg* [The Distinctive Features of the Danes], pp. 338–63. Copenhagen: Hans Reitzel.

Bourdieu, P. 1977. *Outline of a Theory of Practice*. Cambridge: Cambridge University Press.

Bræmer, M. 2017. *Psykolog Advarer: Danskerne Dør Af Dårlig Ledelse Og for Høj Arbejdsmoral* [Psychologist Warns: The Danes are Dying from Bad Management and Work Moral]. Available online, https://www.ugebreveta4.dk/psykolog-advarer-danskerne-doer-af-daarlige-ledere-og_20878.aspx, accessed 26 January 2018.

Briggs, J. 1970. Kapluna Daughter. In P. Golde (ed.), *Women in the Field. Anthropological Experiences*, pp. 19–44. Chicago: Aldine Publishing Company.

Brink, S. 2008. Christianisation and the Emergence of the Early Church in Scandinavia. In S. Brink, and N. Price (eds.), *The Viking World*, pp. 621–28. Abingdon: Routledge.

Browne, K. E. 2009. Economics and Morality: Introduction. In K. E. Browne, and B. L. Milgram (eds.), *Economics and Morality. Anthropological Approaches*, pp. 1–40. Lanham: AltaMira Press.

Bruun, M. H. 2011. Egalitarianism and Community in Danish Housing Cooperatives: Proper Forms of Sharing and Being Together. *Social Analysis* 55 (2): 62–83.

———. 2012. *Social Life and Moral Economies in Danish Cooperative Housing: Community, Property and Value*. Copenhagen: University of Copenhagen.

———. 2016. Om at "følge markedet" og "købe sig ind i fællesskabet" [On "Following the Market" and "Bying Your Way into the Community"]. *Tidsskriftet Antropologi* [Journal of Anthropology] 73: 5-27.

———. 2018. Social Imaginaries and Egalitarian Practices in the Era of Neoliberalization. In S. Bendixen, M. B. Bringslid, and H. Vike (eds.), *Egalitarianism in Scandinavia: Historical and Contemporary Perspectives*, pp. 135–56. London: Palgrave Macmillan.

Bruun, M. H., G. S. Jakobsen, and S. Krøijer. 2011. Introduction: The Concern for Sociality; Practicing Equality and Hierarchy in Denmark. *Social Analysis* 55 (2): 1–19.

Bruun, M. H, S. Krøijer, and M. Rytter. 2015. Indledende Perspektiver: Forandringsstaten Og Selvstændighedsstaten [Opening Perspectives: The Changing State and the Independence State]. *Tidsskriftet Antropologi* [Journal of Anthropology] 72: 11-37.

Budget og Planlægning, Borgemesterens afdeling, Aarhus Kommune [Department of Budget and Planning, the Mayor's Office, Aarhus Commune]. 2014. *Arbejdsstyrke Og Erhvervsfrekvenser i Aarhus Kommune, 2103* [Workforce and Frequencies of Work in Aarhus Commune, 2013].

Buhmann-Holmes, N. 2018. *"Hygge kan ikke oversættes": et kritisk indspark i danskhedsdebatten* ["Hygge Cannot be Translated": A Critical Contribution to the Danishness Debate]. Available online, https://respons.community/kultur/hygge-kan-ikke-overs%C3%A6ttes-et-kritisk-indspark-i-danskhedsdebatten/, accessed 5 September 2018.

Burkart, M., F. Panunzi, and A. Shleifer. 2003. Family Firms. *The Journal of Finance* 58 (5): 2167–2201.

Business Aarhus. 2017. *Fakta Om Aarhus* [Facts About Aarhus]. 2017. Available online, https://businessaarhus.dk/om-aarhus/fakta/, accessed 29 July 2017.

Børne- og undervisningsministeriet [Ministry of Education]. n.d. *SFO*. Available online, https://www.uvm.dk/sfo-klub-og-fritidshjem/sfo/formaal--indhold-og-ansvar, accessed 1 December 2022.

Caillé, A. 2010. Gift. In K. Hart, J.-L. Laville, and A. D. Cattani (eds.), *The Human Economy: A Citizen's Guide*, pp. 180–86. Cambridge and Malden: Polity Press.

Callon, M. 1998a. Introduction: The Embeddedness of Economic Markets in Economics. In M. Callon (ed.), *The Laws of the Markets*, pp. 1–57. Oxford and Malden: Blackwell Publishers/The Sociological Review.

——— (ed.). 1998b. *The Laws of the Markets*. Oxford and Malden: Blackwell Publishers/The Sociological Review.

Carey, M. 2017. *Mistrust: An Ethnographic Theory*. Available online, https://library.oapen.org/handle/20.500.12657/30538, accessed 16 January 2021.

Carrier, J. 1992. Emerging Alienation in Production: A Maussian History. *Man* 27 (3): 539–58.

———. 1995. *Gifts and Commodities: Exchange and Western Capitalism since 1700*. London: Routledge.

———. 1997. Introduction. In J. Carrier (ed.), *Meanings of the Market: The Free Market in Western Culture*, pp. 1-68. Oxford and New York: Berg.

———. 2017. Moral Economy: What's in a Name. *Anthropological Theory* 18 (1): 18–35.

Christensen, B. 2000. *Fortællinger Fra Indre Nørrebro: Solidaritet Og Handlekraft i Det Lokale* [Tales from Inner Nørrebro: Solidarity and Action in the Local Community]. Copenhagen: Jurist- og Økonomiforbundets Forlag [Union of Law and Economy Publishing].

Christensen, C. S. 1997. *Om Begrebet Dannelse* [About the Term *Dannelse*]. Available online, http://static.uvm.dk/Publikationer/1997/dannel3.htm, accessed 1. December 2022.

Christensen, J. 2001. *At være dansk* [To be Danish]. Available online, https://www.fyens.dk/article/383135, accessed 5 September 2018.

Cohen, J. H. 1999. *Cooperation and Community: Economy and Society in Oaxaca*. Austin: University of Texas Press.

Colli, A., F. P. Paloma, and M. B. Rose. 2003. National Determinants of Family Firm Development? Family Firms in Britain, Spain, and Italy in the Nineteenth and Twentieth Centuries. *Enterprise & Society* 4 (1): 28–64.

Cosper, R. 1977. 'Book Review'. *Sociology of Work and Occupations* 4 (2): 235–38.

Curasi, C. F., L. L. Price, and E. J. Arnould. 2004. How Individuals' Cherished Possessions Become Families' Inalienable Wealth. *Journal of Consumer Research* 31 (3): 609–22.

Dahl, H. F. 1986. Those Equal Folk. In S. R. Graubard (ed.), *Norden – The Passion for Equality*, pp. 97–111. Oslo: Norwegian University Press.

Danmarks Statistik. 2014. *Danmark har tredjelaveste andel selvstendige i EU* [Denmark has the Third Lowest Number of Self-Employment in the EU]. Arbejdskraftundersøelsen, Europæisk 2. kvt. 2014 Arbejde løn og indkomst [Labour Survey, European, 2. Quarter 2014 Labour, Wages and Salaries]. Available online, https://www.dst.dk/Site/Dst/Udgivelser/nyt/GetPdf.aspx?cid=18487, accessed 26 September 2022.

———. n.d. *Denmark GDP Annual Growth Rate*. Available online, www.dst.dk, accessed 27 July 2017.

Den Danske Ordbog [The Danish Dictionary]. 2018. *Moral*. Available online, https://ordnet.dk/ddo/ordbog?query=moral&tab=for, accessed 23 March 2018.

Douglas, M. 2002. Foreword: No Free Gifts. In M. Mauss, *The Gift: The Form and Reason for Exchange in Archaic Societies*, pp. ix–xxiii. London and New York: Routledge.

Drachmann, H. 2005. *Danmark er verdensmester i lighed* [Denmark is The Worlds Most Equal Country]. Available online, https://politiken.dk/indland/art5698523/Danmark-er-verdensmester-i-lighed, accessed 25 January 2018.

Dumont, L. 2013. On Value. Radcliffe-Brown Lecture in Social Anthropology 1980. *HAU: Journal of Ethnographic Theory* 3 (1): 287-315.

Durkheim, E. 2010 [1953]. *Sociology and Philosophy*. Oxon and New York: Routledge.

Edel, A. 1962. Anthropology and Ethics in Common Focus. *The Journal of the Royal Anthropological Institute of Great Britain and Ireland* 92 (1): 55–72.

Edel, M. M., and A. Edel. 1959. *Anthropology and Ethics.* Springfield: Charles C. Thomas.

Eriksen, T. H. 2016. *Overheating: An Anthropology of Accelerated Change.* London: Pluto Press.

———. 2017. Conflicting Regimes of Knowledge about Gladstone Harbour: A Drama in Four Acts. In T. H. Eriksen, and E. Schober (eds.), *Knowledge and Power in an Overheated World*, pp. 72–97. Oslo: Department of Social Anthropology.

Esping-Andersen, G. 1990a. The Three Political Economies of the Welfare State. *International Journal of Sociology* 20 (3): 92–123.

———. 1990b. *The Three Worlds of Welfare Capitalism.* Princeton: Princeton University Press.

———. 1996a. After the Golden Age? Welfare State Dilemmas in a Global Economy. In G. Esping-Andersen (ed.), *Welfare States in Transition: National Adaptations in Global Economies*, pp. 2–28. London: SAGE publications.

———. 1996b. Equality or Employment? The Interaction of Wages, Welfare States and Family Change. *Transfer: European Review of Labour and Research* 2 (4): 615–34.

———. 2000. The Sustainability of Welfare States Into The Twenty-First Century. *International Journal of Health Services.* 30 (1): 1–12.

———. 2002. The Generational Conflict Reconsidered. *Journal of European Social Policy* 12 (1): 5–21.

———. 2009. *The Incomplete Revolution.* Cambridge: Polity Press.

———. 2015. Welfare Regimes and Social Stratification. *Journal of European Social Policy* 25 (1): 124–34.

Etzioni, A. A. 1995. The Socio-Economics of Work. In F. C. Gamst (ed.), *Meanings of Work. Considerations for the Twenty-First Century*, pp. 251–60. Albany: State University of New York Press.

Eurostat. 2003. *European Union Labour Force Survey 2014.* Available online, www.ec.europa.eu, accessed 12 February 2017.

Falbe, C. E. 2011. *Lighed gør os lykkelige* [Equality Makes Us Happy]. Available online, https://www.kristeligt-dagblad.dk/danmark/lighed-gør-os-lykkelige, accessed 25 January 2018.

Fassin, D. 2012. Introduction: Toward a Critical Moral Anthropology. In D. Fassin (ed.), *A Companion to Moral Anthropology*, pp. 1–17. Malden: John Wiley & Sons, Ltd.

Firth, R. 1936. *We, the Tikopia: Kinship in Primitive Polynesia.* London and New York: Routledge.

———. 1953. The Study of Values by Social Anthropologists: The Marett Lecture, 1953. *Man* 53: 146–53.

————. 1979. Work and Value: Reflections on Ideas of Karl Marx. In
Sandra Wallman (ed.), *Social Anthropology of Work*, pp. 177–206.
London: Academic Press.

Folketingstiende. 1975. *Lov om Folkeskoleskolen 26. Juni 1975* [Act on the
Folkeskoleskolen 26 June 1975]. Available online,
https://danmarkshistorien.dk/vis/materiale/lov-om-folkeskolen-26-
juni-1975, accessed 30 September 2022.

Formandskabet [Chairmanship]. 2016. Dansk Økonomi, Efterår 2016:
Konjukturvurdering, Offentlige Finanser, Finanspolitisk
Holdbarhed, Investeringskrise? Indkomst- Og Formuefordeling
[Danish Economy, Fall 2016: Conjunctures, Public Finance,
Investment Crisis? Income and Fortune]. Copenhagen: De
økonomiske Råd [The Financial Council].

Fridberg, T. 2004. Velfærdsstaten [The Welfare State]. In P. Gundelach
(ed.), *Danskernes Særpreg* [The Distinctive Features of the Danes],
pp. 119–44. Copenhagen: Hans Reitzel.

Frøystad, K. 2003. Forestillingen Om Det "Ordentlige" Feltarbeid Og Dets
Umulighet i Norge [The Notion of "Proper" Fieldwork and the
Impossibility of Such in Norway]. In M. Rugkåsa, and K. T.
Thorsen (eds.), *Nære Stader, Nye Rom: Utfordringer i
Antropologiske Studier i Norge* [Near Places, New Rooms:
Challenges with Anthropological Fieldwork in Norway], pp. 32–64.
Oslo: Gyldendal Norsk Forlag.

Ganti, T. 2014. Neoliberalism. *Annual Review of Anthropology* 43 (1): 89–
104.

Garsten, C., and M. L. De Montoya. 2004. *Market Matters. Exploring
Cultural Processes in the Global Marketplace.* Basingstoke:
Palgrave Macmillan.

Geertz, C. 1973. *The Interpretation of Cultures: Selected Essays.* (2000th
edition). New York: Basic Books.

Gershuny, J. 1988. Time, Technology and the Informal Economy. In R. E.
Pahl (ed.), *On Work: Historical, Comparative and Theoretical
Approaches.* Oxford: Blackwell.

Gilliam, L. 2016. Nødvendighedens Pædagogik [Necessity of Pedagogics].
*Tidsskriftet Antropologi* [Journal of Anthropology] 73: 59–82.

Goldschmidt, W. 1984. Independence among Pastoralists. In H. Applebaum
(ed.), *Work in Non-Market and Transitional Societies*, pp. 134–42.
Albany: State University of New York Press.

Gómez-Mejía, L. R., K. T. Haynes, M. Núñez-Nickel, K. Jacobson, and J.
Moyano-Fuentes. 2007. Socioemotional Wealth and Business Risks

in Family-Controlled Firms: Evidence from Spanish Olive Oil Mills. *Administrative Science Quarterly* 52: 106–37.

Graeber, D. 2001. *Toward an Anthropological Theory of Value: The False Coin of Our Own Dreams*. New York: Palgrave.

Gräslund, A.-S. 2008. The Material Culture of Old Norse Religion. In S. Brink, and N. Price (eds.), *The Viking World*, pp. 249–56. Abingdon: Routledge.

Graubard, S. R. 1986. Introduction. In S. R. Graubard (ed.), *Norden – The Passion for Equality*, pp. 7–15. Oslo: Norwegian University Press.

Gregory, C. A. 1982. *Gifts and Commodities*. London, New York: Academic Press Inc.

———. 1997. *Savage Money: The Anthropology and Politics of Commodity Exchange*. Amsterdam: Harwood Academic.

———. 2015. *Gifts and Commodities*. (2nd edition). Chicago: Hau Books.

Gregory, C. A., and J. C. Altman. 1989. *Observing the Economy*. London: Routledge.

Greve, B. 2004. Denmark: Universal or Not So Universal Welfare State. *Social Policy & Administration* 38 (2): 156–69.

Griffin, P. 2017. *CDP Carbon Majors Report 2017*. Available online, https://b8f65cb373b1b7b15feb-c70d8ead6ced550b4d987d7c03 fcdd1d.ssl.cf3.rackcdn.com/cms/reports/documents/000/002/327/ori ginal/Carbon-Majors-Report-2017.pdf, accessed 19 February 2018.

Grønborg, U. 2017. *Gaver er ikke arveforskud* [Gifts are not Advance on Inheritance]. Available online, https://www.minadvokat.dk/ pengegaver/gaver-er-ikke-arveforskud/, accessed 26 September 2022.

Gudeman, S. 2008. *Economy's Tension: The Dialectics of Community and Market*. New York and Oxford: Berghahn Books.

———. 2009. Necessity or Contingency: Mutuality and Market. In C. Hann, and K. Hart (eds.), *Market and Society: The Great Transformation Today*, pp. 17–37. New York: Cambridge University Press.

Gullbekk, S. H. 2008. Coinage and Monetary Economies. In S. Brink, and N. Price (eds.), *The Viking World*, pp. 159–69. Abingdon: Routledge.

Gullestad, M. 1984. *Kitchen Table Society: A Case Study of the Family Life and Friendships of Young Working-Class Mothers in Urban Norway*. Oslo, Bergen, Stavanger, Tromsø: Universitetsforlaget.

———. 1986. Equality and Marital Love: The Norwegian Case as an Illustration of a General Western Dilemma. *Social Analysis: The International Journal of Social and Cultural Practice* (19): 40–53.

———. 1989. Small Facts and Large Issues: The Anthropology of Contemporary Scandinavian Society. *Annual Review of Anthropology* 18: 71–93.

———. 1990. Doing Interpretative Analysis in a Modern Large Scale Society: The Meaning of Peace and Quiet in Norway. *Social Analysis: The International Journal of Social and Cultural Practice* (29): 38–61.

———. 1991. The Transformation of the Norwegian Notion of Everyday Life. *American Ethnologist* 18 (3): 480–99.

———. 1992. *The Art of Social Relations. Essays on Culture, Social Action and Everyday Life in Modern Norway*. Oslo: Scandinavian University Press.

———. 1996. From Obedience to Negotiation: Dilemmas in the Transmission of Values Between the Generations in Norway. *The Journal of the Royal Anthropological Institute* 2 (1): 25–42.

———. 1997. From "Being of Use" to "Finding Oneself": Dilemmas of Value Transmission between the Generations in Norway. In M. Gullestad, and M. Segalen (eds.), *Family and Kinship in Europe*, pp. 202–18. London: Pinter.

———. 2002. Invisible Fences: Egalitarianism, Nationalism and Racism. *The Journal of the Royal Anthropological Institute* 8 (1): 45–63.

Gundelach, P. 2004a. *Danskernes Særpreg* [The Distinctive Features of the Danes]. Copenhagen: Hans Reitzel.

———. 2004b. Det Moralske Klima [The Moral Climate]. In P. Gundelach (ed.), *Danskernes Særpreg* [The Distinctive Features of the Danes], pp. 269–92. Copenhagen: Hans Reitzel.

———. 2004c. Det Særligt Danske? [The Distinctively Danish?] In P. Gundelach (ed.), *Danskernes Særpreg* [The Distinctive Features of the Danes], pp. 11–26. Copenhagen: Hans Reitzel.

———. 2011. Stabilitet Og Forandringer [Stability and Change]. In P. Gundelach (ed.), *Små Og Store Forandringer: Danskernes Værdier Siden 1981* [Large and Small Changes: Danish Values since 1981], pp. 11–29. Copenhagen: Hans Reitzel.

Hall, J. A., and J. L. Campbell. 2017. Denmark. In J. A. Hall, and J. L. Campbell (eds.), *The Paradox of Vulnerability: States Nationalism, and the Financial Crisis*, pp. 27–62. Princeton and Oxford: Princeton University Press.

Hann, C. 2015. Goody, Polanyi and Eurasia: An Unfinished Project in Comparative Historical Economic Anthropology. *History and Anthropology* 26 (3): 308–20.

———. 2016. A Concept of Eurasia. *Current Anthropology* 57 (1): 1–27.

———. 2018. Moral(Ity and) Economy: Work, Workfare, and Fairness in Provincial Hungary. *European Journal of Sociology* 59 (2): 225–54.

Hansen, J. F. 1980. *We Are a Little Land: Cultural Assumptions in Danish Everyday Life*. New York: Arno Press.

Hart, K. 1997. Informal Income Opportunities and Urban Employment in Ghana. In R. R. Grinker, and C. B. Steiner (eds.), *Perspectives on Africa: A Reader in Culture, History and Representation*, pp. 142–62. Oxford: Blackwell Publishers.

———. 2005. Formal Bureaucracy and the Emergent Forms of the Informal Economy. *EGDI and UNU-WIDER* 11: 1–19.

———. 2009. Money in the Making of World Society. In C. Hann, and K. Hart (eds.), *Market and Society: The Great Transformation Today*, pp. 91–105. New York: Cambridge University Press.

Hart, K., J.-L. Laville, and A. D. Cattani. 2010. Building the Human Economy Together. In K. Hart, J.-L. Laville, and A. D. Cattani (eds.), *The Human Economy: A Citizen's Guide*, pp. 1–17. Cambridge and Malden: Polity Press.

Hastrup, K. 1987. Fieldwork among Friends: Ethnographic Exchange within the Northern Civilization. In A. Jackson (ed.), *Anthropology at Home*, pp. 94–108. London: Tavistock.

Hastrup, K., and O. Löfgren. 1992. Lykkens Økonomi [Economy of Luck]. In K. Hastrup (ed.), *Den Nordiske Verden* [The Nordic World], pp. 240–57. Copenhagen: Gyldendal.

Hedeager, L. 2008. Scandinavia before the Viking Age. In S. Brink, and N. Price (eds.), *The Viking World*, pp. 11–22. Abingdon: Routledge.

Heintz, M. 2008. Changes in Work Ethic in Eastern Europe: The Case of Romania. *Autrepart* 48 (4): 45–58.

———. 2009a. Introduction. In M. Heintz (ed.), *The Anthropology of Moralities*, pp. 1–19. New York and Oxford: Berghahn Books.

———. (ed.). 2009b. *The Anthropology of Moralities*. New York: Berghahn Books.

———. 2017. *The Social Division of Values – with Reference to Postsocialist Romanian Work Ethic*. Paper at the Conference 'Moral Economies: Work, Values and Economic Ethics'. Lutherstadt/Wittenberg, Gemany.

———. 2020. *The Anthropology of Morality: A Dynamic and Interactionist Approach*. London and New York: Routledge.

Helliwell, J., R. Layard, and J. Sachs. 2016. *World Happiness Report 2016, Update*. New York: Sustainable Development Solutions Network.

Hetter, K. 2016. *Where Are the World's Happiest Countries?* Available online, https://www.cnn.com/travel/article/worlds-happiest-countries-united-nations/index.html, accessed 25 January 2018.

Hobolt, S. B. 2004. Lokal Orientering. In P. Gundelach (ed.), *Danskernes Særpreg* [The Distinctive Features of the Danes], pp. 313–37. Copenhagen: Hans Reitzel.

Højrup, T. 1983. *Det Glemte Folk* [The Forgotten People]. Copenhagen: Inst. Euro. Forlkelivsforsk. Statens Byggeforskningsinstitut (SBI).

———. 2002. *Dannelsens Dialektikk: Etnologiske Utfordringer Til Det Glemte Folk* [Dialectics of Dannelse: Ethnological Problems in The Forgotten People]. Copenhagen: Museum Tusculanums Forlag.

———. 2013. *Life Mode Analysis – the Coming in to Being*. Available online, https://lifemodes.ku.dk/about/Life_Mode_Analysis_the_coming_into_being.pdf, accessed 26 September 2022.

Højrup, T., and K. Schriewer (eds.). 2012. *European Fisheries at a Tipping-Point / La Pesca Europea Ante Un Cambio Irreversible*. Copenhagen: Museum Tusculanum Press.

Hornig, L. 2020. *On Money and* Mettā*: Economy and Morality in Urban Myanmar*. Berlin: LIT.

Hovbakke, L. 2017. *Reformationen Var Den Største Omvæltning* [The Reformation: Our Most Important Upheval]. Available online, http://jyllands-posten.dk/debat/kronik/ECE9506011/reformationen-var-den-stoerste-omvaeltning/, accessed 22 November 2017.

Howell, S. 1997a. Introduction. In S. Howell (ed.), *The Ethnography of Moralities*, pp. 1–24. London and New York: Routledge.

———. (ed.). 1997b. *The Ethnography of Moralities*. London and New York: Routledge.

Hultgård, A. 2008. The Religion of the Vikings. In S. Brink, and N. Price (eds.), *The Viking World*, pp. 212–18. Abingdon: Routledge.

Humphrey, C. 1997. Exemplars and Rules: Aspects of the Discourse of Moralities in Mongolia. In S. Howell (ed.), *The Ethnography of Moralities*, pp. 25–47. London and New York: Routledge.

Ibsen, A. A. 2012. *Amerikanisering* [Americanization]. Available online, http://danmarkshistorien.dk/leksikon-og-kilder/vis/materiale/amerikanisering/, accessed 27 January 2018.

Jakobsen, A. M. 2000. *Danmark har førsteplads i social lighed* [Denmark Tops Social Equality Scales]. Available online, https://finans.dk/artikel/ECE4241843/Danmark-har-f%C3%B8rsteplads-i-social-lighed/, accessed 25 January 2018.

Jakobsen, M. N. 2017. *Den Lutherske Kulturarv i Danmark, ca. 1536-1708* [The Lutheran Cultural Heritage in Denmark, ca. 1537-1708].

Available online, https://danmarkshistorien.dk/vis/materiale/den-lutherske-kulturarv-i-danmark-ca-1536-1708, accessed 15 November 2017.

Jaskiewicz, P., J. G. Combs, and S. B. Rau. 2015. Entrepreneurial Legacy: Toward a Theory of How Some Family Firms Nurture Transgenerational Entrepreneurship. *Journal of Business Venturing* 30 (1): 29–49.

Jenkins, R. 2006. Telling the Forest from the Trees: Local Images of National Change in a Danish Town. *Ethnos* 71 (3): 367–89.

———. 2011. *Being Danish: Paradoxes of Identity in Everyday Life*. Copenhagen: Museum Tusculanum Press.

Jensen, A. H. 2018. *BNP Pr. Indbygger* [GDP per capita]. Available online, https://www.eu.dk/da/fakta-og-tal/statistik/bnp-pr-indbygger, accessed 23 October 2018.

Jensen, C. 2007. Fixed or Variable Needs? Public Support and Welfare State Reform. *Government and Opposition* 42 (2): 139–57.

Jensen, F., D. Knudsen, T. R. Graversen, and M. Mackie. 2011. Bobler Og Finanskrise – Danske Konjukturudsving 1999-2010 [Bubbles and Financial Crisis – Danish Economic Fluctuations]. *Dansk Statistik Tema* [Danish Statistics Special Issue]. Copenhagen: Danmarks Statistik.

Jensen, M. F. 2014. The Question of How Denmark Got To Be Denmark: Establishing Rule of Law and Fighting Corruption in the State of Denmark 1660 – 1900. *QoG Working Paper* Series 2014: 6. Gothenburg: The Quality of Government Institute.

Jessen, C. 2016. *Aarhus*. Available online, https://danmarkshistorien.dk/vis/materiale/aarhus, accessed 26 September 2022.

Johannisson, B., and C. Wigren. 2006. The Dynamics of Community Identity Making in an Industrial District: The Spirit of Gnosjö Revisited. In C. Steyaert, and D. Hjorth (eds.), *Entrepreneurship as Social Change: A Third Movements in Entrepreneurship*, pp. 188–209. Cheltenham: Edward Elgar.

Jonassen, C. T. 1947. The Protestant Ethic and the Spirit of Capitalism in Norway. *American Sociological Review* 12 (6): 676–86.

Jørgensen, T. B., and B. Bozeman. 2002. Public Values Lost? Comparing Cases on Contracting out from Denmark and the United States. *Public Management Review* 4 (1): 63–81.

Kanter, R. M. 1978. Work in a New America. *Daedalus* 107 (1): 47–78.

Kastrup, M. 2013. *M. Albæk: Vi Danskere Er Blevet Dovne* [Have We Danes Become Lazy?]. Available online, http://www.b.dk/kultur/morten-albaek-vi-danskere-er-blevet-dovne, accessed 20 June 2015.

Klitgaard, M. B. 2007. Why Are They Doing It? Social Democracy and Market-Oriented Welfare State Reforms. *West European Politics* 30 (1): 172–94.

Kluckhohn, C. 1951. An Anthropological Approach to the Study of Values. *Bulletin of the American Academy of Arts and Sciences* 4 (6): 2–3.

———. 1956. Some Navaho Value Terms in Behavioral Context. *Language* 32 (1): 140–45.

———. 1958. The Scientific Study of Values and Contemporary Civilization. *Proceedings of the American Philosophical Society* 102 (5): 469–76.

Koch, H. 1943. *Grundtvig*. Copenhagen: Gyldendalske.

Kold, L. F. 2015. *Kanslergadeforliget 1933* [Kanslergade Settlement]. Available online, http://danmarkshistorien.dk/leksikon-og-kilder/vis/materiale/kanslergadeforliget-1933/, accessed 26 January 2018.

Kousholt, D. 2011. Researching Family through the Everyday Lives of Children across Home and Day Care in Denmark. *Ethos* 39 (1): 98–114.

Laidlaw, J. 2002. For an Anthropology of Ethics and Freedom. *The Journal of the Royal Anthropological Institute* 8 (2): 311–32.

———. 2014. *The Subject of Virtue: An Anthropology of Ethics and Freedom*. Cambridge: Cambridge University Press.

Landström, H. 2005. *Pioneers in Entrepreneurship and Small Business Research*. Boston: Springer Science and Business Media, Inc.

Larsen, A. 2013. *Hver 5. dansker: Mennesker i nød er dovne* [Every 5. Dane: People in Need are Lazy]. Available online, http://www.ugebreveta4.dk/hver-5-dansker-mennesker-i-noed-er-dovne_13968.aspx, accessed 20 June 2015.

Larsen, B. R. 2011. Drawing Back the Curtains: The Role of Domestic Space in the Social Inclusion and Exclusion of Refugees in Rural Denmark. *Social Analysis* 55 (2): 142–58.

———. 2018. Ridling Along in the Name of Equality: Everyday Demands on Refugee Children to Conform to Local Bodily Practices of Danish Egalitarianism. In S. Bendixen, M. B. Bringslid, and H. Vike (eds.), *Egalitarianism in Scandinavia: Historical and Contemporary Perspectives*, pp. 247–68. London: Palgrave Macmillan.

Larsen, C. A., and J. G. Andersen. 2009. How New Economic Ideas Changed the Danish Welfare State: The Case of Neoliberal Ideas and Highly Organized Social Democratic Interests. *Governance* 22 (2): 239–61.

Larsen, K. K. 2017. *Bedrifter Efter Areal, Bedriftstype, Enhed, Område Og Tid* [Businesses According to Size, Branche, Area, Unit, Place and

Time]. Available online, https://www.statbank.dk/statbank5a/SelectVarVal/Define.asp?Maintable=BDF11&PLanguage=0, accessed 5 February 2018.

Lee, R. B. 1984. Hunting among the !Kung San. In H. Applebaum (ed.), *Work in Non-Market and Transitional Societies*, pp. 69–83. Albany: State University of New York Press.

Lien, M. E. 1997. *Marketing and Modernity*. Oxford and New York: Berg.

———. 2001. Latter Og Troverdighet: Om Antropologi i Hjemlige Egne [Laughter and Credibility]. *Norsk antropologisk tidsskrift* [Norwegian Journal of Anthropology] 12 (1–2): 68–74.

———. 2004. The Virtual Consumer: Constructions of Uncertainty in Marketing Discourse. In C. Garsten, and M. L. De Montoya (eds.), *Market Matters: Exploring Cultural Processes in the Global Marketplace*, pp. 46–66. Basingstoke: Palgrave Macmillan.

Lien, M. E., H. Lidén, and H. Vike. 2001. *Likhetens Paradokser: Antropologiske Undersøkelser i Det Moderne Norge* [Paradoxes of Equality: Anthropological Studies in Modern Norway]. Oslo: Universitetsforlaget.

Linnet, J. T. 2011. Money Can't Buy Me Hygge: Danish Middle-Class Consumption, Egalitarianism, and the Sanctity of Inner Space. *Social Analysis* 55 (2): 21–44.

———. 2012a. The Social-Material Performance of Cozy Interiority. *Ambiances in action /Ambiances en acte(s) – International Congress on Ambiances*: 403–8. Montreal, Canada, 2012.

———. 2012b. The Value of Atmosphere. *Advances in Consumer Research* 40: 28–31.

Lodberg, P. 2001. *Dansker Først Og Kristen Så – Overvejelser Om Nationalitet Og Kristendom* [Danes First, then Christian – Considerations about Nationality and Christianity]. Aarhus: Aros Forlag.

Løkke, A., and A. F. Jacobsen. 1997. *Familieliv i Danmark: 1550 Til År 2000*. [Familiy Life in Denmark: 1550 to Year 2000]. (3rd edition). Århus: Systime.

Luckman, T. 1967. *The Invisible Religion: The Problem of Religion in Modern Society*. New York: Macmillan.

Lundkvist, A. (ed.). 2009a. *Dansk Nyliberalisme* [Danish Neoliberalism]. Copenhagen: Frydenlund.

——— 2009b. Indledning [Introduction]. In A. Lundkvist (ed.), *Dansk Nyliberalisme* [Danish Neoliberalism], pp. 7–12. Copenhagen: Frydenlund.

————. 2009c. Den Danske Kapitalisme Og Demokratiets Forfald [The Danish Capitalism and the Decay of the Welfare State]. In A. Lundkvist (ed.), *Dansk Nyliberalisme* [Danish Neoliberalism], pp. 13–94. Copenhagen: Frydenlund.

————. 2017a. *Dansk Kapitalisme – Gennembrud, Storhed Og Stagnation, 2. Del: Klasserne Og Den Socialistiske Strategi* [Danish Capitalism – Breakthrough, Greatness and Stagnation, Part 2: The Classes and the Socialist Strategy]. Available online, https://anderslundkvist.net/ dansk-kapitalisme-gennembrud-storhed-og-stagnation-2-del-klasserne-og-den-socialistiske-strategi/, accessed 5 November 2017.

————. 2017b. *Dansk Kapitalisme: Gennembrud, Storhed Og Stanation* [Danish Capitalism: Breakthrough, Greatness and Stagnation]. Copenhagen: Hovedland.

Malinowski, B. 1922. *Argonauts of the Western Pacific: An Account of Native Enterprise and Adventure in the Archipelagoes of Melanesian New Guinea.* London: Routledge and Kegan Paul Ltd.

————. 1935. *Coral Gardens and Their Magic: A Study of the Methods of Tilling the Soil and of Agricultural Rites in the Trobriand Islands.* London: George Allen & Unwin Ltd.

————. 1984. Trobrians Gardeners and Their Magic. In H. Applebaum (ed.), *Work in Non-Market and Transitional Societies*, pp. 161–67. Albany: State University of New York Press.

Marcus, G. E. 1998. Ethnography in/ of the World System: The Emergence of Multicited Ethnography. In G. E. Marcus, *Ethnography through Thick and Thin*, pp. 79–104. Princeton: Princeton University Press.

Marx, K. 1995. *Capital: An Abridged Edition.* Oxford: Oxford University Press.

————. 2007. *Capital: A Critique of Political Economy – The Process of Capitalist Production.* (ed. by F. Engels). New York: Cosimo, Inc.

Maurer, B. 2009. Afterword: Moral Economies, Economic Moralities: Consider the Possibilities! In K. Browne, and B. Lynne (eds.), *Economics and Morality: Anthropological Approaches*, pp. 257–70. Plymouth: Altamira Press.

Mauss, M. 1966. *The Gift: Forms and Functions of Exchange in Archaic Societies.* London: Cohen & West LTD.

————. 2002. *The Gift: The Form and Reason for Exchange in Archaic Societies.* London and New York: Routledge.

McCloskey, D. N. 2006. *The Bourgeois Virtues: Ethics for an Age of Capitalism.* Chicago: University of Chicago Press.

Melhuus, M. 1999. Insisting on Culture? *Social Anthropology* 7 (1): 65–80.

Melhuus, M., and T. Borchgrevink. 1984. Husarbeid: Tidsbinding Av Kvinner [Housework: Time Bonding of Women]. In I. Rudie (ed.), *Myk Start – Hard Landing: Om Forvaltning Av Kjønnsidentitet i En Endringsprosess*, Kvinners levekår og livsløp [Soft Start – Hard Landing: About Gender Identity Management in a Process of Change, Women's Living Conditions and Life Cycle], pp. 319–38. Oslo: Universitetsforlaget.

Metz, G. 2014. *Pusling-landet ærligt talt* [Wimp-Country, Honestly]. Available online, https://www.information.dk/debat/2014/09/pusling-landet-aerligt-talt, accessed 5 September 2018.

Mollona, M. 2005a. Factory, Family and Neighbourhood: The Political Economy of Informal Labour in Sheffield. *Journal of the Royal Anthropological Institute* 11 (3): 527–48.

———. 2005b. Gifts of Labour. *Critique of Anthropology* 25 (2): 177–98.

Mønnesland, J. 1995. Regional Development in the Nordic Periphery. In H. Eskelinen, and F. Snickars (eds.), *Competetive European Peripheries*, pp. 131–50. Berlin: Springer-Verlag.

Moth, L. 2016. *Hvad Koster En Medarbejder* [How Much Does an Employee Cost]. Available online, www.moth-adv.dk, accessed 1 January 2017.

Mühlfried, F. 2019. *Mistrust: A Global Perspective*. Tbilisi: Palgrave Macmillan.

Munn, N. 1986. *The Fane of Gawa: A Symbolic Study of Value Transformation in a Massim (Papua New Guinea) Society*. Durham and London: Cambridge University Press.

Murphy, Y., and R. F. Murphy. 1985. *Women of the Forest*. New York: Columbia University Press.

Narotzky, S., and N. Besnier. 2014. Crisis, Value, and Hope: Rethinking the Economy: An Introduction to Supplement 9. *Current Anthropology* 55 (S9): S4–16.

Nielsen, A. M. 2014. Accommodating Religious Pluralism in Denmark. *European Journal of Sociology/Archives Européennes de Sociologie* 55 (2): 245–74.

Nielsen, J. P. 2014. *Generationsskifte Af Virksomheder Og Fast Ejendom - Overblik Og Status* [Generation Change of Companies and Real Estate – Overview and Status]. Available online, https://www.plesner.com/insights/artikler/2014/12/generationsskifte%20af%20virksomheder%20og%20fast%20ejendom%20-%20overblik%20og%20status?sc_lang=da-DK, accessed 12 January 2016.

Nielsen, K., and S. Kesting. 2003. Small Is Resilient: The Impact of Globalization on Denmark. *Review of Social Economy* 61 (3): 365–87.

Nielsen, M. E. 2010. *Små Og Mellemstore Virksomheders Adgang Til Finansiering* [Small and Medium Sized Firms Access to Financialization]. Copenhagen: Danmarks Statistik.

OECD (Organisation for Economic Co-operation and Development). 2015a. *Gross National Income*. Available online, https://data.oecd.org/natincome/gross-national-income.htm, accessed 26 September 2022.

———. 2015b. *National Accounts at a Glance*. Available online, https://www.oecd-ilibrary.org/economics/national-accounts-at-a-glance-2015_na_glance-2015-en, accessed 26 September 2022.

———. 2016a. *OECD Economic Surveys: Denmark 2016*. Paris: OECD Publishing.

———. 2016b. *Social Spending*. Available online, https://data.oecd.org/socialexp/social-spending.htm, accessed 3 August 2017.

———. 2017. *Unemployment Rate (Indicator)*. Available online, https://data.oecd.org/unemp/unemployment-rate.htm, accessed 26 September 2022.

———. 2018a. *OECD Labour Force Statistics 2017*. Available online, https://www.oecd-ilibrary.org/employment/oecd-labour-force-statistics-2017_oecd_lfs-2017-en, accessed 26 September 2022.

———. 2018b. *General Government Debt (Indicator)*. Available online, https://data.oecd.org/gga/general-government-debt.htm, accessed 9 August 2017.

Olesen, T. L. 2013. *Rigtige fiskehandlere er en sjældenhed* [Real Fish Mongers is a Rarity]. Available online, https://www.dr.dk/nyheder/regionale/syd/rigtige-fiskehandlere-er-en-sjaeldenhed, accessed 7 June 2016.

Olwig, K. F. 2011. Children's Sociality: The Civilizing Project in the Danish Kindergarten. *Social Analysis* 55 (2): 121–41.

Olwig, K. F, and K. Pærregaard. 2011. Introduction: "Strangers" in the Nation. In K. F. Olwig, and K. Pærregaard (eds.), *The Question of Intergration: Immigration, Exclusion and the Danish Welfare State*, pp. 1–29. Cambridge: Cambridge Scholars Publishing.

Østergård, U. 2012. The Danish Path to Modernity. In J. P. Árnason, and B. Wittrock (eds.), *Nordic Paths to Modernity*, pp. 49–68. New York: Berghahn Books.

Oxford Dictionary. n.d. *Hygge*. Available online, https://en.oxforddictionaries.com/definition/hygge, accessed 7 June 2018.

Pahl, R. E. 1988. Epilogue: On Work. In R. E. Pahl (ed.), *On Work. Historical, Comparative and Theoretical Approaches*, pp. 743–52. Oxford: Blackwell.

Paine, R. 1972. Entrepreneurial Activity Without Its Profits. In F. Barth (ed.), *The Role of the Entrepreneur in Social Change in Northern Norway*, pp. 33–55. Bergen: Norwegian University Press.

Pallesen, A. D. 2014. *Lykken Er... at Være Selvstændig i Aarhus Og Hovedstaden* [Happiness is... to be Self-Employed in Aarhus and the Capital]. Available online, https://www.dr.dk/nyheder/regionale/ hovedstadsomraadet/lykken-er-vaere-selvstaendig-i-aarhus-og-hovedstaden, accessed 29 July 2017.

Parry, J., R. Taylor, and M. Glucksmann. 2005. Confronting the Challenges of Work Today. New Horizons and Perspectives. In L. Pettinger, J. Parry, R. Taylor, and M. Glucksmann (eds.), *A New Sociology of Work?*, pp. 3–18. Malden: Blackwell.

Parry, J. 1986. The Gift, the Indian Gift and the "Indian Gift". *Man* 21 (3): 453–73.

———. 1989. On the Moral Perils of Exchange. In J. Parry, and M. Bloch (eds.), *Money and the Morality of Exchange*, pp. 64–93. Cambridge and New York: Cambridge University Press.

———. 1999. Lords of Labour: Working and Shirking in Bihlai. In J. Parry, J. Breman, and K. Kapadia (eds.), *The Worlds of Indian Industrial Labour*, pp. 107–40. London: SAGE Publications.

Parry, J., and M. Bloch (eds.). 1989. *Money and the Morality of Exchange*. Cambridge and New York: Cambridge University Press.

Pedersen, O. K. 2011. *Konkurrencestaten* [The Competitive State]. Copenhagen: Hans Reitzel.

Petersen, J. 2013. *Er danskerne nogle dovne stoddere?* [Are the Danes some Lazy Stutterers?] Available online, http://politiken.dk/debat/ profiler/jesper-petersen/ECE2098183/er-danskerne-nogle-dovne-stoddere/, accessed 24 June 2017.

Ploug, N. 2003. The Recalibration of the Danish Old-Age Pension System. *International Social Security Review* 56 (2): 65–80.

Polanyi, K. 2001 [1944]. *The Great Transformation. The Political and Economic Origins of Our Time*. (2nd edition). Boston: Beacon Press.

———. 2005. The Self-Regulating Market and the Fictitious Commodities: Labor, Land, and Money. In M. Eldman, and A. H. Maiden (eds.), *The Anthropology of Development and Globalization: From Classical Political Economy to Contemporary Neoliberalism*, pp. 99–104. Malden: Blackwell Publishing Ltd.

Prakash, R. 1993. *Danes Are like That! Perspectives of an Indian Anthropologist on the Danish Society*. Grevas: Mørke.

Rapport, N. 1997. The Morality of Locality: On the Absolutism of Landownership in an English Village. In S. Howell (ed.), *The Ethnography of Moralities*, pp. 49–74. London and New York: Routledge.

Raudvere, C. 2008. Popular Religion in the Viking Age. In S. Brink, and N. Price (eds.), *The Viking World*, pp. 235–43. Abingdon: Routledge.

Reeh, N. 2013. Danish State Policy on the Teaching of Religion from 1900 to 2007. *Social Compass* 60 (2): 236–50.

Rehling, D. 2005. *Du Pusling-Land, Som Hygger Dig i Smug, Mens Hele Verden Brænder Om Din Vugge* [You Wimp-Country who Enjoy *Hygge* in Secret, While the Whole World is on Fire Surrounding Your Cradle]. Available online, https://www.information.dk/2005/02/pusling-land-hygger-smug-mens-hele-verden-braender-vugge, accessed 12 January 2018.

Rehn, G. 1986. The Wages of Success. In S. R. Graubard (ed.), *Norden – The Passion for Equality*, pp. 143–75. Oslo: Norwegian University Press.

Reinertsen, M. B., and H. M. L. Solbø. 2018. Det Er Problemer i Ekteskapet Mellom Kapitalismen Og Demokratiet [Are There Problems in the Marriage Between Capitalism and Democracy?]. *Morgenbladet* [Morning Magazine]: 6–8.

Rerup, L. 2017. Danmark - Historie (1945–2001) [History of Denmark 1945–2001]. *Den Store Danske*. Available online at https://denstoredanske.lex.dk/   Danmarks_historie_1945-2001, accessed 19. December 2019

Ritzau. 2015. *Danmark topper i Vesten med størst lighed* [Denmark is Number One Most Equal in The West]. Available online, https://www.information.dk/telegram/2015/05/danmark-topper-vesten-stoerst-lighed, accessed 25 January 2018.

———. 2017a. *Dronningen, Løkke Og Kjærsgaard Fejrer Luther* [The Queen, Løkke and Kjærsgaard are Celebrating Luther]. Available online, http://jyllands-posten.dk/indland/ECE9989418/dronningen-loekke-og-kjaersgaard-fejrer-luther/, accessed 22 November 2017.

———. 2017b. *Pia Kjærsgaard: Reformationen Har Formet Danmark* [Pia Kjærsgaard; The Reformation has shaped Denmark]. Available online, http://jyllands-posten.dk/kultur/historie/ECE9990462/pia-kjaersgaard-reformationen-har-formet-danmark/, accessed 22 November 2017.

Rivers, W. H. 1912. Part III. Sociology. In B. Freire-Marreco, and J. L. Sir Myres (eds.), *Notes and Queries on Anthropology*, pp. 108–27. London: The Royal Anthropological Institute.

Robbins, J. 2009. Morality, Value and Radical Cultural Change. In M. Heintz (ed.), *The Anthropology of Moralities*, pp. 6280. New York: Berghahn Books.

———. 2012. Cultural Values. In D. Fassin (ed.), *A Companion to Moral Anthropology*, pp. 117–32. Chichester: Wiley-Blackwell.

———. 2013. Beyond the Suffering Subject: Toward an Anthropology of the Good. *Journal of the Royal Anthropological Institute* 19 (3): 447–62.

Rømhild, L. P., and M. Schack. 2018. *Janteloven. Gyldendal – Den Store Danske* [The Law of Jante, Gyldendal the Great Dane]. Available online, http://denstoredanske.dk/Kunst_og_kultur/Litteratur/Nyere_motivskikkelser/Janteloven, accessed 27 January 2018.

Ronco, W., and L. Peattie. 1988. Making Work: A Perspective from Social Science. In R. E. Pahl (ed.), *On Work. Historical, Comparative and Theoretical Approaches*, pp. 709-721. Oxford: Blackwell.

Rosesdahl, E. 2008. The Emergence of Denmark and the Reign of Harald Bluetooth. In S. Brink, and N. Price (eds.), *The Viking World*, pp. 652–64. Abingdon: Routledge.

Sahlins, M. 1972. *Stone Age Economics*. Chicago: Aldine Atherton, INC.

———. 1976. *Culture and Practical Reason*. Chicago: University of Chicago Press.

———. 2002. *Waiting for Foucault, Still*. Oxford: Prickly Paradigm Press.

Salaman, G. 1974. *Community and Occupation: An Exploration of Work/Leisure Relationships*. Cambridge: Cambridge University Press.

Sampson, S. 1985. Italienske Tilstande Eller Utopi? [Italian Circumstances or Utopia?] *Stofskifte Tidsskrift for Antropologi* [Journal of Anthropology]: 83–105.

Sand, A. 2011. *Medarbejdere Og Ferie - Hvem Bestemmer Hvad?* [Employees and Holiday: Who Decides What?] Available online, https://www.d-i-f.dk/2011/10/18/medarbejdere-og-ferie-hvem-bestemmer-hvad-1070/, accessed 25 July 2016.

———. 2013. *Hvad Koster En Medarbejder?* [How Much Does an Employee Cost?] Available online, https://www.d-i-f.dk/2014/02/20/hvad-koster-en-medarbejder-1162/, accessed 25 July 2016.

de Sardan, Oliver J.P. 1999. A Moral Economy of Corruption in Africa? *The Journal of Modern African Studies* 37 (1): 25–52.

Schnack, K. 2016. *Arbejde* [Work]. Available online, http://denstoredanske.dk/Sprog,_religion_og_filosofi/Filosofi/Menneskets_grundvilkår/arbejde, accessed 26 January 2018.

Schultz-Jørgensen, P., and R. S. Christensen. 2011. Den Fleksible Familie [The Flexible Family]. In P. Gundelach (ed.), *Små Og Store Forandringer: Danskernes Værdier Siden 1981* [Small and Large Changes: Danish Values since 1981], pp. 30–56. Copenhagen: Hans Reitzel.

Schumpeter, J. A. 1943. *Capitalism, Socialism and Democracy*. London and New York: Routledge.

Shore, C. 2018. *International Accountancy Firms and Contemporary Capitalism: Collusion, Revolving Doors and State Capture*. Paper at Conference 'The Space and Time of Capitalism in Crisis'. Oslo, Norway.

Smart, A., and J. Smart. 2005a. Introduction. In A. Smart, and J. Smart (eds.), *Petty Capitalists and Globalization: Flexibility, Entrepreneurship, and Economic Development*, pp. 1–22. Albany: State University of New York Press.

———. (eds.). 2005b. Petty Capitalists and Globalization: Flexibility, Entrepreneurship, and Economic Development. Albany: State University of New York Press.

Stenius, H. 1997. The Good Life Is a Life of Conformity: The Impact of the Lutheran Tradition on Nordic Political Culture. In Ø. Sørensen, and B. Stråth (eds.), *The Cultural Construction of Norden*, pp. 161–73. Oslo: Scandinavian University Press.

———. 2010. Nordic Associational Life in a European and an Inter-Nordic Perspective. In R. Alapuro, and H. Stenius (eds.), *Nordic Associations in a European Perspective*, pp. 29–86. Baden-Baden: Nomos Verlagsgesellschaft.

Stewart, A. 1998. *The Ethnographer's Method*. London: Sage.

Stjernfelt, F. 2017. *Syv Myter Om Martin Luther* [Seven Myths about Martin Luther]. Copenhagen: Gyldendal.

Stoller, P. 1989. Eye, Mind and World in Anthropology. In P. Stoller, *The Taste of Ethnographic Things. The Senses in Anthropology*, pp. 37–55. Philadelphia: University of Pennsylvania Press.

Stråth, B. 2012. Nordic Modernity: Origins, Trajectories, Perspectives. In J. P. Árnason, and B. Wittrock (eds.), *Nordic Paths to Modernity*, 25–48. New York: Berghahn Books.

———. 2018. The Cultural Construction of Equality in Norden. In S. Bendixen, M. B. Bringslid, and H. Vike (eds.), *Egalitarianism in*

*Scandinavia: Historical and Contemporary Perspectives*, pp. 47–64. London: Palgrave Macmillan.

Styrelsen for Arbejdsmarked og Rekruttering [Department of Work and Employment]. 2017. *Efterløn* [Pension]. Available online, *https://www.borger.dk/pension-og-efterloen/efterloen-fleksydelse-delpension/efterloen,* accessed 12 June 2018.

Sundqvist, O. 2008. Cult Leaders. Rulers and Religion. In S. Brink, and N. Price (eds.), *The Viking World*, pp. 223–26. Abingdon: Routledge.

Suzman, J. 2020. *Work: A History of How We Spend Our Time*. London: Bloomsbury Circus.

Svansø, V. L., and T. Larsen. 2017. *Danmark er blandt de bedste i verden til at skabe både vækst og lighed* [Danes Are Among The Best in The World in Both Economic Growth and Equality]. Available online, https://www.business.dk/content/item/419968, accessed 25 January 2018.

Swedberg, R. 2000. The Social Science View of Entrepreneurship: Introduction and Practical Application. In R. Swedberg (ed.), *Entrepreneurship: The Social Science View*, pp. 7–44. Oxford: Oxford University Press.

Tagiuri, R., and J. Davis. 1996. Bivalent Attributes of the Family Firm. *Family Business Review* 9 (2): 199–208.

The World Bank. 2017. *Denmark GDP*. Available online, https://data.worldbank.org/indicator/NY.GDP.MKTP.KD.ZG?locations=DK, accessed 2 August 2017.

Thompson, E. P. 1963. *The Making of the English Working Class*. New York: Vintage Books.

Thorkildsen, D. 2006. Scandinavia: Lutheranism and National Identity. In S. Gilley, and B. Stanley (eds.), *World Christianities c. 1815 - c. 1914*, pp. 342–58. Cambridge: Cambridge University Press.

TNS Gallup. 1960. *Gallup 1960: Har ungdommen for løse tøjler?* [Are the Youth on a Loose Strap?] Available online, http://danmarkshistorien.dk/leksikon-og-kilder/vis/materiale/gallup-1960-har-ungdommen-for-loese-toejler/, accessed 26 January 2018.

Tsing, A. L. 2005. *Friction: An Ethnography of Global Connection*. Princeton: Princeton University Press.

Tulinius, B. 2016. *Uffe Østergård Er Historikeren, Der Blev Indhentet Af Virkeligheden*. [Uffe Østergård is the Historien that Was Caught Up by Reality]. Available online, https://www.kristeligt-dagblad.dk/danmark/historikeren-der-blev-indhentet-af-virkeligheden, accessed 22 November 2017.

Udenrigshandel [Foreign Trade]. 2014. *Danmarks Statistik*. Available online, http://www.dst.dk/en/Statistik/emner/udenrigshandel.aspx#, accessed 12 October 2017.

Vacher, M. 2011. Consuming Leisure Time: Landscapes of Infinite Horizons. *Social Analysis* 55 (2): 45–61.

Vestergaard, H. 2018. *»Du puslingland«* [You Weak Country]. Available online, /artikel/du-puslingland, accessed 5 September 2018.

Vestergaard, J., and M. Linneberg. 2018. *Competitive Patterns in the Danish Organic Industry & Its Usefulness in Predicting Development in Other EU Markets*. Aarhus: Aarhus School of Business.

Vike, H. 2004. *Velferd Uten Grenser: Den Norske Velferdsstaten Ved Veiskillet* [Welfare Without Boarders: The Norwegian Welfare State at Crossroads]. Oslo: Akribe.

———. 2016. Forord: Antropologien Og Den Skandinaviske Velferdsstaten [Preface: Anthropology and The Scandinavian Welfare State]. *Tidsskriftet Antropologi* 72 [Journal of Anthropology 72]: 5–10.

———. 2018. The Protestant Ethic and the Spirit of Political Resistance: Notes on the Political Roots of Egalitarianism in Scandinavia. In S. Bendixen, M. B. Bringslid, and H. Vike (eds.), *Egalitarianism in Scandinavia: Historical and Contemporary Perspectives*, pp. 111–34. London: Palgrave Macmillan.

Wadel, C. 1979. The Hidden Work of Everyday Life. In S. Wallman (ed.), *Social Anthropology of Work*, pp. 365–84. London: Academic Press.

———. 1991. *Feltarbeid i Egen Kultur* [Fieldwork in Native Culture]. Flekkefjord: SEEK.

Wallerstein, I. 1983. *Historical Capitalism with Capitalist Civilization*. London and New York: Verso.

———. 2004 *World-Systems Analysis: An Introduction*. Durham and London: Duke University Press.

Weber, M. 1904. *The Protestant Ethic and the Spirit of Capitalism*. London and New York: Routledge.

———. 1999. The Beginnings of the Firm. In R. Swedberg (ed.), *Essays in Economic Sociology*, pp. 80–82. Princeton: Princeton University Press.

———. 2001. *The Protestant Ethic and the Spirit of Capitalism*. London and New York: Routledge.

Widding, A. J. 1997. "I Lied, I Farted, I Stole...": Dignity and Morality in African Discourses on Personhood. In S. Howell (ed.), *The Ethnography of Moralities*, pp. 49–74. London and New York: Routledge.

Widlok, T. 2009. Norm and Spontaneity: Elicitation with Moral Dilemma Scenarios. In M. Heintz (ed.), *The Anthropology of Moralities*, pp. 20–45. New York and Oxford: Berghahn Books.

Wikan, U. 1992. Beyond the Words: The Power of Resonance. *American Ethnologist* 19 (3): 460–82.

Williams, C. C. 2004a. Cash-in-Hand Work: The Underground Sector and the Hidden Economy of Favours. Hampshire and New York: Palgrave Macmillan.

———. 2004b. Cash-In-Hand Work: Unravelling Informal Employment from The Moral Economy of Favours. *Sociological Research Online* 9 (1): 34-45.

Winther-Jensen, T. 2017. *Dannelse*. Available online, http://denstoredanske.dk/index.php?sideId=61304, accessed 23 August 2018.

Yanagisako, S. J. 1979. Family and Household: The Analysis of Domestic Groups. *Annual Review of Anthropology* 8: 161–205.

———. 2002. *Producing Culture and Capital: Family Firms in Italy*. New Jersey: Princeton University Press.

———. 2019a. Family Firms as Kinship Enterprises. *Economics Discussion Papers* 2019 (12): 1–9.

———. 2019b. On Generation. In L. Rofel, and S. J. Yanagisako (eds.), *Fabricating Transnational Capitalism: A Collaborative Ethnography of Italian-Chinese Global Fashion*, pp. 227–63. Durham and London: Duke University Press.

Zigon, J. 2011. Multiple Moralities: Discourses, Practices, and Breakdowns in Post-Sovjet Russia. In J. Zigon (ed.), *Multiple Moralities and Religions in Post-Sovjet Russia*, pp. 3–15. New York and Oxford: Berghahn Books.

———. 2012. Narratives. In D. Fassin (ed.), *A Companion to Moral Anthropology*, pp. 204–20. Malden: John Wiley & Sons, Ltd.

# Index

# Halle Studies in the Anthropology of Eurasia

1  Hann, Chris, and the "Property Relations" Group, 2003: *The Postsocialist Agrarian Question. Property Relations and the Rural Condition.*

2  Grandits, Hannes, and Patrick Heady (eds.), 2004: *Distinct Inheritances. Property, Family and Community in a Changing Europe.*

3  Torsello, David, 2004: *Trust, Property and Social Change in a Southern Slovakian Village.*

4  Pine, Frances, Deema Kaneff, and Haldis Haukanes (eds.), 2004: *Memory, Politics and Religion. The Past Meets the Present in Europe.*

5  Habeck, Joachim Otto, 2005: *What it Means to be a Herdsman. The Practice and Image of Reindeer Husbandry among the Komi of Northern Russia.*

6  Stammler, Florian, 2009: *Reindeer Nomads Meet the Market. Culture, Property and Globalisation at the 'End of the Land'* (2 editions).

7  Ventsel, Aimar, 2006: *Reindeer,* Rodina *and Reciprocity. Kinship and Property Relations in a Siberian Village.*

8  Hann, Chris, Mihály Sárkány, and Peter Skalník (eds.), 2005: *Studying Peoples in the People's Democracies. Socialist Era Anthropology in East-Central Europe.*

9  Leutloff-Grandits, Caroline, 2006: *Claiming Ownership in Postwar Croatia. The Dynamics of Property Relations and Ethnic Conflict in the Knin Region.*

10 Hann, Chris, 2006: *"Not the Horse We Wanted!" Postsocialism, Neoliberalism, and Eurasia.*

11 Hann, Chris, and the "Civil Religion" Group, 2006: *The Postsocialist Religious Question. Faith and Power in Central Asia and East-Central Europe.*

12 Heintz, Monica, 2006: *"Be European, Recycle Yourself!" The Changing Work Ethic in Romania.*

**13** Grant, Bruce, and Lale Yalçın-Heckmann (eds.), 2007: *Caucasus Paradigms. Anthropologies, Histories and the Making of a World Area.*

**14** Buzalka, Juraj, 2007: *Nation and Religion. The Politics of Commemoration in South-East Poland.*

**15** Naumescu, Vlad, 2007: *Modes of Religiosity in Eastern Christianity. Religious Processes and Social Change in Ukraine.*

**16** Mahieu, Stéphanie, and Vlad Naumescu (eds.), 2008: *Churches Inbetween. Greek Catholic Churches in Postsocialist Europe.*

**17** Mihăilescu, Vintilă, Ilia Iliev, and Slobodan Naumović (eds.), 2008: *Studying Peoples in the People's Democracies II. Socialist Era Anthropology in South-East Europe.*

**18** Kehl-Bodrogi, Krisztina, 2008: *"Religion is not so strong here". Muslim Religious Life in Khorezm after Socialism.*

**19** Light, Nathan, 2008: *Intimate Heritage. Creating Uyghur Muqam Song in Xinjiang.*

**20** Schröder, Ingo W., and Asta Vonderau (eds.), 2008: *Changing Economies and Changing Identities in Postsocialist Eastern Europe.*

**21** Fosztó, László, 2009: *Ritual Revitalisation after Socialism. Community, Personhood, and Conversion among Roma in a Transylvanian Village.*

**22** Hilgers, Irene, 2009: *Why Do Uzbeks have to be Muslims? Exploring religiosity in the Ferghana Valley.*

**23** Trevisani, Tommaso, 2010: *Land and Power in Khorezm. Farmers, Communities, and the State in Uzbekistan's Decollectivisation.*

**24** Yalçın-Heckmann, Lale, 2010: *The Return of Private Property. Rural Life after the Agrarian Reform in the Republic of Azerbaijan.*

**25** Mühlfried, Florian, and Sergey Sokolovskiy (eds.), 2011. *Exploring the Edge of Empire. Soviet Era Anthropology in the Caucasus and Central Asia.*

**26** Cash, Jennifer R., 2011: *Villages on Stage. Folklore and Nationalism in the Republic of Moldova.*

**27** Köllner, Tobias, 2012: *Practising Without Belonging? Entrepreneurship, Morality, and Religion in Contemporary Russia.*

**28** Bethmann, Carla, 2013: *"Clean, Friendly, Profitable?" Tourism and the Tourism Industry in Varna, Bulgaria.*

**29** Bošković, Aleksandar, and Chris Hann (eds.), 2013: *The Anthropological Field on the Margins of Europe, 1945-1991.*

**30** Holzlehner, Tobias, 2014: *Shadow Networks. Border Economies, Informal Markets and Organised Crime in the Russian Far East.*

**31** Bellér-Hann, Ildikó, 2015: *Negotiating Identities. Work, Religion, Gender, and the Mobilisation of Tradition among the Uyghur in the 1990s.*

**32** Oelschlaegel, Anett C., 2016: *Plural World Interpretations. The Case of the South-Siberian Tyvans.*

**33** Obendiek, Helena, 2016: *"Changing Fate". Education, Poverty and Family Support in Contemporary Chinese Society.*

**34** Sha, Heila, 2017: *Care and Ageing in North-West China.*

**35** Tocheva, Detelina, 2017: *Intimate Divisions. Street-Level Orthodoxy in Post-Soviet Russia.*

**36** Sárközi, Ildikó Gyöngyvér, 2018: *From the Mists of Martyrdom. Sibe Ancestors and Heroes on the Altar of Chinese Nation Building.*

**37** Cheung Ah Li, Leah, 2019: *Where the Past meets the Future. The Politics of Heritage in Xi'an.*

**38** Wang, Ruijing, 2019: *Kinship, Cosmology and Support. Toward a Holistic Approach of Childcare in the Akha Community of South-Western China.*